Police Violence
in America, 1869–1920

SELECTED OTHER WORKS BY KERRY SEGRAVE
AND FROM McFARLAND

The Hatpin Menace: American Women Armed and Fashionable, 1887–1920 (2016)

Chewing Gum in America, 1850–1920 (2015)

Wiretapping and Electronic Surveillance in America, 1862–1920 (2014)

*Beware the Masher: Sexual Harassment in American
Public Places, 1880–1930* (2014)

Policewomen: A History, 2d ed. (2014)

Extras of Early Hollywood: A History of the Crowd, 1913–1945 (2013)

Parking Cars in America, 1910–1945: A History (2012)

*Begging in America, 1850–1940: The Needy, the Frauds,
the Charities and the Law* (2011)

*Vision Aids in America: A Social History of Eyewear
and Sight Correction Since 1900* (2011)

Lynchings of Women in the United States: The Recorded Cases, 1851–1946 (2010)

*America Brushes Up: The Use and Marketing of Toothpaste and
Toothbrushes in the Twentieth Century* (2010)

Film Actors Organize: Union Formation Efforts in America, 1912–1937 (2009)

Parricide in the United States, 1840–1899 (2009)

*Actors Organize: A History of Union Formation
Efforts in America, 1880–1919* (2008)

Obesity in America, 1850–1939: A History of Social Attitudes and Treatment (2008)

*Women and Capital Punishment in America, 1840–1899: Death Sentences
and Executions in the United States and Canada* (2008)

Women Swindlers in America, 1860–1920 (2007)

Ticket Scalping: An American History, 1850–2005 (2007)

America on Foot: Walking and Pedestrianism in the 20th Century (2006)

Suntanning in 20th Century America (2005)

Endorsements in Advertising: A Social History (2005)

Women and Smoking in America, 1880 to 1950 (2005)

Foreign Films in America: A History (2004)

Lie Detectors: A Social History (2004)

Product Placement in Hollywood Films: A History (2004)

Piracy in the Motion Picture Industry (2003)

Jukeboxes: An American Social History (2002)

Vending Machines: An American Social History (2002)

Age Discrimination by Employers (2001)

Shoplifting: A Social History (2001)

Police Violence in America, 1869–1920

256 Incidents Involving Death or Injury

KERRY SEGRAVE

McFarland & Company, Inc., Publishers
Jefferson, North Carolina

LIBRARY OF CONGRESS CATALOGUING-IN-PUBLICATION DATA

Names: Segrave, Kerry, 1944– author.
Title: Police violence in America, 1869–1920 : 256 incidents involving death or injury / Kerry Segrave.
Description: Jefferson, North Carolina : McFarland & Company, Inc., Publishers, 2016. | Includes bibliographical references and index.
Identifiers: LCCN 2016031814 | ISBN 9781476664835 (softcover : acid free paper) ∞
Subjects: LCSH: Police brutality—United States—History. | Serial murders—United States—History. | Murder—United States—History.
Classification: LCC HV8141 .S385 2016 | DDC 363.2/32—dc23
LC record available at https://lccn.loc.gov/2016031814

BRITISH LIBRARY CATALOGUING DATA ARE AVAILABLE

ISBN (print) 978-1-4766-6483-5
ISBN (ebook) 978-1-4766-6483-5

© 2016 Kerry Segrave. All rights reserved

No part of this book may be reproduced or transmitted in any form or by any means, electronic or mechanical, including photocopying or recording, or by any information storage and retrieval system, without permission in writing from the publisher.

Front cover image is of a 1918 Newark, New Jersey, Police Officer (Library of Congress)

Manufactured in the United States of America

McFarland & Company, Inc., Publishers
  Box 611, Jefferson, North Carolina 28640
    www.mcfarlandpub.com

Contents

Preface		1
Introduction		3
ONE	• 1869–1879	7
TWO	• 1880–1889	18
THREE	• 1890–1899	44
FOUR	• 1900–1909	77
FIVE	• 1910–1920	156
Chapter Notes		203
Bibliography		218
Index		233

Preface

This book looks at all the examples I could find in the old newspapers online of cases where unarmed citizens have come to their deaths or have been assaulted by the police in the period 1869–1920. Excluded are private police such as railroad officers and the like. Also excluded are cases where the reports appeared to show that the citizen who died or was assaulted was using or trying to use a weapon on the police. Cases are included whether the officer in question was on duty or off duty, in uniform or out of uniform. Also included are instances where a policeman killed another policeman. In those cases both parties were virtually always armed. Not included as well are instances where large numbers of police were gathered together to go out in large numbers to break up something such as a labor disturbance or a racial disturbance. Police in such cases did regularly kill and assault unarmed citizens, although, of course, that was the point.

Information is sketchy in many of the cases, with only a brief item and no follow-up. Some cases were covered by the press for a period of time and then suddenly disappeared from sight. Therefore, for many of these incidents the outcome is unknown. The material is presented chronologically, by decade. The majority of cases portrayed involve single police officers out on the beat, supposedly keeping the peace and protecting citizens. Quite a few of the incidents involve cops killing other cops and some saw policemen killing one or more of their family members.

Research for this book was conducted using online databases, with the most important ones being the Library of Congress' Chronicling America database and newspaperarchive.com.

Introduction

One of the more obvious conclusions to draw from this book is the amount of dreadful injustices inflicted upon citizens, which can be compared to what is happening in contemporary America with injustices inflicted on the black community by rogue cops. It did not start in the 21st century; that type of police behavior goes back to at least 1869 and continues to the present. In the period covered by this book those injustices were imposed on whites also, but proportionally blacks were more affected. As you read through this book look carefully for the same tactics used over and over again by the police to whitewash their criminal behavior. Think of how Michael Brown (Ferguson, Missouri, in 2014) was demonized by the police and then look at the large number of examples scattered through these pages of the same behavior, that of demonizing the victim. Consider the case of Freddie Gray in Baltimore (2014) and watch out herein for other equally egregious example of police lying; there are many. The opposite also takes place—the sanctifying of the villain. When a citizen died or was assaulted it was almost automatic for someone in the department to laud the officer's record.

Innocent bystanders were gunned down in the street with no apparent punishment for the offenders. A two-year-old child standing beside her mother, was shot dead because nearby a "Cowboy Bob"-style cop was rushing after supposed felons and firing his gun wildly in the air and managed to kill the innocent child. In a different place at a different time another Cowboy Bob shot to death a 19-year-old standing in front of his father's store. It was at noon on a busy shopping street.

Another item for the reader to watch for is the sometimes appallingly poor prosecution that took place in some of these cases. On one or two occasions the prosecution was of such low quality that the judge felt obliged to remark on it. In the aforementioned case of the young man shot in front of the family business the cop, on the stand, claimed the street was empty. He was exonerated, but it would have been very easy for the prosecution to show how busy the street was and how foolish it was for a cop to be firing wildly in the air.

Due to little or no information many of the case descriptions are limited to a paragraph or a sentence or two. That would be the preliminary information and almost always it would have come from the police and thus should be viewed suspiciously. The police lied, regularly and egregiously.

Still, there were cases where the police were punished, and perhaps that sets this time apart from the current era, when there seems to never be any punishment of any kind for the rogue cops. In two of the cases described the peace officer involved was executed. However, the circumstances were somewhat unusual. One of them was executed for murdering his wife, while the other was put to death because he had orchestrated the death of a gambling den operator after the latter had complained to the police that the cop, Charles Becker, had been shaking him down for a share of his profits. Becker was a part of a corrupt segment of the NYPD involved in various illegal practices. Even when punishment was handed out it could be negated to some extent when a pardon or commutation was issued by the state governor. There were many points within the justice system where it could break down and allow the officer to escape: manipulation of a coroner's jury; use of the grand jury, or not, and manipulation of that body. The severed trial was another method to allow the cop off. There are only a handful of incidents cited in this book where more than one cop was charged at the same time with the same offense. And many of those involved severed trials; that is, the individuals were tried one by one, if any trials came after the first one. That increased the likelihood of escape. And, in the end, mount a sloppy prosecution so that the felonious cop walks away.

As well, there are many examples of the police killing children (under 18) for no reason or very trivial reasons. Then there were the large number of peace officers who were in fear for their lives and shot only in self-defense; each shot his victim in the back. Perhaps the most obvious excuse for killing an unarmed citizen was for the cop to claim the citizen was "resisting arrest." The fact that the arrest was unwarranted or illegal in the first place was almost never mentioned. There are more examples in this book of deaths than assaults when one would expect the reverse. However, a death always left a body that had to be explained. The assault victim was alive and all he could do to seek justice was complain to the very group that assaulted him. That is not a very successful or wise move today; it was likely even more difficult in the period covered by this book. Thus it was only the bravest, or most foolish, who would launch a complaint against the police back in the old days.

There are 57 cases herein where an unarmed citizen was assaulted by the police. The exact number of individuals attacked in those instances is impossible to determine. Several of the cases are brief summaries from various proceedings. For example, #58 is the summary of a government hearing during which it was revealed that approximately 90 NYPD officers had been convicted of assaulting citizens (in internal police trial board proceedings that were not public). Almost none of those men were sanctioned and few of those incidents, if any, were ever reported in the press.

There are 199 cases herein where death was the result for an unarmed person in an interaction with the police. In 34 (17 percent) of those 199 cases a policeman was reported as having been sent to jail. A pardon or commutation was given in six of those cases. With respect to the victims, those 199 incidents can be broken down into five categories; police victims, children, family members, blacks, and citizens. In seven cases children were the victims, with only one report of a cop being sent to jail (14 percent). Ten cases of family murders are included herein with four (40 percent) of those killers being jailed (including one who was executed), with one pardon/commutation issued. Also, six of those killers were not available for punishment, as five committed suicide and the sixth was shot to death by another policeman who came to arrest the family member killer. Seventeen cases of police killing other police are included herein, with eight (47 percent) of those killers being imprisoned. A total of 138 cases of citizens meeting their deaths at the hands of the police are reported, with 18 (13 percent) of those cops sent to jail (including one who was executed), and four pardons/commutations issued. Last, in the category of black victims there are 27 cases, with only three (11 percent) of the involved officers being sent to jail (one pardon/commutation), the lowest percentage of all the categories. Also, cases involving black victims tended to have less coverage than other cases, with the coverage being usually briefer and there being much less follow-up. Of those three, one served probably less than a year before being pardoned. A second case involved a white cop who shot his black mistress or "concubine," as one article described the victim. Public sentiment went against him and he pled guilty to the crime—it was almost unheard of for a cop in one of the cases reported in this book to plead guilty, to anything. The third cop jailed for killed a black was given a long prison term, but he was a black cop himself.

ONE

1869–1879

1869 August 24 *[1] Cincinnati, death.*

On the afternoon of August 25 in Cincinnati the coroner held an inquest into the death of John Bebb, who was killed on the morning of August 24 by blows from the mace of police officer John Cottle. According to a report, "The evidence tended to show that the police officer was utterly unjustifiable not only in dealing blows but in making an arrest." Witnesses swore that the murdered man up to the time of the assault was sitting quietly on the steps of his own house. One witness saw Bebb sitting there a minute before the assault and he then turned away. That witness was drawn back by the noise of the assault. When he went to his window he saw Officer Cottle strike Bebb with three blows from his club. Several other witnesses swore the murdered man did not say a word all the time during the assault, and after it was all over Bebb walked to the police station, escorted by Cottle, and remained there until the morning, at which time he was taken to the hospital where he died, some 15 hours after the beating. A postmortem revealed Bebb had suffered a fractured skull. Bebb was 27 years old and left a wife and three small children. He was intoxicated at the time of the beating. Cottle was then under arrest after the coroner's jury pronounced him the murderer.[1]

When information about a case was brief and presented very soon after the event it usually meant that information was obtained from the police and it, of course, tended to put them in the best possible light. It was often very inaccurate, to say the least. All too often that information was all that was ever published, with no follow-up material ever surfacing. Thus the victim was often left portrayed in a very bad light even if that was not the case. The police regularly set out to demonize the victims of their assaults and murders, even if it meant blatantly lying. That tendency could be seen in the present day (for example, Michael Brown in Ferguson Missouri in 2014), but it started long ago and can be seen herein in the case of John Cottle The reverse also happened regularly—the villain was sanctified. Whenever a cop came under scrutiny one of the usual responses was to laud the cop's good, or excellent, record, even if it was not. Those first early reports about the clubbing to death of Bebb all mentioned that he was intoxicated. And so it was published at the very end of December 1869 when the conviction of Cottle was announced. One report observed, on December 30, that the policeman found Bebb "drunk in the door, or on the pavement of a boarding house."[2]

Yet a piece published in a single newspaper some six days after the murder told a different story, mainly that the victim had not been drunk at all. According to that piece, Bebb left his wife and three children with a total of a $13 estate for their support. His employer had been about to promote him and "he was a sober man—never got drunk." On the day of his death Bebb's wife and children were away visiting friends in the country. It had been a very hot day in Cincinnati and Bebb had trouble getting to sleep. He took a pillow and went downstairs from the third-floor apartment in the house where he lived with his family and lay down in the hallway near the front door with that door left open in order to try to escape some of the heat. Officer Cottle saw that open door as he passed the house and a man lying in the doorway. Apparently he thought the man was drunk and "roused him with violence." The newspaper editor who presented the above facts thought two things should be done. The first thing was that the wife and children should be cared for and, "second, the policeman whose blows caused the death of Bebb must be fairly tried and not be permitted to get out on straw bail and run off." The editor added: "The policeman must have the same right as unofficial persons who beat people to death with clubs have, and no more." Then the journalist went on to address police violence against citizens in a more general way by saying: "In addition to Cottle, two other policeman are now under arrest upon similar charges—one at Hudson, N.Y., and the other at Jersey City, N.J. So many of these police murders occurring almost simultaneously in different portions of the country may well arouse public attention to the subject of the powers and duties of policemen. It is one worthy of the considerations of Judges and legislators."[3]

Nearly eight months after the beating and several months after Cincinnati policeman John Cottle was convicted of manslaughter and sentenced to five years in the penitentiary, a journalist observed that Cottle "was so overcome by his sentence of five years in the Penitentiary that his hair has turned white, and he lost fifty pounds in weight within six weeks of his arrest."[4]

Apparently Cottle served most of his sentence and he was next heard from in January 1875 when he appeared in court in Cincinnati on a charge of "cutting with intent to kill." He went on trial later that month and on January 25 he was convicted on a second count in the indictment, namely, cutting with intent to wound. A motion for a new trial was denied in this case and on February 15, 1875, Judge Murdock sentenced the ex-cop to a term of one year in the penitentiary. Back on the streets of Cincinnati Cottle was once again on trial. This time, in October 1876, he was charged with assault with intent to kill.[5]

1869 summer? *[2] Hudson, New York, death.*

A policeman was placed under arrest in Hudson, New York, for causing the death of a citizen in circumstances similar to the Cottle case [1] mentioned earlier, around the same time.[6]

1869 summer? *[3] Jersey City, New Jersey, death.*

A policeman was placed under arrest in Jersey City, New Jersey, for causing the death of a citizen in circumstances similar to the Cottle case [1] mentioned earlier, around the same time.[7]

1870 April 27 *[4] Philadelphia, death.*

About 10:00 a.m. on April 27, 1870, Philadelphia police officer Mox arrested a man who was said to be being disorderly on a public street when Mox was attacked by another man who attempted to rescue the first man. The officer drew his revolver and shot and killed the two men, who were identified as Hugh Murthrough and James Welsh. The coroner was immediately summoned to investigate the matter. It was also said that Mox had been "severely beaten" before he fired his revolver. Investigation was said to have shown that the officer's assailants were engaged in a fight together when Mox interfered and then they both joined in on an assault upon the policeman: "It is reported that they belonged to a party of young men who occasion much trouble to the officers and about two weeks ago officer Long had a difficulty with two of the gang, in which he shot and slightly wounded one of them. It is said that the deceased were indulging in a sham fight, their object being to find an opportunity to beat officer Mox." Two days later it was reported that Officer Mox had been committed for trial.[8]

1871 May 22 *[5] Chicago, death.*

According to a brief report that appeared in several newspapers, "A policeman killed a youth at Chicago yesterday."[9]

1871 July 22 *[6] Chattanooga, death.*

John Holmes, an employee of the Roane County Iron Works, was killed by policeman Talty in Chattanooga, Tennessee, at about 10:00 p.m. Saturday, July 22. One newspaper account stated that Holmes was being taken to jail by the officer, who, for some unknown cause, drew his pistol and fired his weapon twice, killing the man instantly. Two days later it was reported that the grand jury found a true bill for murder in the first degree, on July 26, against Officer Talty.[10]

An editor with that newspaper observed on the same day that the Talty case would soon come to trial and "there is great feeling over this case, and we think the policeman will suffer severely for his offense." The editor went on to comment that he thought policemen in Chattanooga were dealt with "as severely as common folk. We suppose this is right. The wearing of a blue coat and brass buttons, and the privilege of carrying a pistol don't necessarily imply the right to shoot or beat men on slight provocation, and a little wholesome punishment would teach them the necessity of being prudent and cool in the discharge of their duties."[11]

1872 March *[7] Charleston, South Carolina, assault.*

A dispute between a policeman and a driver that took place in March 1872 over the removal of a carriage at the Northeastern Railroad depot, to make way for the U.S. mail wagon, was tried before Justice Woolf and was decided on March 27. The policeman had the driver arrested on the charge of assaulting him and of cutting a bystander with a knife. The driver had the officer arrested for striking him with his club. Woolf found the cop guilty of assault and battery and sentenced him to pay a fine of $20 and costs or go to jail for 30 days. That officer appealed the decision, with the case expected to come up before the criminal court.[12]

1872 July 15 *[8] Washington, D.C., death.*

At about 11:00 p.m. on the night of July 15, 1872, an incident took place that a newspaper described as a "terrible tragedy" and which resulted in the death of Samuel A. Cunningham, who resided in the Georgetown section of Washington. During the afternoon and evening of that day a large gathering of about 200 people had taken place that included a picnic and games—it was the fraternal gathering of a club. By 10:00 p.m. most of the people at the picnic had gone home. After that hour policeman Charles H. O'Brien of the Third Precinct, who was on duty at the park, became involved in a quarrel with Mr.

and Mrs. Cunningham a little after 10:30, which ended a bit later in the shooting to death of Cunningham. It was reported that neither man had been drinking to excess. O'Brien was 26 years old, had served in the American Civil War and had spent eight months in Andersonville Prison as a prisoner of war. He had been on the police force for about four years and, it was reported, "had always borne a good reputation, although of a somewhat hasty temper," and he had always "rendered satisfactory service" as a police officer. He had married a Miss Wood some 18 months earlier and had an eight-month-old child. O'Brien came from a large family, "all of whom are respectable." A journalist remarked: "In personal appearance O'Brien is rather prepossessing. He has none of the characteristics of the rough but, on the contrary, possesses a pleasant, gentlemanly address and a modest demeanor."

Cunningham, the victim, was 29 years old, had been born in Georgetown, was employed as a laborer at a coal wharf "and had the reputation of being a quiet industrious man." He left a wife and two children, aged seven and eight. His brother William was a policeman attached to the Third Precinct.[13]

The journalist who reported the preceding facts also interviewed O'Brien on the morning of July 16 at the Third Precinct Police Station, where the officer was locked up. O'Brien told the reporter that he went on duty at noon on July 15 and during the afternoon he met Cunningham frequently and conversed pleasantly with him, as they had been friends since childhood. O'Brien had recently been trying to obtain employment for Cunningham and had recently succeeded in getting the promise of a watchman position for him. He related those facts to Mr. and Mrs. Cunningham at 10:30 p.m. on July 15 and said jokingly, "Now, Mrs. Cunningham, as I have got your husband a position, you must be good to 'the appointing power.'" Mrs. Cunningham reportedly took offense to that remark and replied, "If you mean anything bad by that I want you to know that your wife is a bigger w___e than I am." Then Cunningham also became indignant and also disparaged O'Brien's wife, as the officer continued to explain to the reporter. Feeling compelled to protect his wife's honor, O'Brien knocked Cunningham down. Policeman Lieutenant John Essex, who was nearby, then came up and took O'Brien's badge and baton from him and sent him away to a nearby house, apparently to cool down. After that, O'Brien continued, he said he remembered nothing until he was arrested by fellow officer Harry Volkmann. O'Brien said he had a vague recollection of being taken to the station by Essex and Volkmann, but that he had no recollection of the shooting. He said also that he meant no offense to Mrs. Cunningham, whom he described as a "free-talking" woman with whom he had often joked before, without any show of resentment on her part.

Cunningham died at around 1:30 a.m. on July 16 and the inquest was held at 10:00 a.m. that day. Volkmann swore that at around 11:00 p.m. he saw O'Brien come to the pavilion in the park and soon thereafter he heard the report of a pistol. At that point he rushed to the pavilion and seized O'Brien, taking a pistol from his hand, but, Volkmann added, he had not seen the shooting. A witness named Christian Beck testified he saw Essex take the badge and baton and send O'Brien away, but 15 minutes later he saw O'Brien reappear and that he heard him say, "You are a son of a bitch." Beck also swore he saw the revolver in O'Brien's hand and saw him shoot Cunningham and then saw the victim fall to the ground. Other witnesses testified to the fact they also saw O'Brien shoot Cunningham down. The coroner's jury reached a verdict that Cunningham died from a gunshot wound delivered by O'Brien and, noted a journalist, "the general sentiment is that the shooting was unjustifiable and that O'Brien was the original aggressor."[14]

One day later Mrs. Cunningham delivered a statement. She declared she had not spoken to O'Brien since the previous summer, owing to "a difficulty between the two families," until the night of July 15. At that point the policeman spoke to her about the new job that was pending. "Now that I have got Sam a place I expect you to grant me some privileges," he said to her, according to Mrs. Cunningham. She then told him she wanted nothing more to do with him. He then told her not to put on airs with him and that he knew all about her. Cunningham asked O'Brien to explain and the latter said he had visited her alone "and if I had chosen I might have taken liberties with her." Cunningham then admonished the cop and got up and left the area, seeming to want to avoid any quarrel. O'Brien insulted Mrs. Cunningham some more and then left. Fifteen minutes later Cunningham returned and told his wife that O'Brien had knocked him down with his club. The pair then decided to go home and got up to leave the pavilion. Then O'Brien returned to the pavilion and seemed ready to strike the man. But then she saw the revolver in O'Brien's hand and he fired past her, hitting her husband with the shot.[15]

On July 25 at a meeting of the Washington, D.C., Board of Police Commissioners Officer Charles H. O'Brien was dismissed from the police force on the charge of felonious homicide in the killing of Samuel G. Cunningham.[16] When O'Brien was tried for murder later in 1872 he was convicted on that charge and sentenced to be executed, with the date for his hanging set for the last Friday in February 1873. As he sat in his cell waiting for his date with the hangman his lawyers were working to try to secure a commutation of the sentence from the U.S. president. Arguing in favor of a commutation, said his lawyers, was the fact that he had given long and faithful service in the Union Army and had been a prisoner at Andersonville, where, his friends believed, his mental faculties became somewhat impaired. His execution was postponed from February 28 to March 28. Then, on March 24, U.S. president Ulysses S. Grant commuted the sentence of O'Brien to imprisonment at hard labor in the penitentiary at Albany, New York, for the term of the rest of his natural life. On November 30, 1878, O'Brien was pardoned and released from confinement.[17]

1874 January? [9] Philadelphia, assault.

The court case involving Philadelphia officer Jackson and James Morgan came before a judge in early February of 1874. Sometime earlier, perhaps in January, Officer Jackson went to Morgan's house to serve a warrant on another party who was believed to be resident at that home. Morgan, who thought his home was being assailed by intruders, seized an ax and swung it through the closed vestibule door, striking Jackson in the face and inflicting a "fearful gash." The police officer then fired two shots at Morgan, who fled from his house by a back door. In the court case each party had charged the other with assault. The jury acquitted Morgan of the charges against him but convicted Officer Jackson. On February 5 in the Philadelphia Court of Quarter Sessions on six bills of indictment preferred by James Morgan and his family charging Jackson with assault and battery and intent to kill the jury convicted the cop. Jackson was sentenced to 18 months' imprisonment.[18]

1877? [10] Philadelphia, death.

A newspaper story that appeared in print on January 5, 1877, related that a Philadelphia policeman who had been convicted of murder was to have a new trial because at the time of the deed, in the words of the judge, "his reason had been torn up by the roots and judgment jostled from her throne."[19]

1878 February 7 [11] Cincinnati, death.

According to a newspaper story, the police in Cincinnati, since the fairly recent murder of Cincinnati policeman Kunkle, had been armed with Navy revolvers and on Thursday morning, February 7, 1878, a policeman by the name of Thomas Butler had shot to death a young "outlaw" named Edward Norton, whom he was trying to arrest. A different newspaper published a brief editorial in which it fumed: "The unjustifiable fatal shooting of one Edward Norton by policeman Butler at Cincinnati, on Thursday morning last, should call down on the head of that rash officer the legal pains and penalty for murder."[20]

1878 February 18 *[12] Cincinnati, death.*

On Monday morning, February 18, 1878, it was reported that a Cincinnati policeman killed a fleeing prisoner. The man had been placed under arrest by the officer for being disorderly but had started to run away. According to the story, the policeman stubbed his toe and fell down, allowing the suspect to get farther away, with the result that "the negro gained distance and, for obeying the very natural impulse, the policeman shot him, and was not even suspended from duty."[21]

1878 November 14 *[13] Pittston, Pennsylvania, death.*

Pittston, Pennsylvania, was reported to be the scene of "terrible excitement" on November 17, 1878, owing to the arrest of the town's Police Chief Sullivan and two other members of the police force on the charge of killing a young man named Michael Walsh who died on the evening of November 16 from the effects of a pistol shot that he received on Thursday, November 14, at the hands of the police during a street brawl. The arrested officers were conveyed to the Wilkes-Barre lockup and were followed by a number of "reputable citizens" in carriages for the purpose of having them released on a writ of habeas corpus. It was also reported that "the streets of Pittston have been filled all day with crowds of excited and indignant people, and popular feeling is running so high that violence is hourly expected." The ante-mortem statement of Walsh was to the effect that he was downtown with some friends; they had some beer and on reaching the corner of Water and Main Streets Walsh saw Chief Sullivan and other policemen arresting his brother. He went over to intercede and Sullivan, drawing a pistol, told him to stand back. Walsh also pulled out a revolver and said he discharged it twice into the air. The officers then let the brother of Walsh go and the brothers retired to a nearby saloon. They were followed by the police and on seeing them Walsh started to leave the saloon. Officers Brown and Searle were in pursuit and the latter drew a revolver and fired. Walsh said that was the shot that struck him. He was arrested and placed in the lockup and attended by Dr. Rice, who declared the man was mortally wounded. At that point Walsh was taken home. Officer Brown stated that when he arrived on the scene it was a chaotic one with pistol shots being fired promiscuously. Chief Sullivan told Brown that Walsh had cornered him twice with his revolver. Brown also stated that shots were fired by himself, Sullivan and Officer Kern. According to Brown, the entire affair grew "out of what is known as a pay-day spree." Such events were said to be regular happenings on days that men were paid. According to a reporter, "The town has about 70 special Police, and the business men say they will stand by them in the discharge of their duty."

Arrested officers were James Kern and Frank Morley. Brown had yet to be arrested. All three of the men arrested were released after posting bail of $3,000 each.[22]

1879 June 22 [14] Columbia, South Carolina, death.

In Columbia, South Carolina, on Sunday night, June 22, 1879, a planter by the name of John English had a fight with a policeman named Rose in which the planter was badly beaten. English died from those injuries on the morning of June 24. Joe English, brother of the victim, subsequently met Rose in the street and several shots were exchanged, but without effect.[23]

A more detailed account related that at about 8:30 p.m. Sunday English was taken to the lockup in an "insensible" condition by policemen Rose and Daniels. English remained in the lockup until about daylight on June 23, when he was conveyed to the Central Hotel by his brother. He was cared for there until he died early the next day. At the inquest Fred Rice testified he saw Rose and another cop standing together on the street and then he heard a sound and saw a man fall to the ground, whom he recognized as English. Rose had a club in his hand and was in the act of striking again. English was then put in a cart and driven away by Rose and the other officer. Rice had heard Rose say he would kill English. Monroe Smith testified that either Rose or the other cop, Daniels, struck English with a club. Smith saw the victim spin around and fall and saw Rose attempt to strike him again after he fell. Smith also heard Rose threaten to kill English. Witness L. H. Embleton heard a blow and saw Rose and Daniels standing over English and heard Daniels exclaim, "Don't hit him again!" It was also said that English had been lying drunk in front of a house. The coroner's jury was in session all afternoon on June 24 and arrived at the following verdict on that afternoon: "that the deceased came to his death by a blow inflicted by some person unknown to the jury." Rose was arrested and lodged in jail on a charge of murder. Daniels was required to give a $500 bond to answer to the charge of assault and battery with intent to kill. Rumors circulated to the effect that Rose would be taken out of his cell and lynched. That information was conveyed to the governor of South Carolina, who ordered out the militia. A couple of days later that rumor was said to have been without foundation. However, three companies of militia guarded the jail all of one night, but nothing happened.[24]

The jury in the case of William Rose (by this time an ex-cop) charged with the murder of John English delivered a verdict in which they found the defendant guilty of manslaughter, on November 7, 1879, with a recommendation for mercy. A week or so later Judge Mackey sentenced Rose to two years at hard labor in the penitentiary. That was the lowest possible sentence to impose on someone convicted of manslaughter. Later in November it was announced that a decision had been made by the authorities to not prosecute in the case of Daniels.[25]

1879 August 23 [15] Toledo, Ohio, death.

On Thursday evening, August 21, 1879, Toledo police sergeant Jacob Nohl arrested a man named Ross Saulsbury, an old offender who had served terms in various penitentiaries for offenses such as burglary. On that particular night Saulsbury was arrested on a charge of being a "suspicious person." Soon released from custody, Saulsbury had a highly critical letter published in a local paper, on Saturday, August 23, in which he attacked Nohl and how he conducted himself as a police officer. Around eleven that morning Nohl went and located Saulsbury and demanded the former make a formal retraction of his letter. When Saulsbury refused to do so Nohl shot him twice and then shot himself. Both men died within a short time. According to a journalist, "Nohl was a faithful and efficient officer and was greatly respected by members of the police force and citizens generally."[26]

During this decade a few editorials appeared that dealt in a general way with police violence against citizens. One that appeared in October 1875 declared: "No officer should be permitted to shoot at prisoners in our streets who escape from custody. It endangers the lives of citizens, and if the prisoner was killed it would be murder. Policemen and Constables must remember this."[27]

A New York City editor declared, in January 1878, that "there is a widespread impression that police officers can be prosecuted only by complaints before the Police Commissioners. It is an error, and an error that helps many policemen guilty of violating the law to escape the penalty of the law. A police officer who assaults a citizen is just as liable as any private person to prosecution in a police court and before a jury."[28]

The longest editorial on the subject appeared in the press on September 17, 1879, and was a reprint from a New York State law journal. According to the piece, the subject of police violence was one to which attention was constantly drawn by convictions and sentences at various criminal courts. It was in all such cases to be considered whether the policeman, whether by common law or by statute, had any power to touch the party, either by pushing him or taking him into custody, "for if not, then the man would have a right to resist him and defend himself from an assault, and if death ensued in the struggle the man, if he killed the policeman, would not be guilty of murder, and perhaps not even of manslaughter, and if the policeman killed the man he would be guilty of murder. If a policeman without a warrant, endeavors to arrest a man for a mere misdemeanor not committed in his presence, the man may resist even to death." As far as this editorial writer was concerned, it was clear that where a policeman attempted to arrest, without having legal justification, "resistance to him to any extent necessary will be lawful and justifiable and cannot form subject of a criminal charge." However, the editorial writer acknowledged that magistrates constantly allowed a very "loose and arbitrary" application of those statutory powers of the police; that is, they allowed the police to get away with abuses.[29]

TWO

1880–1889

1880 March 8 *[16] New Orleans, death.*

The subhead of this article declared: "Another Police Officer Kills a Man in Attempting an Arrest." The victim was a black man named Ellick Harris, while the man who took Harris' life was New Orleans court officer H. B. Jackson of the First Recorder's Court. Early in March 1880 in New Orleans Harris had allegedly used a pistol to assault a black woman. She went to the First Recorder's Court on March 8 and remained there all day, waiting for one of the court officers, whose duty it was to arrest Harris upon his being identified by the woman. Around 4:00 p.m. Jackson left the office with the woman and a few minutes later he confronted Harris with his warrant of arrest. Harris responded by saying that nobody was going to arrest him. Jackson then tried to arrest him, but, reportedly, Harris resisted violently. Deeming his life in peril at the hands of Harris, Jackson pulled his pistol and shot Harris in the back. (Note the egregious police lying involved. Jackson was afraid for his life, so he shot Harris in the back. It was a "rationale" that would recur over time.) A few minutes after being shot, Harris was dead. Jackson then surrendered himself at the police station. On the advice of his counsel Jackson refused to say anything to reporters except that he committed the deed in self-defense. On March 9 Officer H. B. Jackson was arraigned in the First Recorder's Court on the charge of manslaughter. He was released on bonds of $3,000.[1]

1880 May *[17] St. Louis, death.*

A brief one-sentence report noted that a St. Louis police officer killed a young man who refused to tell him where he was going late at night.[2]

1880 August 6 *[18] Brooklyn, New York, assault.*

Capt. J. W. Bennett and Officer Dennis Conkling of the Sea Beach Police in Brooklyn, New York, were arraigned before Justice Walsh on August 17, 1880, charged with assaulting Thomas Mead, a waiter at the Sea Beach Palace, on August 6. The two cops had been doing police duty at the Coney Island resort. Walsh found the policeman guilty and deferred sentence for a few days. When the men returned for sentencing, the lawyer for Bennett argued that Walsh could not impose any sentence inasmuch as his judicial jurisdiction did not extend outside the city limits. Judge Walsh had already considered that point and, agreeing with the lawyer, he dismissed the complaint and discharged the accused.[3]

1881 December 31 *[19] Louisville, Kentucky, death.*

According to this report, "A policeman killed a Chinaman at Louisville, Ky., Saturday."[4]

1882 September 21 *[20] Nashville, death.*

Joseph Russell was killed by policeman Fields in Nashville, Tennessee, on the night of September 21, 1882, while, it was said, Fields was trying to arrest the man. Russell was a steamboat pilot on the Cumberland River.[5]

1883 March 11 *[21] New York City, death.*

At 11:30 a.m. on March 11, 1883, Officer Patrick Casey of the New York City Police Department killed one of his superior officers, namely, Roundsman Richard Comisky. The latter was sitting at his desk in the station conversing with two cops when Casey entered the area. It was noticed, with hindsight, that he was under the influence of liquor and acted strangely. He went into a rear room in the office and called in the two officers to help him fix his pistol. They did so and he shoved the weapon back into his pocket. Casey then walked out to where Comisky sat and when he was within some two feet of the unsuspecting Comisky said, "What do you follow me so for?" Comisky replied that it was to make him do his duty. Without another word Casey drew a revolver and fired, hitting his superior in the head. The victim fell back dead. Casey was instantly secured by other officers in the area and hurried off to the county jail. Comisky was unmarried, while Casey had a wife and two children. A reporter commented: "It is supposed Casey was in a state on insanity when he shot Comisky." The position of roundsman existed long ago, with the duty of a man holding that rank to go around in the streets to ensure that patrolmen (beat cops) were actually out where they should be and were indeed walking their beats. It was not uncommon for beat cops of this era to enter, for example, saloons, not to check on things but to while away hours in friendly drinking and socializing, rather than out walking their beat.[6]

That shooting took place in Long Island City, with Patrolmen Edward O'Brien and Jeremiah O'Connor being in the station house at the time of the killing, both being on reserve duty. Police Commissioner Joseph McGee, who lived nearby, was summoned to the station and he placed Casey under arrest. They took him to the Queens County Jail, a short distance away, as the station was deemed insecure. It was said that no direct act led to the murder, and no one seemed able to ascribe a motive to it. A huge crowd gathered at the station, but, by this account, they were curious only and not a threatening crowd. Killer and victim had known each other for 17 years and were said to have been on good terms until a year or so earlier. The remark Casey addressed to Comisky was explained by an incident that took place one week earlier. Since the reduction to the police force in Long Island City, owing to economy, roundsmen had been dispensed with and the sergeants had performed their duties. Comisky had recently been moved to acting sergeant but still did a roundsman's duty some of the time. On the evening of March 8 Comisky saw Casey, while the latter was on duty, enter a saloon with a man. Comisky entered and detected Casey in the act of taking a drink of liquor. He ordered Casey back out on duty and demanded the other man's name as a witness. Casey complied with the order. It was also noted that "Comisky and Casey had not been on good terms for a long time, and rarely spoke to each other." With respect to the March 8 incident, Comisky told his brother James to tell Casey that he did not intend to report him over the incident. However, James did not see Casey and did not have the opportunity to tell Casey what his brother had said. Casey had made statements to several people that Comisky followed him around trying to detect him in things that would enable him to prefer charges against the patrolman. Casey had been appointed to the force nine years earlier, compared to Comisky, who had started seven years earlier. Said a journalist: "That Casey was jealous of Comisky, who enjoyed the favor of the Police Commissioners to a greater degree than himself was certain. He had the idea that Comisky had put himself forward and secured a place that in the line of promotion belonged to him." Casey's mother had died on February 5, 1883, and at the wake Casey, under the influence of liquor, said to James Comisky (who was a fireman) that he would get even with the acting sergeant. James said at the inquest into his brother's death that he could give no reason for that threat. Comisky had been 32 years old, while Casey was 36 and had three daughters, with the oldest being seven.

Reportedly, threats of lynching Casey had been made and that was one of the reasons for the removal of Casey, when arrested, to another holding facility.[7]

When Coroner Robinson held an inquest, on March 15, Casey was not present due to the continuing threats of violence uttered against him. The coroner's jury returned a verdict that Comisky came to his death by a pistol shot inflicted by Casey. His trial quickly followed and on April 25, 1883, the jury came back into the courtroom to tell Judge Barnard that there was no possibility of their agreeing on a verdict. Barnard dismissed the jury and set the case down to a new trial on May 21. That dismissed jury was hung with 11 in favor of a verdict of guilty of murder in the first degree while the twelfth juror held out for a verdict of not responsible for the shooting. The jury in the second trial returned with their verdict on May 23, 1883. It was a verdict of guilty of murder in the first degree and had been reached after deliberations that lasted not quite two hours. On May 24 Judge Barnard sentenced Casey to be hanged on July 13, 1883.[8]

Various appeals and motions dragged on and the execution did not take place. In the spring of 1884 the Court of Appeals ordered a new trial for Casey. A journalist wrote: "His friends say that he was on a protracted spree for weeks before the murder. Comisky, who was his superior officer, had repeatedly threatened to have Casey dismissed from the force, and it is said that this caused Casey to become temporarily insane. In this condition he committed the murder." Of course, none of those things were true. None of them had been mentioned in any of Casey's earlier trials. There was also an example here of demonizing Comisky by making him appear more and more of a monster as time passed. Casey was found guilty again and this time sentenced to a life term of imprisonment. By this time Casey was, of course, an ex-cop, having been removed from the force much earlier by the Board of Police Commissioners. On June 23, 1884, Casey, along with two police escorts, took the first available train from New York's Grand Central Station to Sing Sing prison.[9]

1883 August 29 [22] *New York City, death.*

New York City police officer Maurice McNamara was arrested on August 29, 1883, for causing the death of John Smith by clubbing the victim. Earlier in the day on August 29 McNamara had appeared before the city's Board of Police Commissioners to answer to a charge of clubbing "a respectable citizen" a few weeks earlier. Captain Petty was in command of the police precinct to which McNamara was attached and he remarked, "I am sorry to say I have men under me I would not believe under oath. They are a shame and disgrace to the city, and if I had the power they would not remain on the force twenty-four hours. They reflect upon good men, several of whom are ashamed to be known as being connected with my precinct." When a reporter asked Petty why he had not make formal complaints against such officers the captain replied, "I have done this time and again, but those complaints still lie there. I don't feel like giving my opinion of the death of Smith last night as it would not be exactly right, but McNamara is a bad man. He had a bad record on the force and his conduct in arresting Ross Randolph, for which he was tried yesterday, was simply outrageous." Petty was then asked why he didn't suspend such men pending an investigation of such cases. To that query Petty said, "What good would that do? They would still receive their pay just the same, and be doing nothing for it." McNamara was arrested after his attack on Smith while patrolling his beat. Petty told McNamara he would be held in custody pending the examination of witnesses by the coroner. McNamara was then lodged in jail.[10]

On September 3 Coroner Kennedy held an inquest into the death of John Smith. McNamara was brought from the Tombs prison in civilian clothes, escorted by a cop. He had a lawyer with him. Witness Celia Lyon testified she saw McNamara hit Smith twice on the head with his club. Smith exclaimed, "My God! I am killed!" and then collapsed backwards to the ground. Several other eyewitnesses testified to having seen the officer punch and club Smith, for no obvious reason. McNamara testified and said Smith used foul language when he roused Smith from a doorway in which he was lying, The jury of eight men deliberated for 45 minutes before returning a verdict that Smith came to his death by a blow from a club wielded by Officer McNamara. Coroner Kennedy committed McNamara to the Tombs prison without bail. However, on September 10 the officer was admitted to bail in the amount of $5,000 by Judge Donohue, with the consent of the District Attorney.[11]

Around September 12 McNamara was taken before the New York City Police Commissioners to answer to a charge of "conduct unbecoming an officer." That charge had been made against him before he clubbed John Smith to death, but when the case had been previously called it had been postponed until September. On August 1, 1883, McNamara arrested Ross Randolph (the "respectable citizen") of Brooklyn on a Third Avenue elevated train and dragged him by a circuitous route to the Elizabeth Street police station. When they reached that station, Randolph was discharged and released. Randolph said he had noticed the officer on the train, apparently intoxicated and wearing his hat the wrong way around so that the officer's number was not visible. When Randolph turned the hat around on the cop's head McNamara arrested him. McNamara explained that he thought Randolph intended to rob him on the train, and denied he was intoxicated when he made the arrest. Thereafter followed the long march to the police station, called a "humiliating parade" through the streets. The police commissioners voted unanimously to dismiss McNamara from the New York City Police Department.[12]

On that fateful night of August 29 John Smith, a 21-year-old sailor, was sleeping off the effects of a night of carousing on the front steps of a tenement house. He was lying in such a way that people coming and going had their path blocked and had to step over him to enter or leave the building. A Mrs. Hughes sought out a patrolman and it was McNamara who answered the summons. The officer began by clubbing the soles of Smith's boots. Then he slapped Smith on the face and hit him on the legs with his club. That roused the sailor who got up, gathered his coat and vest and went off with McNamara, heading for the police station. As they walked along, Smith threw the clothing he was carrying at an Italian. Thereupon, McNamara, according to witnesses, struck Smith two or more blows with the club, to the head or to the back of the neck. He fell to the sidewalk. Other officers happened by and Smith was conveyed to the station and then to a hospital where he was pronounced dead—his neck had been broken, McNamara was reportedly sober and he told Captain Petty that he had found the man asleep on the steps of a building and arrested him for drunkenness. On the way to the station, according to McNamara, Smith called out to friends to come and kill the officer and McNamara gave him "a push" with his club and he fell against an iron railing and thus got injured. However, several eyewitnesses all saw McNamara brutally club Smith for no apparent reason. The 38-year-old officer had been appointed to the police force on June 23, 1882, and during his 14-month career he had been brought to trial before the police board several times for minor breaches of disciple, for which he was fined a day's pay. In January 1883 he was fined 20 days' pay for being asleep in the station when he should have been out on the streets on duty. In September 1882 he was accused of assaulting a citizen and placed on trial, before the police board, but the case was dismissed.[13]

McNamara stood trial in criminal court for two days in October 1883. On October 18 the jury found him guilty of manslaughter in the third degree. It was reported that "the verdict took every one in the court by surprise." McNamara was sentenced to one year's imprisonment and a fine of $500. The degree of outrage expressed at that egregious example of injustice was summed up in the headline on the story that reported the verdict. That headline stated: "A Brute Gets Off with a Ridiculous Sentence."[14]

1883 November 3 *[23] New York City, death.*

On November 3, 1883, New York City policeman William Conroy brought to the station house a prisoner named Peter Keenan, a 34-year-old furniture mover. Keenan's head was covered with flowing blood and blood was also dripping from the cop's club. In the injured man's abdomen was a bullet wound. Keenan was removed to the hospital where he soon died. Conroy explained that he had arrested the man for being drunk and disorderly and that a mob formed up as a result of that arrest and it had assaulted him and, in self-defense, he was obliged to use his club and revolver. Conroy was placed under arrest. From information obtained by detectives and witnesses at the coroner's preliminary examination it appeared Conroy had been drinking heavily and that in a saloon at 322 East 36th Street he assaulted several people without cause and finally attacked Keenan, who was quietly standing near the bar, interfering neither with the cop nor with anybody else. After shooting Keenan without warning Conroy dragged him out of the saloon and clubbed him long after he became unconscious." It was also noted that "Conroy made several contradictory statements about the matter."[15]

Another newspaper gave a fuller account. On that evening a political meeting had ended in that saloon, operated by Patrick Cody. A laborer by the name of John Bulkley was leaving the saloon when he bumped into Conroy, who was in uniform and on duty. Bulkley said to the cop, "Tom Murphy's [a political candidate] paid for a drink for you. Come in and get it." Conroy did so. Then the officer offered to stand the drinks. There was then an argument between Conroy and Cody over the exact cost of those drinks that the cop had offered to pay for. Conroy then turned on Peter McGinnis and asked him if he had drank. When he got an answer he did not like, Conroy struck McGinnis in the face, knocking him down. Then Conroy clubbed the prone man. Next, he turned on others in the same general group and began to club them. Following that, he broke a window in the saloon and drew his gun. All the noise had awakened Mrs. Cody, who appeared in a doorway with a baby in her arms. Standing near her at the bar was Keenan. Conroy raised his pistol and when Bulkley saw it pointed at Mrs. Cody and her baby he struck the cop's arm, knocking it downward. A second later Conroy fired the weapon, hitting Keenan in the abdomen. Conroy then went outside to the sidewalk where there were a dozen or so men lounging around. He wildly emptied his pistol and used his club until that group had scattered. At that point he returned to the inside of the saloon and informed Keenan that he was going to take him to the station house. Keenan managed to get up, moving with great difficulty. It was also alleged that Conroy clubbed him on the head on the way to the station. As they moved along the sidewalk Keenan finally fell and could not get up again. It was then about 11:30 p.m. and a citizen who witnessed the procession of the cop and his prisoner ran into the nearest police station and told Sergeant McDonald there had been a shooting on 36th Street. McDonald sent a number of officers to investigate.

On their way they came across Conroy trying to drag Keenan to the station. Conroy directed some of the cops to the saloon where they arrested three men and marched them off to the station. One of the officers saw that Keenan was in a bad way and called an ambulance, which took Keenan to the hospital. However, the victim died on the way and the ambulance continued on to the morgue.[16]

By that time Conroy was at the station, where he was told he was in trouble. He asked for permission to leave the station in order to get a coffee; that permission was granted. Sergeant Walsh relieved Sergeant McDonald at midnight, at which time Conroy had not returned. When he was still not back at 1:00 a.m. when Captain Riley arrived it raised alarm bells and Ryan went out personally to find Conroy. They found him in the middle of a crowd of people on 35th Street, where he was talking about the shooting. Back at the station house Conroy declared he had arrested Keenan for being drunk and disorderly and while he was taking his prisoner to the station he had been attacked and pelted with stones by friends of Keenan. When asked how Keenan came to be shot Conroy replied, "He got into the way. It was a mistake." However, by then a dozen or so witnesses were in the police station with their testimonies to show Keenan was shot in the saloon. One of them was Bulkley, who said, "There was no cause for Conroy to club or shoot anyone. Everyone was peaceable until he started in. He had taken a good deal [to drink] during the night. I had had four drinks with him." Bulkley added, "I think Conroy took a second aim before he fired at Keenan." Other witnesses testified to the unprovoked nature of the attack. The other three men arrested were held overnight in cells, even though they had done nothing, but were released immediately in the morning when they got to court. Conroy was formerly a conductor on the Second Avenue horse cars. Two years earlier he had been arrested with one Mr. Bradley on a charge of shooting policeman Fahey—that was before Conroy joined the police force. At that time he demanded a separate trial, from Bradley, and was acquitted of the charge. Bradley was convicted. Conroy had been made a police officer some eight months earlier. In his short time on the force he had only one mark on his record; he was once fined for standing in a doorway when he should have been walking his beat.[17]

Other testimony about that night indicated that McGinnis had been clubbed over the head and while he was down on the floor Conroy had kicked him in the abdomen and groin until he was almost unconscious. When Conroy fired the remaining rounds in his weapon some, or all, were said to have been directed at Mrs. Cody, who still had her nine-month-old child in her arms. None hit her. Conroy was 25 years old and it was also alleged that some years earlier he was arrested on a charge of highway robbery but that he was never brought to trial on that charge. With respect to the shooting of Officer Fahey, for which Bradley drew a term of two and a half years in prison, it was said that "Conroy, through political influence was given his freedom." To a newspaper reporter Conroy stated he had fired only one shot and that the supposed crowd that attacked him had been firing weapons and perhaps one of their bullets hit Keenan. Yet one hour later Conroy told the same reporter that he had not touched a drop of liquor since his appointment to the police force and that he had not even fired a single shot on the night in question.[18]

Coroner Levy's inquest into the death of Keenan concluded on November 8. It declared that the victim came to his death from the effects of a pistol shot inflicted by policeman William Conroy while on duty and at his post on the night of November 3, 1883, between 11:00 p.m. and 12:00 p.m. Another conclusion arrived at by the coroner's jury was that "the said officer William Conroy, after thus wounding the said Patrick Keenan, with brutal violence dragged the deceased to the police station and there preferred untrue charges against him. From the evidence before us we have become convinced that Officer William Conroy was a totally unfit person to be entrusted with such an important position as that of a police officer and we deplore that such a man could be appointed on the police force by the City of New York."[19]

The nature of the Keenan case prompted an editorial. The editor began by stating one rule was that a policeman shall not drink on duty on his beat. He added: "William Conroy had been disciplined for that very offense only a few weeks before, and had been reprimanded and mulcted three days' pay: more than that, he had been arrested for robbery once, and once for murder, but by hook or by crook—and I think it was by crook—he managed to slip through the clutches of the law." Sarcastically, the newsman declared: "Of course this is exactly the proper kind of timber to make policemen of." He declared that Conroy was a heeler (political worker) for Paddy Kinney, the alderman of the 18th Ward, "and Paddy had him put on the police two years ago. It is true the antecedents of Conroy were rather unsavory, but he could serve his friend Paddy, one of Tammany Hall's magnates, better as a policeman than a common tough." It was a custom around election time for elected officials to leave small sums of money around at the saloons "for the boys to take a drink ... and our admirable police are never neglected." In conclusion the editor declared: "It is a terrible thing to reflect that our lives and all we have are at the mercy of protectors like these, whose mugs are found in our rogues' galleries and who if they had their desserts, would be inside the walls of our penitentiary or State prison. It is to be hoped that some effort will be made to sever the connection of our police with politics."[20]

Conroy stood trial in December 1883 and on December 12 two physicians who were presented as experts by the defense argued that Conroy was insane—driven so by drinking. One, Dr. Hannon, testified that on the night of the shooting Conroy was, in his opinion, suffering from "acute alcohol mania. Persons under the influence of this mania frequently displayed great violence and exhibited much cunning before and after the outbreak."[21]

Conroy's trial, on a charge of murder in the first degree, ended on December 15. One day earlier the jury had returned from some six hours of deliberations to tell the judge that they could not agree. However, the judge held them overnight and told them to try again. On that final day three ballots were cast, with the first one standing 10–2 in favor of a verdict of guilty of murder in the first degree, with two holding out for murder in the second degree. The second vote stood 11–1 before the third and final voted rendered a unanimous verdict of guilty of murder in the first degree. A few days later Conroy was sentenced to be executed by hanging, on February 8, 1884.[22]

Motions and appeals dragged the final disposition of the case out to the spring of 1885, when it was ruled that the absence of premeditation, a necessary condition for conviction of murder in the first degree, meant he could not be executed. On April 22, 1885, Conroy entered a plea of guilty of murder in the second degree and Judge Van Brunt sentenced him to a life term of imprisonment.[23]

1883 December 4 [24] *Danville, Virginia, death.*

In Danville, Virginia, on December 4, 1883, a black man by the name of Green Miller was beating his wife. Police officer Kennedy arrived on the scene and tried to arrest Miller but was also assaulted by Miller. Kennedy's call for help brought policeman Ditrion Williams to the scene. Williams said he found Miller beating and choking Kennedy. Williams then threatened to shoot Miller if he did not relax his grip, but Miller simply cursed him and called out for him to shoot. Finally, Miller consented to go to jail, but as the two cops escorted Miller to jail the latter broke loose from Kennedy and attacked Williams, swearing he would not be arrested, and Williams shot him. A different account gave a different version of the events that took place after Miller agreed to go to jail. In that version Miller agreed to go to jail if Williams did not accompany them. But when Miller saw Williams following him and Kennedy he rushed upon Williams and was shot. Officially Miller was listed as having died while "resisting arrest." Williams was held for the grand jury with bail set at $3,000. On March 5, 1884, the grand jury brought in a verdict of "not a true bill" and Ditrion Williams, who was described then as "formerly" a cop, was exonerated.[24]

1884 June 8 [25] *Washington, D.C., assault.*

At about five o'clock on the morning of June 8, 1884, in Washington, D.C., three young men were out in a neighborhood disturbing the peace by ringing various doorbells, and so forth. The three disorderly youths were William Barnes, W. H. Parks, and Salvador Hobbs. When Barnes spotted a mockingbird on the balcony of a house he climbed up, stole it, and climbed back down to the street, whereupon all three men ran off, pursued by Officer Samuel H. Ellis and Special Officer Lloyd. The three men were too fast for the police and Ellis fired "several shots at them," one of which hit Barnes in the thigh and dropped him to the ground. All three were captured and taken into custody, with a charge of larceny being laid against Barnes. That charge against Barnes was continued, as he could not appear in court due to his injury. Parks was charged with disorderly conduct and fined $5. Hobbs disappeared and forfeited his collateral on the same charge. The case against Barnes came up in police court on July 18, at which time Barnes was convicted and fined $50 or 60 days in jail. He appealed and subsequently swore out a warrant against Officer Ellis, charging him with assault to kill. When his appeal was heard in October 1884 Barnes was acquitted in the criminal court of the charge of larceny.[25]

In the criminal court in Washington, D.C., on December 17, 1884, police officer Samuel H. Ellis was tried before Judge Wylie on the charge of assault with intent to kill William Barnes on the night of June 8 and was "promptly" acquitted when the case reached the jury. The officer saw Barnes descending from the second-floor balcony of the house and tried to arrest him, but he ran off. When he did not heed an order from Ellis to halt, the cop fired three times, twice into the air; the third shot struck Barnes in the back. In his charge to the jury Wylie drew the line where the citizen's right ceased and the officer's authority commenced and also the duty of an officer as to arresting night prowlers, burglars and thieves. Wylie said that a policeman had a right to arrest any person who had committed a felony in his sight without a warrant, either day or night: "If the perpetrator of the felony attempts to make his escape and the officer cannot overtake him, or if he had caught him and the felon has broken away from him, and he is of the opinion that the felon is likely to get off, the officer may shoot him and if the jury are satisfied that the felon was likely to escape, an officer exercising a reasonable discretion had a right to take his life rather than the felon should escape. He had a right to shoot at him and if he happened to take his life, the officer is not responsible." Wylie continued by declaring, "It is all the better if he only shoots him in the leg or body, but the law applies where no felony has been committed in fact but where from appearances of the act the officer had reasonable grounds to believe that felony had been committed." All that was necessary was that there should be the appearance of a crime having been committed and that the felon or party by whom the crime seemed to have been committed refused to submit to arrest and was endeavoring to make his escape, with every appearance of being able to accomplish that escape. Judge Wylie concluded his address to the jury by saying, "If an officer sees the crime of felony committed and declines on account of some risk to himself, or for some other reason, to arrest an offender, he should not only lose his office, but ought to be indicted. The law therefore gives him power to perform his duties, and it requires on the other hand the public or person charged to submit to that authority."26

An editorial in a New York City newspaper that appeared in February 1885 and was reprinted in other papers addressed the same issue as Judge Wylie, but in a general sense; it was not about the Ellis case specifically. While Wylie had outlined what he likely saw as the natural order of things, the journalist was clearly opposed. He said that "property commands much more jealous protection than life, and that the most striking inequality exists in the punishment of crime against the person and crimes of robbery and theft." The editorial writer continued: "A policeman kills a man for not stopping when summoned to do so, and the homicide is justified."27

1885 May [26] Salt Lake City, assault.

Salt Lake City police officers George Hilton and F. Thomas were indicted by the grand jury in May 1885 for assault and battery on a man named Harvey, described as the black murderer of Captain Burt. The prosecution alleged that while Harvey was in the marshal's room undergoing a search prior to being taken to jail he was beaten by Officers Hilton and Thomas. Hilton told a reporter that he was not on the regular police force. On the night in question he had come to town to collect his pay and while he was there he ran into Burt. The pair then spent some time in a saloon and then parted. When Hilton had walked a little way he heard two shots fired. When he ran back he found the wounded Burt had staggered into a drugstore and collapsed. Policeman Thomas was then struggling with Harvey. Thomas called for Hilton to help him and the latter did so. They took Harvey away, fighting off a crowd that wanted to lynch the black man. Thomas and Hilton got him into the marshal's room and began to search him while the lynch crowd milled around outside the building. According to Hilton's account, that crowd spilled over into the building and before the two cops realized what had happened Harvey was on the floor being kicked and punched. It was at that point Hilton said he understood that it was alleged that he and Thomas struck Harvey with brass knuckles. Two reporters from two different newspapers had each stated they saw the knuckles in the hands of the two cops. Hilton claimed that what they probably saw were the handcuffs, which at that moment had been removed from Harvey's wrists. Harvey never made it to the jail cell, as the crowd swarmed in, took the black man out and lynched him. How the crowd managed that was something Hilton claimed not to know.[28]

The trial of policeman Thomas took place on May 14, severed from the co-defendant, Hilton. The defense argued any force used was necessary. A defense witness said he was in the marshal's office when two cops brought Harvey in; at the time eight to ten other people were in the room. Harvey was searched by Thomas, assisted by Hilton. When the money was taken from the suspect and counted and the amount verbally announced, Harvey called Thomas a liar and a thief. Defense attorneys admitted that at that point Thomas struck Harvey in the face and then the officer helped him up from the floor where he had fallen, and afterward he was taken to a cell. That witness added that when Harvey was brought to the office his face was bloody. Then, once Harvey was lodged in a jail cell, the mob surged in, overpowered Thomas and Hilton and removed the prisoner. Dr. Jeter Clinton testified that Thomas did his best to try to prevent the mob from removing the prisoner. On cross-examination it was learned that the door to the marshal's room was closed and that Harvey was not violent during the search, but he had used some abusive language. When the prosecution presented its case it merely introduced a policeman's club in evidence and then announced that it rested.[29]

When the case went to the jury at 11:45 a.m. it was widely believed that the verdict would be delivered before the 12:30 p.m. lunch recess. However, the deliberations lasted almost five hours before the expected verdict of not guilty was rendered. Five ballots were needed, with the first one being 8–4 in favor of acquittal and then moving one vote at a time on each ballot until it was 12–0 on the fifth ballot. There was then speculation by reporters whether there would be a trial in the case of Hilton, "in which the evidence is infinitely weaker than in the Thomas case." Of course, there was no trial for Hilton. At the conclusion of the case a reporter declared: "The judge rendered a fair and impartial decision but the tone of which, in the opinion of the lawyers, learned slightly to the side of the prisoner."[30]

1885 December 19 *[27] New York City, assault.*

Bail in the amount of $2,000 was accepted by Justice White in the Harlem Police Court on December 22, 1885, in the case of Park Policeman Matthew McInerney, who was charged with assaulting and attempting to rob Joseph Schwarzler on the night of December 19. Schwarzler had gone to the Harlem Police Court to prefer charges against two men; the second was an ex–park policeman by the name of John J. McDonald (he was not a policeman at the time of the assault).[31]

At the trial of the two men New York Police Department officer James

Finnegan, who made the arrest of the accused, told his story. Finnegan found the three men in close proximity to one another. McInerney admitted he was a cop, but he gave the wrong badge number to Finnegan. Schwarzler said he was assaulted by the two men but said nothing about being robbed. The face of the complainant was in "terrible condition" and he was bleeding from the mouth and nose. When the two prisoners were at the Park Police station Schwarzler was asked if he had been robbed and he said no. Another witness was Edward Hatch, a Wall Street broker who said he was attracted to the scene by the noise, and he agreed that Schwarzler was in very bad physical condition. Hatch went along to the station house with all the others. He also thought the complainant was unfairly treated by Police Sergeant Harroden, who was in charge of the desk when the arrest was made and the group arrived at the station. According to Hatch, the sergeant refused to listen to Schwarzler and seemed to favor the accused. The sergeant did not even take the trouble to enter the case on the police blotter until the prisoners were brought back there from the Park Police station. On the stand Harroden explained his reasons for not entering the arrest on the blotter at first, as he thought it was his duty to turn over the prisoners to the custody of the Park Police. Several character witnesses were called who testified as to the good character of McInerney.[32]

On February 19, 1886, the two men were convicted of robbery in the first degree. That assault took place at the outskirts of Central Park. A large number of Park Police were in the courtroom when the verdict was delivered. On the stand McDonald said he had been a member of the Park Police but had been discharged for intoxication (sometime before the assault) and on the night of the assault, he said, he met McInerney and the pair went for a stroll. They heard a cry and ran across the street to find Schwarzler standing near a tree. He denied either assaulting or robbing the man. McInerney testified he had been a member of the Park Police for the past two years. He admitted that Officer Finnegan struck a match to look at his shield, but he denied giving that man the wrong badge number. The jury deliberated for one hour before reaching a verdict. Penalty for the crime was a term in prison of from 10 to 20 years.[33]

On February 26, 1886, Recorder Smyth sentenced McInerney to 12.5 years' imprisonment in Sing Sing prison. Smyth remarked that since McInerney "was in the uniform of one who had sworn to preserve the public peace that was sufficient reason why his sentence should be more severe than that imposed upon McDonald," who was not a member of the police at the time of the assault. McDonald was sentenced to 10.5 years in Sing Sing.[34]

On July 29, 1886, Justice Peckham of the New York State Supreme Court released Matthew McInerney and John J. McDonald on $7,000 bail each, because an appeal was pending in their case.[35]

1885 December 24 *[28] Newark, New Jersey, death.*

On the night of December 24, 1885, in Newark, New Jersey, policeman August Baumer (maybe John Baummer, or Banner) shot and killed Bartley Rice, who was said to have been attempting to escape arrest. That evening Rice had entered a saloon and tried to steal a keg of beer. Saloon keeper J. Bateo caught him in the act and chased him off. Bateo found Rice in the house of a woman named Lizzie Killen and pointed him out to Officer Baumer. Rice ran off again with the cop in pursuit. Baumer told him to stop and when he did not the policeman shot him in the back. Rice collapsed on the sidewalk and died on the way to the hospital. A day later, by the direction of prosecutor Keene of Newark, a complaint was made against policeman John Baummer for manslaughter in the death of Rice.[36]

However, when a coroner's jury met in Newark on December 31 that body decided the shooting of Rice by cop Banner was accidental. Banner testified that after he told Rice to stop and his command went unheeded he fired one shot into the ground and the second shot to the left of the fleeing suspect; it was that shot that killed Rice.[37]

1885 ? *[29] Buffalo, death.*

It was reported at the beginning of January 1886 that Buffalo, New York, mayor Becker, the new Republican magistrate of that city, had begun the work of "stirring up" the police department. Reportedly, in 1885 two policemen on that city's police force had killed escaping prisoners, in two separate incidents. Becker lectured the police captains and lieutenants and told them that they had to do "better work."[38]

1886 November 13 *[30] Hamilton, Ohio, death.*

John Ryan, a policeman on the Hamilton, Ohio, police force, shot and killed William Long, an alleged thief, on the night of November 13. Long had been placed under arrest by Ryan but managed to break away from the officer's custody and ran off. When the suspect refused to obey the policeman's command to halt, Ryan fired his gun and shot William Long in the back.[39]

1887 January 21 *[31] New York City, death.*

A case of manslaughter was assembled against policeman Charles Adams of the Sixth Precinct in New York City on January 21, 1887. Adams was conveying a couple of boys to the Tombs prison and through his own carelessness one of them got away from him. Adams ran after the boy through Centre Street—one of the most crowded streets in the city, according to this account—and shot at him. When the first shot missed, Adams fired again, striking and killing a young man who happened to be standing in front of his father's store. An editorial writer on a New York City newspaper then commented: "This kind of recklessness on the part of policemen is criminal. It is getting far too frequent. Nobody knows when some fool whom the law entrusts with a pistol is going to blow an inoffensive citizens' brains out. Policemen who have so little sense should be punished with a severity which will teach well the lesson that firearms must never be resorted to except when an officer's very life is in danger or when there is no possibility of killing other people. It is far better that a picayune rogue who pilfers a watch or an overcoat should escape than for a half a hundred people to run the risk of being killed."[40]

Early on the morning of January 21 Charles Adams was making his rounds when he came upon a man leaving a clothing store laden down with clothes, a circumstance that aroused his suspicions. He soon discovered the store had been broken into and clothes stolen. He took the man, whom he had placed under arrest, to the Elizabeth Street police station, where another of Adams' prisoners—who had stolen a watch from a man—was awaiting his trip to the Tombs. In due course on that same morning Adams marched both his prisoners into the presence of Justice Duffy, who committed them both for trial. The man who stole the clothes gave his name as James McCarthy (sometimes Murray), age 19, while the boy who took the watch was Timothy Tehan, age 13. Having a grip on McCarthy's coat sleeve, Adams prepared to escort the man downstairs while he allowed the boy's father to escort Tim. Near an open door McCarthy slipped away from Adams and rushed into the street. The officer followed him into Centre Street. As the time then was about noon, the street was very busy and crowded. Taking out his revolver, Adams fired a shot into the air, supposedly to attract the attention of other cops; at least that was what Adams said later. Still running after McCarthy, the cop fired a second shot. While he saw McCarthy enter a building a search of it by Adams and several other officers—who by then had arrived on the scene—failed to find McCarthy. Attracted by the noise and the commotion, many people stood at doors of shops on Centre Street, watching the case. The shop at 84 Centre Street was operated by Louis Canale. In the doorway of that shop, watching the activity, stood the son of the shopkeeper, Pantalini Canale, and a friend of his by the name of Henry Schucci. They heard the first shot fired and a moment after the second shot was fired Pantalini put his hands to his head and cried out, "My God, I'm shot," and fell to the ground. The 21-year-old died soon thereafter. Adams later fired a third shot. When Adams returned to his station house he was told what happened by Sergeant Strong, who said, "He was doing his duty. It was certainly justifiable homicide. I don't see why Adams should be arrested." But he was. Captain McCullagh suspended him from duty and later in the afternoon of January 21 he was arrested and himself taken to the Tombs.[41]

On January 26 the coroner held an inquest into the death of Canale. According to a reporter, "there were few persons in the street" during the chase and shooting. Apparently the journalist came to this bizarre, and false, conclusion because "the officer took the stand and swore that this was so." Captain McCullagh testified that Officer Adams had a good record and that he was justified in acting as he did. The coroner's jury took the same view and exonerated policeman Charles Adams.[42]

1887 June 2 *[32] New York City, death.*

The first report of this murder of a citizen by the police carried the subhead "Cowardly Attack Which Was Unprovoked—the Gallant Victim Likely to Die of His Wound." The victim was the gate keeper at Castle Garden, a man by the name of John Hussey, better known as "Captain Jack" "and widely known as a courageous and bemedaled life saver." (Compare this early description with the latter descriptions of the man given during the trial. It is one of the best examples of victim demonization. It is also one of the better examples of the police soldiering together and lying as a group.) On June 2 policeman Edward Hahn was off duty and in civilian clothes. He had attended a picnic earlier in the day and by the evening he was described as being "full of beer and quarrelsome." In a saloon Hahn picked a quarrel with Hussey, but the latter tried to avoid any further trouble by leaving the saloon and walking toward his home. However, he stopped and went into a second saloon before he reached home. Hahn followed him into that second saloon and continued to abuse Hussey verbally and challenged him to fight. Hussey became angry and told Hahn to keep away and that he was not fighting "boy cops." Hussey left that saloon, Hahn followed, and shots were heard. Later, with Hahn at the police station, reporters were denied access to the cop and it was asserted that he had made no other statement other than that he was drunk and he had acted in self-defense and, said a journalist, "there was an evident disposition at the station house to keep the facts of the shooting from the newspapers." Hussey came to New York City in 1853 and had worked as a laborer and longshoreman, although at the time of his death he had been the gatekeeper at Castle Garden for some time. Over the years he had reportedly saved the lives of three women, three boys, 32 men and seven horses and had several medals that had been awarded to him by various organizations. He had saved all those people and animals from drowning. He was noted to such an extent that he had his life dramatized, had appeared on the stage, had been lauded in the U.S. Congress and was considered "as brave as a lion and Warm-hearted and generous." No article explained why Hussey had been in a position to save so many people. It was, perhaps, due to his position at Castle Garden. It was an immigrant reception center in the last half of the nineteenth century for people arriving in America and had a large number of people coming and going. It was located at the water's edge. Several brief articles appeared about Hussey's lifesaving exploits in the 1880s and two specifically were about saving recently arrived immigrants at Castle Garden. A couple of the articles also mentioned him receiving medals.[43]

One day later and the lying and victimization of Hussey began. Hahn declared he had been drinking with Hussey and kept telling him to go home. Hussey said okay but kept staying on for one more drink. Then Hussey grew quarrelsome and wanted to fight with Hahn, said the cop. To avoid a fight Hahn backed out of the saloon, but Hussey followed him onto the sidewalk. When Hussey advanced toward the policeman Hahn declared he fired a shot in the air. Hussey then rushed Hahn and again the cop fired into the air, but it did not deter Hussey. Hahn continued by saying he ran away, but Hussey ran after him and "as he was gaining on me I turned and fired two shots at him, which felled the man." Then, Hahn said, he went to give himself up. (This was, of course, all lies. But compare this version of the incident and later versions when more and more people, not present in any early accounts, miraculously appear, always making Hussey more villainous and dangerous). Since he had been appointed to the police force on March 6, 1886, Edward Hahn had been fined twice for being absent from his post and in liquor stores. According to the reporter who wrote this piece, "He is a tall, athletic young man, and could have easily handled an old man like Hussey without resorting to his revolver." Hussey was in his late fifties.[44]

Edward Hahn stood trial for murder in October 1887 in the Court of General Sessions in New York City. While Jack Hussey was shot on June 2, he did not die

A set of sketches of Jack Hussey, the courtroom and the shooting. Note the medals on his chest. They were lifesaving awards and the sketch was done at a time when Hussey was still a good guy, before the police got finished demonizing him.

until 19 days later in the hospital. On June 2 Hussey had worked all day at Castle Garden. Hahn had been on the force for about nine months and was enjoying a day off at the policemen's picnic earlier in the day. When he met Hussey at a saloon that evening Hahn was, reportedly, "flushed with drink." The two men drank together for a time, but then Hahn grew quarrelsome and when Hussey declined to drink anymore the pair exchanged verbal insults. Then Hussey left the saloon and started for home. Hahn followed and once in the street drew a revolver and fired. The shot missed. Hussey turned to see what was happening and as he turned the second shot entered his abdomen. The police arrested Hahn. Hussey insisted on walking home and did so, accompanied by friends. From there he walked three more blocks to the hospital. An operation was performed, but Hussey did not recover. He lingered in the hospital before he died on June 21. Hussey was 59 years old and had four children. Hahn stood trial for murder in the first degree.[45]

When Hahn got on the stand at his trial for murder was the time the lies really got going. The officer testified that he had known Hussey for many years and that his reputation among the policemen was that while he was under the influence of liquor he was "a violent and dangerous man." The 26-year-old Hahn said he did not drink much at the picnic he attended earlier in the day. He then reiterated that he was actually a kind and caring person who was trying to get the intoxicated Hussey to stop drinking and to go home. In this version of the story Hahn insisted that when Hussey came running at him he had two or three men who were running at the cop with Hussey. Hahn fired in the air, but the "mob" fired missiles at the officer. During the hour and a half the defense used to present a summation at the trial, a reporter observed that most of that time was devoted to "a review of that part of the testimony given which showed Capt. Hussey to have been a violent and dangerous man."[46]

During the trial all of the past record of Hussey being a lifesaver of renown and a generally decent man was forgotten. His character was attacked incessantly, apparently with no general objections from the prosecution. It was alleged that he had been the leader of the anti-draft riots (opposed to conscription in the U.S. Civil War) in New York City in 1863. It was also alleged that he had a serious and known reputation for assaulting police officers. Other officers testified to that fact. None of that was true. And, in fact, no specific evidence was introduced to back up such allegations, even though if what was said was true then there should have been plenty of police records to verify the allegations. Leading questions were used repeatedly, with no apparent objections from the prosecution. One of Hahn's lawyers directed the following question to the officer: "Have you heard that Hussey had often assaulted other policemen and citizens?" To which the cop replied, "Yes." Another such question was: "Have you heard that Hussey was a leader of the draft riots?" That question was too much for the judge, who disallowed it—he had allowed the earlier one. Those draft riots took place almost 25 years before the shooting. At the trial Hahn had been presented as a man who feared for his life and never meant to kill Hussey but only to wound him. The officer thought that as many as a dozen missiles—bricks or stones—had been thrown at him by the "mob" that accompanied Hussey as they all rushed the cop. Strange that when Hahn told his story back in June no mob or missiles existed.[47]

On the morning of October 14, 1887, Judge Cowing charged the jury in the trial of Hahn. Cowing said, "This man was a policeman, but he must be shown no partiality because he was a policeman; he must be treated as a citizen on trial for the same time." The jury was out for just one hour before they returned to announce they had acquitted Hahn. The first ballot was nine votes for acquittal, with two for manslaughter in the first degree and

A sketch of Jack Hussey. His case represented several ways in which the police conspired against the victim. He was demonized to an egregious extent, the police lied as a group, and the prosecution was woefully negligent. It was hardly a surprise the verdict was justifiable homicide.

one vote for manslaughter in the second degree. The second vote was 11–1 and the third and last ballot was unanimous. Hahn, who had been under suspension from the force pending the outcome of the case, would not be allowed back onto the force until Superintendent Murray received an official copy of the acquittal, and then Hahn was to be tried by the police commissioners for being off post and drunk. One police commissioner said to a reporter, "The evidence showed that he was more agile than Hussey, had from fifteen to twenty feet start on him and could have avoided shooting if he had cared to." As far as the jury was concerned, it had been a justifiable homicide.[48]

On January 11, 1888, Hahn was on trial before Police Commissioner Voorhis at police headquarters for being absent from roll call. Hahn admitted being guilty of the charge but gave as an excuse that he missed his commuter train. He was then back on active duty but attached to a different station house.[49]

During Hahn's trial one of the tactics that had been used was to try to show that Hussey had died not from the bullet wound received from the cop's gun but from something else, such as poor medical care; remember that Hussey had lingered for 19 days in the hospital. One who testified at the trial was a man named Joseph O'Neil, who testified he had been outside the hospital on the street and had seen Hussey walking about in his room, passing by the window, and so forth. There was much wrong with O'Neil's testimony. For one thing, he identified a room that was not that of Hussey and was not in use at that time. Another problem was that the date O'Neil gave as the date he saw Hussey moving about in his hospital room was one month after he died. Nonetheless, when O'Neil appeared in court in May 1888 charged with perjury the jury quickly acquitted him.[50] A brief report published on September 5, 1895, noted that at a meeting of the Board of Police Commissioners on the previous day three policemen were dismissed from the force. One was Edward Hahn, who was dismissed for being discovered in liquor stores in full uniform while on duty.[51]

1887 November [33] *Memphis, Tennessee, assault.*

On November 26, 1887, a jury in a criminal court in Memphis, Tennessee, found policeman C. M. Bevell guilty of assault and battery upon a drummer (traveling salesman) by the name of R. A. Givens. The jury also recommended the officer to the mercy of the court. But two days later when he was sentenced that recommendation for mercy found no response in the heart of Judge DuBose. Based on the mercy recommendation, the lawyers for Bevell confidently expected a sentence of just a $10 fine. Instead the judge imposed a fine of $10 and imprisonment in the county workhouse for 11 months and 29 days. Friends of Bevell thought it was a sentence that was too severe. Bevell received $60 a month in pay for patrolling a beat a mile or more square for 12 hours per day. As well, the officer faced a judgment for $500 for a blow inflicted upon Nick Dodds that same day as that upon which Bevell assaulted Givens. That was a separate assault case. Even then it was reported that a petition for a pardon was being circulated.[52]

That petition proved to be successful and on March 14, 1888, Memphis policeman Bevell, who stood convicted of assault and battery in two separate cases that involved two separate individuals, was pardoned by the governor of Tennessee on the recommendation of the jury "and prominent Memphis citizens."[53]

1887 December 31 [34] *Evansville, Indiana, death.*

At 3:00 a.m. on December 31, 1887, Evansville, Indiana, policeman Joseph Ziegler of that city's police force shot and killed Abe Smock, another officer from the same force. Ziegler was walking his beat when he observed two men leaving a residence. When the men saw him they broke into a run. He chased them into an alley where he ordered them to halt. When they ignored his command Ziegler fired into the ground. That stopped one of the men, but thinking he was about to be fired upon, Ziegler shot and killed Smock. On reaching the side of the fallen man Ziegler discovered it was a fellow officer. At that point the other man identified himself as still another cop on that force, Officer Cahill. He and Smock were off duty and had been out "skylarking." They did not want Ziegler to know who they were and it was for that reason that they tried to evade Ziegler. Reportedly, no arrests were made.[54]

However, a few days later, on January 3, 1888, Superintendent Newitt filed an affidavit against Ziegler, charging him with the murder of Smock. When a preliminary examination of the policeman was held that afternoon Ziegler was acquitted on the ground of self-defense.[55]

1888 September 26 [35] *San Francisco, assault.*

San Francisco policeman J. F. Glennon shot a man named Willie Burke on the morning of September 26, 1888, in what was described as an unprovoked attack. Glennon was immediately arrested and held in lieu of $4,000 bail to await trial on a charge of assault to commit murder. On October 2, 1888, the Board of Police Commissioners dismissed Glennon from the city police force. At his trial it was alleged the assault took place while the cop was under the influence of liquor. On February 6, 1889, Glennon was found guilty of assault to commit murder.[56]

On February 9 ex-cop Glennon was sentenced to ten years at San Quentin for that assault to murder Burke. Glennon, it was claimed, while under the influence of liquor walked up to Burke and, after a remark or two, fired at him with his pistol. Burke's first impulse was to save himself and he made a dash at the drunken cop. In the effort to get the weapon away from him a struggle ensued in which the slight 17-year-old Burke was no match for a muscular 250-pound man. The result was that the officer got his victim down on the ground, shot him twice, and then beat him about the head with his weapon, completely destroying the hearing of one of Burke's ears, as well as leaving several gashes in the youth's head, in addition to the two bullet wounds.[57]

1888 October 27 [36] *Elkhart, Indiana, death.*

Joseph Barrett was a police officer in Elkhart, Indiana, who, on the afternoon of October 27, 1888, shot and instantly killed a brother officer named

William Burton. Barrett had been on the force for several years, but on the 26th his superior officer, Major Goldwaith, had reprimanded him for drunkenness. Later in the evening of the 27th, in a spirit of revenge, Barrett waylaid Goldwaith and gave him a severe beating. That day police officers attempted to arrest Barrett, but he resisted. During the scuffle he pulled his revolver and began shooting, with the second shot piercing the brain of Burton and with the following three shots wounding three bystanders. Barrett then took refuge in the saloon where he was under threat of being lynched by angry citizens until policemen managed to extract him. He was taken to the town of Goshen for safekeeping.[58]

Barrett stood trial six months later and in Elkhart on April 26, 1889, he was sentenced to three years in the penitentiary. Reportedly, there was considerable angry feeling about the sentence among the citizenry. Most strongly felt the sentence was far too lenient.[59]

1888 December 5 *[37] San Francisco, death.*

In San Francisco on the evening of December 5, 1888, William S. Thompson, a member of that city's police force, shot Christopher Rosenbrock, who died not long after being shot. Thompson was off duty at the time and described as being "filled with wine." He was walking along a street and stopped to talk with a prostitute. Then he dragged one of the brothel inmates out of a ground-floor window and began to beat her. One or two men intervened and came to the aid of the woman; one of them was Rosenbrock. A struggle ensued and the two men fell to the sidewalk, whereupon the cop pulled out his pistol and shot Rosenbrock in the stomach. Rosenbrock then arose and ran off, but Thompson followed and shot him twice more. As he was running away and before the fatal shots were fired Rosenbrock came upon two policemen and screamed for help, explaining that he had been shot by a man. At that point Thompson appeared from around the corner and shot his victim again. The two officers subdued and arrested Thompson. On December 9 the inquest into the death of Rosenbrock was held. The coroner's jury deliberated for about one hour before returning a verdict that charged Thompson with murder.[60]

The trial of the by then ex-cop William S. Thompson for the murder of Christopher Rosenbrock began before Judge Murphy on April 22, 1889. On May 12, after being convicted of murder, Thompson was sentenced to a term of ten years to be served at San Quentin Prison.[61]

1889 April? *[38] Washington, D.C., assault.*

In the criminal court in Washington, D.C., on July 4, 1889, the case of W. J. Rogers, a Washington policeman, was heard. He was charged with assault on a man named Roger McBride and the case that day was tried on an appeal from the police court, where a verdict of guilty was found. The assault had taken place "a few months" earlier. Once again Rogers was found guilty of the charge and the sentence was set the same as had been imposed earlier in police court. Rogers was fined $10.[62]

1889 May 17 [39] *Joliet, Illinois, death.*

A drunken man shot and seriously wounded a woman named Della Hart on the night of May 17, 1889, in Joliet, Illinois, as she was walking along the street. The man then ran off into a nearby railroad yard. By this time the police were on the scene and were in the railroad yard carefully searching the boxcars. As a freight train was pulling out, a man appeared at an open door of one of the cars and policeman Babb (black), believing the man in the doorway to be the wanted man, fired at him, killing him instantly. It was subsequently discovered that the dead man was not the wanted man, who remained at large. The dead man was William Hansen, a 17-year-old from Chicago. Hansen and a friend named Lewis Larsen (also in the train car) had left Chicago a day or so earlier and were heading to Oklahoma by hopping freight cars. The man who shot Hart was captured on the following day. Officer Babb (perhaps Bibb) was then under arrest.[63]

1889 October 21 [40] *New York City, death.*

Policeman Patrick T. Morris shot William F. Campbell in the saloon operated by John Campbell late on the night of Monday, October 21, 1889, in New York City. The next evening New York coroner Levy was summoned to the hospital to take an ante-mortem statement from Campbell. The fatally wounded man told Levy he knew of no trouble between himself and the policeman. Campbell added that he had been drinking to excess that night and did not know who shot him. The next thing he knew was when he awoke in the hospital. On the evening in question, he told the coroner, he had no quarrel with anyone before being shot.[64]

Ten days later Coroner Levy concluded his inquest into the death of William Campbell. Levy determined that Campbell went into the saloon and created a disturbance. Officer Morris was called in to arrest the man. Witness Edward O'Connor, a fireman, was in the bar at the time and testified that Campbell drew a revolver, whereupon Morris drew his revolver and told Campbell to put his weapon down or he would shoot him. Campbell put the gun down and then Morris arrested him and handed him over to Patrolman Moody. Morris then picked up Campbell's revolver and walked toward the end of the bar. He raised the revolver and it immediately discharged and Campbell fell to the floor. Other witnesses testified to the same effect, but none could say whether or not the shooting was accidental. Morris claimed he took the revolver intending to hand it to the barkeeper. As Morris was passing down the bar with the revolver in his hand he raised his arm to remove an obstruction and his revolver discharged. It was entirely accidental, said the cop. The coroner's jury rendered a verdict of accidental death, but Morris was taken to the Tombs lockup to await action by the grand jury.[65]

About two weeks after that, Morris stood trial before the Board of Police Commissioners. Morris told the same story as he had at the coroner's inquest. His tale was corroborated at this hearing by policeman Moody, to whom Morris had handed over his prisoner on that fateful night. Bartender Patrick Rice was on duty in the saloon at the time of the shooting and he told the police board that Campbell had his pistol on the counter behind the bar and that Morris reached around with a drawn club and revolver to get that pistol. Campbell met Morris at the end of the counter and was placed under arrest. He was then given to Moody to take charge of the prisoner. Continued Rice: "Morris got the revolver and when within three feet of the prisoner fired at him." One day earlier there was also activity that involved the police board. Captain Slevin asked that Morris be returned to duty, as he had been exonerated by the coroner. Police Superintendent Murray endorsed that recommendation but asked that Morris be transferred to another station. The board postponed any action on that request, as Morris was due to appear for a board trial on the following day.[66]

Morris went on trial in February 1890 for killing Campbell. However, the jury could not reach a verdict and was discharged on February 12, 1890, by Judge Cowing. They stood 11 votes for conviction on a charge of manslaughter and one vote for acquittal. As he awaited a second trial Morris remained free on $15,000 bail and he was reported to be much disconcerted at the action of the jury, as he expected to be acquitted. His defense remained that the shooting was accidental. On May 2, 1894, Judge Cowling dismissed the charge of murder against Morris on a motion made by Assistant District Attorney O'Hare.[67]

1889 October 21 [41] *New York City, assault.*

In the early-morning hours of October 21, 1889, in New York City a chase took place in which Patrolman Edward Walsh shot and wounded a "suspicious" character named John Coleman. The streets of the city were left in total darkness, according to a reporter, "by the suspension of electric lighting." An editorial comment stated: "It is a serious question whether the policeman who fired the bullet was justified in doing it.... His own explanation shows that he fired recklessly." He did not take aim and his object was to attract other cops. The man being chased was a prowler and wanted on suspicion. As the suspect seemed about to get away from the pursuing officer the latter yelled for the suspect to stop or be shot. He did not heed the command and was shot at. Reportedly the shot ricocheted off an elevated railroad pillar and struck the fleeing suspect. Walsh had been on the force for 20 years and was said to have an "excellent record." Walsh was suspended and arrested but was soon exonerated in the police court. On November 13, 1889, Police Superintendent Murray and Captain Siebert recommended to the police board that Edward Walsh be restored to duty, as he had been discharged in the police court. Police Commissioner Voorhis did not agree with the recommendation and said so at the meeting. Commissioner Martin remarked that Walsh had shot at a "suspicious person without justification" and had hit Coleman. By a unanimous vote of the police commissioners Edward Walsh was dismissed from the New York City police force.[68]

1889 November *[42] New York City, assault.*

On that November 13, 1889, day in New York City when the city's police board discussed the cases of Patrick Morris and Edward Walsh (as noted earlier) they also dismissed two other city policemen from the force for violent conduct. Officer James A. Costello, who clubbed Peter Mogin and Peter Seaman, was dismissed and so was Officer Henry Kayler, for handcuffing and clubbing an Italian fruit vendor.[69]

THREE

1890–1899

1890 January 20 *[43] Washington, D.C., assault.*

In the criminal court in Washington, D.C., on January 22, 1890, Judge Bingham had before him Richard L. Dean, a city policeman, who had been convicted on January 20 of an assault on a citizen. Dean's lawyer asked for a suspended sentence. Bingham said that, taking the officer's own evidence into account, he was guilty of an assault. That Dean had no good reason for throwing his baton at the boy and the injury might have been serious. However, in view of the recommendation for mercy from the jury and in light of the officer's "good standing" Bingham would impose a sentence of a fine of $10 and he would suspend that sentence during the officer's good behavior.[1]

Dean, however, soon returned to the attention of the justice system. A young black man by the name of Sam Hutchinson was before the police court on June 4, 1890, charged with disorderly conduct. Sam had been arrested a few weeks earlier by a policeman, Richard L. Dean, who had clubbed him. An "indignation meeting" was held at the Second Baptist Church in Washington and Hutchinson's trouble was on the program "for ventilation." Hutchinson had set out to attend that meeting, but policeman Grant had arrested him before he reached the church and locked him up on a charge of disorderly conduct. Judge Miller did not think the facts made out a case of disorderly conduct and dismissed the charge "with a little advice to Hutchinson to bring his cases of assault to court and not try them in the street."[2]

The trial of Officer Richard L. Dean, charged with assaulting Sam Hutchinson, began in police court on July 10. Sam testified that on May 24 he was standing on a street corner with a number of other people and a cop came up and spoke to one of them—a man named Simms. The policeman then walked past them but turned around and came back, whereupon Dean arrested Simms and Hutchinson. The pair were not doing anything at the time. The three started to walk toward the police station, but on the way Sam ran off, trying to escape. Dean chased him and fired two shots to frighten him. When Dean overtook Hutchinson he struck him on the back of his head with his pistol. They walked across the street when the officer struck him another blow with his pistol, this one over the eye. A third blow was delivered to his head and Hutchinson fell unconscious to the ground, A minister who witnessed the incident corroborated Sam's story and even added that the cop kicked Sam in the ribs when he was down on the ground and unconscious.[3]

Dean's trial finished on July 12. A reporter who covered the trial stated that the testimony for the prosecution was very conflicting, with witnesses contradicting one another: "The case was brought about by agitation among the colored people over an alleged brutal assault by Officer Dean on a prisoner named Samuel Hutchinson, whom he arrested for disorderly conduct. Hutchinson resisted arrest, broke away from the officer, and ran. When recaptured he attempted to assault the officer." Among those who testified were Bishop Johnson, the Rev. Dr. Gaines, Preacher Loanes, and a number of "other colored residents" of the neighborhood where the assault took place. "Many of the witnesses did not seem to understand that they were under oath, for each had a different and brutal story of the affray, and each located the various occurrences at different points," declared a journalist. Most of the differences in the testimony related to minor points such as whether the victim was struck two or three times by Dean's club, not whether Hutchinson was struck or not struck. Another example of a difference was whether the pair were in the middle of a specific block when the assault occurred or they were closer to the corner of the block. "The court-room was crowded, and prominent in the throng were the agitators who worked up the affair," added the reporter. In going over the case, Judge Miller said malice had to be shown and none had been shown and in his judgment the officer did not exceed his authority. Also, Miller said he could not find "one particle" that would justify a conviction. Dean was acquitted of the charge. Miller concluded that Dean had struck one blow and the only thing to be determined was whether it was justified and necessary to maintain the arrest. Judge Miller concluded by saying the case should have been taken to the police trial board (Internal Affairs) and should never have been brought to his court. Concluded the journalist: "Officer Dean, who is regarded as one of the best officers on the force, was the recipient of many congratulations at the finish of the trial." (Just as a victim was often demonized so was the villain often sanctified.)[4]

When the Law and Order League held a meeting at the Second Baptist Church on the evening of July 17, Sam Hutchinson was not, as usual, the hero of that gathering. As far as the league was concerned, he was the black who had sworn out the warrant against Dean and then did not testify to the facts as he had related them to the league. He was denounced by several members of the league at the meeting that night and Chairman Ruffin of the committee on grievances moved that the Dean-Hutchinson case be dropped by the league. That motion was adopted. It was true that Sam's testimony had changed somewhat. In court he stated that Dean had struck him only once, while when he spoke to the League members before the trial he spoke of being clubbed several times. (There were independent witnesses who testified to multiple blows being struck—but they were all black.) Each of the black clergymen at that meeting denounced Hutchinson as a bad man and the Reverend Johnson thought he had probably been bought. Perhaps, or threatened by the police into changing his testimony. Sam had been picked up for no reason whatsoever before the trial to prevent him from attending an indignation meeting. He, of course, did not make that meeting and he was not released from custody until the next morning. What happened to him during 12 hours or so of false custody? In any event, the whole affair was another example of demonizing the victim with the victim being shunned in the end and all attention diverted from the assaulting cop.[5]

1890 June 18 [44] New York City, assault.

New York City police officer George B. Bourne was arraigned in the Yorkville Police Court on the morning of June 21, 1890, on a charge of attempting to assault 15-year-old Jennie Tanfie (perhaps Mamie Teaffe). The girl was being held in a cell of the police station to which Bourne was attached. She was in a cell there because her parents complained that the girl was "incorrigible." Jennie was arrested on the night of June 17 and lodged in a cell. Early on the morning of June 18, she alleged, Bourne visited her cell on some pretense and attempted to assault her. She cried out in alarm and Bourne left the cell. Later on June 18 she was committed to the care of a child welfare agency and it was to that agency that she told the story of her treatment at the hands of Bourne. While he denied the charge, Bourne admitted that he had gone into the girl's cell, but he said it was only to make her comfortable. He was held for trial.[6]

When he appeared in criminal court before Judge Martins on July 8, Bourne pled guilty to assault in the third degree with respect to his attempt to "outrage" the child. The official charge under which Jennie was held was that of disorderly conduct. Martins told the prisoner that he would impose the heaviest sentence possible "and that it would be of no use for Bourne's companions on the force to try to get the sentence alleviated." Martins sentenced Bourne to pay a fine of $250 and to be imprisoned for a term of one year.[7]

1890 September 30 *[45] Boston, death.*

When policeman Thomas F. Kearney, of the Boston police force, was patrolling Winthrop Street about 10:00 p.m. on September 30, 1890, he heard someone prowling in the rear of the house occupied by Mrs. Eliza J. Laws and proceeded to investigate. As Kearney entered the yard he saw indistinctly the forms of two people who fled as he approached. He called upon them to stop but was not obeyed. He then drew his gun and fired, into the air, he said, to frighten them. His bullet killed 11-year-old John Davenport. The child's companion was 15-year-old L. F. Green, who was found soon thereafter. Green said the two boys were stealing grapes in the yard when they were surprised by the policeman.[8]

A coroner's inquest was held into the child's death on October 9 and 10. Judge Bolster reported on that inquest and observed that the verdict was that the death of Davenport was caused by a pistol shot delivered by Kearney. Bolster declared, "From all the evidence I am unable to find any justification for the firing of the pistol, and I cannot see any reason for the firing of the pistol at that time. I think said Davenport came to his death by an unlawful act committed by Thomas F. Kearney.[9]

Kearney was charged with manslaughter and his trial began on December 29, 1890. The officer pled not guilty. With respect to his appearance and demeanor a journalist remarked: "His general appearance was that of a man who had suffered much mentally and feared somewhat for the future. There was nothing of the braggart about him, and it is needless to say he would be one of the last men a criminal taker would pick out from a crowd as a law breaker." Kearney's story on the stand was the same one he had told earlier: that he fired a warning shot into the air but somehow hit and killed the child. Green, on the stand, insisted the cop had come within ten or so feet of them and then fired directly at them. With respect to his performance on a stand a reporter commented that the cop gave way to tears as he testified and that "has won for him more public sympathy than he could otherwise have hoped to gain" and "No doubt his emotions and distressing situation have not been without their effect upon the jury."[10]

The jury deliberated for 19 hours before it returned a verdict of not guilty of manslaughter, on January 3, 1891. Kearney had faced a second charge at that trial, that of "wanton and gross negligence in using his pistol." On that charge the jury could not reach a verdict—it was hung. He was not tried again on that count. Kearney had never been suspended from duty (which would have been unpaid time) but rather was given a leave of absence pending the trial and its outcome. Speculation was that the officer would be fully paid for the time he was on leave. One more problem remained for him. On January 5, 1891, he had to appear before the Board of Police Commissioners to answer charges with reference to the violation of the rules of the police manual that pertained to the use of weapons. Under the cop's own admission in court during his trial he had violated those rules and quite possibly could have been dismissed from the force. However, in the morning of January 5 Thomas Kearney tendered his resignation, to take effect immediately. It was accepted by the commissioners.[11]

1890 October 15 *[46] Chicago, death.*

On the morning of October 15, 1890, in Chicago Officer Thomas Madden of that city's police department shot and killed brother officer Albert Junge, allegedly for reporting him for drinking while on duty. The men had patrolled adjoining beats and there had been bad blood between them for some time. At roll call in the evening of October 14 Lieutenant Kane summoned the pair before him and questioned them as to what the trouble was between them. Madden refused to answer his superior's question and instead took off his badge and club and threw them on the floor, saying he would resign, and then left the station muttering threats against Junge. Around 3:00 a.m. on October 15 while Junge was on patrol in his area Madden came up and fired three shots at him. Then Madden walked away. Another report related that a few nights before the shooting the pair had a violent quarrel and Junge reported Madden for drinking while on duty. When Madden refused to answer his superior on the previous evening he was informed, before he stomped out, that his behavior would bring him before the police trial board of commissioners. After stomping out of his station and before shooting his fellow policeman, Madden was seen drinking in several saloons. Other officers at the station house said the pair had first quarreled about religious matters. Madden accused Junge of being a member of the United Order of Deputies, which was an anti–Catholic society, while Junge retorted that Madden was a Clan na Gael man, which was an Irish republican organization. Out of this, the other officers said, the trouble grew. Several days after the killing Madden had still not been located.[12]

1890 December *[47] Pittsburgh, assault.*

Pittsburgh policemen Edward Cross and Michael Hanley pled guilty in court on December 10, 1890, to assault and battery on Hugh McClure. The plea was afterward withdrawn and the case went to trial. The officers, it was alleged, beat McClure with their clubs while arresting him for not "moving on" when told to do so on the street. Both men were found guilty. In criminal court on December 20 Judge Stowe sentenced a number of convicted prisoners. One of them was Edward Cross, upon whom Stowe imposed a sentence of a fine of $100 and a 30-day term in the workhouse. Another cop appeared for sentencing with Cross. W. J. McDonough was charged and convicted on an offense similar to that of Cross and was sentenced to a term of four months. According to the reporter, "Judge Stowe was very emphatic in his denunciation of unnecessary beating of prisoners with clubs, which he thought was too common." Added the journalist: "Assistant City Attorney Burleigh stated that out of 16,000 arrests in the past year, but 12 cases of this kind had come into court, and these two convictions were the only ones terminating in this way."[13]

Apparently none of that chastising had any effect on Cross, because less than two years later he was in trouble again for the same offense. On the night of February 27, 1892, Cross placed William Hickey under arrest and because he, reportedly, offered some resistance, the officer attacked him with his club and "beat him in a terrible manner." One week later Hickey was still confined to bed because of the injuries he sustained during that beating. Information charging aggravated assault and battery was lodged against the Pittsburgh policeman and a warrant was issued for his arrest. In the meantime Cross was suspended by Police Superintendent O'Mara for too-free use of his mace. In July 1892 Cross was convicted of assault on William Hickey and was fined six cents and costs.[14]

1890 December 23 *[48] New York City, assault.*

Policeman John Holsworth of the New York City Police Department was arraigned before Justice Walsh on December 24, 1890, charged with assault with a pistol upon his fellow policeman Joseph Riley, whom he blazed away at on December 23 in the afternoon in a saloon in New York. Riley told the court he saw his fellow cop was drinking too much and gave him "friendly advice" to stop. Holsworth called him names and Riley then struck Holsworth, who then fired seven shots, one of which hit Riley in the hip. Riley managed to run out of the saloon and escape. Holsworth then put his revolver away and went to his mother's house, where he was arrested shortly afterward. Riley swore out a complaint on December 24 charging Holsworth with assault. The latter pled not guilty and was committed to jail in default of $1,500 bail. Riley was in the bar in civilian clothes and had been drinking with policeman Madigan, also in civilian clothes. Holsworth came in, wearing his uniform, and, according to the bartender, after taking two drinks pulled out his pistol and started firing at Riley. Holsworth said that he had a row with Riley, who had "smashed him in the mouth," whereupon he had drawn his gun and fired. Reportedly, Holsworth had been on the force for four years and had a good reputation.[15]

When Holsworth appeared on court on January 30, 1891, charged with assault in the second degree the policeman pled guilty. Judge Moore sent him to the penitentiary for a term of two years.[16]

1891 January 1 *[49] New York City, death.*

On January 9, 1891, New York City Coroner Levy ordered city policeman William Smith of the 29th Precinct to be placed under arrest on suspicion of having killed his wife, Mary. It was alleged that on January 1 the couple argued and the cop gave his wife a "brutal beating." That beating was so severe that day by day her medical condition grew worse. Police officials sent Coroner Levy to go immediately to her residence to take her ante-mortem statement. However, by the time he got there she was already dead—passing way at around 1:00 p.m. on January 9. Smith and his wife were each 34 years old. He had been on the force for about six years. William Smith was placed in the lockup to await the inquest into Mary Smith's death.[17]

In April of that year Smith went on trial for manslaughter before Judge Barrett and a jury. It had been ascertained that Mary was beaten to death with Smith's nightstick. One of those who testified was the couple's eight-year-old son, Johnnie Smith. Judge Barrett ruled the child was competent to testify after questioning him and hearing him say, among other answers, that if he told a lie he would go to hell and if he told the truth he would go to heaven. Johnnie testified that at about 9:00 p.m. on New Year's Eve he and his mother went to a saloon where his father was drinking. His mother asked for money when his father came outside from the saloon, but his only reply was to hit her in the face. Then they walked along the street for a bit and then Johnnie's father drew his club and struck his mother on the head. She did not scream but went home, put a cloth on her head and lay down. The official cause of death was listed as tetanus caused by the wounds on her head. No other witnesses testified to the clubbing. Dr. Charles E. Phillips, for the prosecution, was allowed by Barrett to tell the jury what Mary Smith said just before she died. Phillips said he asked her if her husband had clubbed her. At first she refused to answer, but then she said, "Yes." Phillips asked her where and she put her hand on her head. She also told the doctor that she had been well before the assault.[18]

When Smith took the stand at his trial he said he never struck his wife with his club or with his fist because he "had no need to." He also declared his son was not with him and his wife on the night in question. He denied telling anyone he had given his wife a slap. When he met Mary that evening he said she was "under the influence [of liquor] a bit."[19]

On December 31 Smith had been drinking in that bar with two companions. One was a man named Gillespie, who at the trial refused to say what his business was at that time because it was illegal, and a woman by the name of Mrs. Stewart, with whom Smith was said to have been infatuated. Mary Smith called her husband out of the bar and when he returned a few minutes later to his companions he said he had given her "a slap on the jaw that would keep her from troubling him anymore." The jury was out for less than 30 minutes of deliberations before returning with a verdict of guilty of manslaughter in the first degree. That conviction carried a sentence in the penitentiary of from five to 20 years.[20]

Later in April 1891 the Board of Police Commissioners dismissed him from the force. In May Smith was sentenced to 11 years and six months in the state prison. On application of Smith's lawyer, Judge Barrett granted a stay pending an appeal. On June 19, 1891, Judge Barrett vacated the temporary stay granted to William Smith. The ex-cop was then set to go to prison.[21]

1891 April 13 *[50] Pittsburgh, death.*

Giuseppe Manzello went out of his house in Pittsburgh to kill a little time while waiting for his supper but was clubbed by a black police officer and was taken to a hospital where he died some days after the clubbing. The officer involved was under arrest. Manzello was 40 years old and came to the United States from Italy with his sister Maria two years earlier and went to Mahoning, Pennsylvania, to settle. He obtained employment there as a laborer and hoped to save up some money and return to live in his native city of Naples. Maria was employed as a domestic. Both saved as much as they could and were nearing their goal of having enough money to live in Naples in some comfort when Manzello suddenly became unemployed. He moved to Pittsburgh about three weeks before he was assaulted and rented a room in Angelo Sabill's boardinghouse. On the afternoon of April 13, 1891, Manzello went out for that fatal walk before his evening meal. He ran into a dozen or so of his countrymen standing on the sidewalk talking; he joined their conversation. Then Pittsburgh policeman Matthew Bell came up to them and ordered them to move on. The men understood English imperfectly and hesitated. Bell called upon fellow officers Robert Bagley and Charles Allen (these two were also black) and proceeded to arrest the crowd. The patrol wagon was sent for and 11 men were taken to the central station. One of them was Manzello. In the morning they each paid a small fine and were released. Later in the day on April 14 Manzello went to the office of Dr. Jacobs to have a wound on the back of his head attended to. Jacobs saw that the scalp was cut but was unable then to determine if the skull was fractured. On the next day Manzello's mind began to wander and it was at once seen that he needed medical treatment. A number of his countrymen joined together and raised $20 to send him to a hospital where it was found that his skull was fractured. When he had seen Jacobs the day before Manzello told the physician that a tall black patrolman had pounded him over the head with his mace. Manzello lingered and died in that hospital on April 23, with erysipelas (acute bacterial infection) being listed as the cause of death.[22]

As soon as the death of Manzello was reported the Pittsburgh coroner began an investigation and found ten Italian men who each claimed to have seen the assault. At once the coroner notified the police to go and arrest Bell. However, when Bell heard he was wanted he surrendered himself. Five of the Italians positively identified Bell as the cop who clubbed Manzello. Bell claimed that he did not use his mace on the night of the arrest and he further stated he did not arrest Manzello at all. He said he was assisted in the arrest by Officers Allen and Bagley and did not know if they clubbed any of the men or not, but he insisted he had clubbed nobody. Some of the Italian witnesses said there were only two officers present for the arrest, while the others corroborated Bell's statement that three cops were present. The coroner had decided he would not ask for the arrest of the other policemen unless there were new developments in the case. Bell had been a member of the Pittsburgh police force off and on for several years, a situation that was also true for Bagley. Allen was described as a "new man" on the force. Allen and Bell were suspended from the force on April 21 by Inspector McAleese for clubbing a black man whom they arrested for shooting at another man, on the street, on April 20.[23] A day or so later Bell was in jail charged with the murder of Manzello and a coroner's jury was dealing with the case. Jacobs declared the victim's death was due to the wound on his head. One Italian witness stated he saw Manzello come out of a store and Bell hit him on the head. Another Italian said he saw Bell hit Manzello with his club when the latter was doing nothing. A non–Italian witness by the name of William Shoulmann said he saw Manzello standing between two men when Bell came up, remarking that there was no use fooling with such people, and hit him with his mace. Officer Bagley was present, but he declared he did not see Bell hit anybody. The coroner's jury returned a verdict of death due to a wound on the head inflicted by policeman Bell.[24]

On June 6, 1891, the grand jury returned a true bill against Matthew Bell and he was indicted for involuntary manslaughter for the killing of Giuseppe Manzello. A week later the grand jury returned a true bill against Robert Bagley for aggravated assault and battery (a separate case from Manzello's). Bagley was later tried and convicted of assault and battery on James Jones, an assault by Bagley with his club upon the man after he had arrested him. On October 4, 1891, Bagley was sentenced to 90 days in the workhouse.[25]

The trial of Bell began on July 15, 1891. After the doctors testified, said a reporter, "then a number of witnesses were put on the stand, who mixed things up in a woeful manner." Some of them testified Bell ran up and hit Manzello when two other officers had hold of him. Others testified no other officers were at the scene. Some testified Manzello struggled and refused to be arrested, while others said he did not struggle "and altogether the Italians contradicted each other in the most glaring manner."[26]

In his summation speech on July 16 the lawyer for Bell said that his client struck the blow with his club when he was "in great peril of his own life. Three policemen testified to Bell's good character." Inspector McAleese stated it was the duty of all officers to carry their maces in their hands and a failure to do so meant suspension. Bagley testified that he saw Manzello resist arrest but did not see any blow struck. Bagley also claimed he took a knife from Manzello at the lockup. That knife was produced in court and, said a reporter, "it was an ugly looking weapon." Sergeant Cochran, present at the lockup on April 13 when the 11 Italians were brought in, testified he took a knife from one of the Italian prisoners but could not remember if it was Manzello or not. When Bell testified he said that on the night in question a citizen had complained that he could not cross the pavement because of a crowd of Italians. Bell went there and ordered them to move on, but they refused. He said he arrested one man who resisted and he hit that man "lightly" on the head with his mace. Bell admitted the man he hit did not have a knife in his hand "but seemed to be trying to get one out." When he was cross-examined Bell admitted to being "in trouble once or twice" with respect to his police service. On July 16 Bell was acquitted on a charge of murder after the jury deliberated for just 30 minutes. However, he was still in jail, having a charge of involuntary manslaughter to answer to.[27]

That case for involuntary manslaughter was called to the bar on July 20. When Bell appeared, District Attorney Burleigh addressed the court and stated that inasmuch as Bell had been acquitted of murder and the evidence adduced showed that he was merely acting in the line of duty as a police officer he would ask that the charge of involuntary manslaughter not be prosecuted. That motion was allowed by Judge Slagle and the prisoner was discharged.[28]

One of those times that Bell was trouble appeared to have taken place in August 1890. Bell then faced a charge of assault and battery upon Ross Morrison, who had sworn out an affidavit regarding the alleged assault. Morrison said Bell had arrested him without a warrant and then the policeman used his club on Morrison. On the evening of August 8 Bell was given a hearing, with the policeman being exonerated.[29]

1891 July 13 *[51] Jersey City, New Jersey, death.*

On Sunday evening, July 12, 1891, Mary Boulger, a niece of William Brennan, was married to Charles Wilson. After the ceremony they went to Brennan's house to celebrate. Other people arrived to join the party and it soon became noisy enough that neighbors were annoyed. Then a fight broke out between two of the people at the party. Jersey City policeman John Ryerson was called in to quell the disturbance. The moment Brennan saw Ryerson attempt to arrest John Lawless (one of the fighters) he went to his rescue. Ryerson broke away from Brennan to chase Lawless into the house. In the kitchen the policeman was overtaken by Brennan again. Two men held him while Mrs. Elizabeth (Lizzie) Brennan hit him. Brennan had once been arrested by Ryerson on an assault charge and kept shouting that now that he had the opportunity he intended to kill him. Ryerson was finally beaten to the floor, whereupon all three, reportedly, began to kick him, while Mrs. Brennan grabbed his throat with her fingers. Ryerson finally freed himself and managed to draw his pistol. He shot twice, hitting Brennan, but the crowd was still at him; he fired for a second time and hit Mrs. Brennan, at which the crowd was said to have scattered. Brennan and his wife, Lizzie, both died from their gunshot wounds. There were some contradictions in the story, as doctors thought Lizzie must have been lying on the floor when she was shot. Brennan had been in the custody of the police several times, it was said, for crimes of violence, once for beating his wife. Ryerson was then in custody.[30]

Other newspapers were quick to accept the theme of the preceding story, whether true or not. One paper stated that Ryerson claimed he had to use his pistol to save his own life while the tragedy came "out of a murderous assault by Brennan on the policeman who killed him. Mrs. Brennan also took part in the assault upon Ryerson." Another newspaper noted that the Brennans often appeared in police court and "were quarrelsome and violent." However, it was admitted that the couple were "not improvident" and their five young children were not left destitute. The couple had a comfortable two-story house and owned it free of a mortgage. They also had money in the bank.[31]

William and Elizabeth Brennan were buried on July 17. Relatives had intended to bury them in a Catholic cemetery but officials of the Catholic Church refused to allow any services in their churches and denied permission to bury them in a Catholic cemetery. Noted a journalist; "This was because the ill-fated couple had neglected their religious duties; had not lived up to the rules of the church, and therefore could not be buried in consecrated ground." They were buried in a Protestant cemetery.[32]

When the inquest was held in the deaths of the couple John Lawless (the other fighter) testified that Ryerson did not fire shots while on the floor, as he said, but that he was on his feet during the entire fight.[33]

1892 January [52] Paris, Tennessee, death.

According to this very brief report that appeared in newspapers at the end of January 1892, Bob Nelson, a policeman from Paris, Tennessee, killed Doc Alexander, who was drunk and resisting arrest: "This is Nelson's fourth killing."[34]

1893 June 16 [53] San Francisco, assault.

An assault took place in San Francisco on June 16, 1893, when Dennis Daly insulted a niece of city policeman Edgar B. Harper. In response to that slur Harper slapped Daly in the face. A month later Harper was tried and convicted of the offense of battery upon Daly, although the jury, after finding him guilty, recommended him to the mercy of the court. On July 18 Judge Low sentenced Harper to pay a fine of $20 or be imprisoned for 20 days.[35]

1893 November 22 [54] Washington, D.C., death.

Around 3:40 a.m. on November 22, 1893, in Washington, D.C., two policemen in civilian clothes were walking their beat. They, and other officers in the city, were on special alert for an attacker who had been plaguing the area in recent times, a man who had been dubbed "Jack the Slasher." At that time policeman Charles B. Terry (one of the two) spotted what he believed to be a suspicious character. He fired at the figure and wounded a 19-year-old black man named Willis Washington who was on his way to work. When Terry reached the wounded man Washington said to him, "I ain't done nothin', boss. I was on my way to work." It was reported that Washington had a good reputation, being described as hardworking, honest, industrious, and so forth. The landlady at the house where he had roomed for over a year explained that he was in the habit of leaving the house at around 4:00 a.m. to head for work. First he went to his brother's house, where he got his breakfast and a packed lunch from his sister-in-law, and then he proceeded to work from there. He left somewhat earlier than usual that morning (he was shot a few hundred feet from where he lived) because the clock in the house was fast. Terry had been a member of the force for "a few months." During that time he was tried in the police court on a charge of shooting at a black man and also figured in the arrest of a man named Meany "whom he clubbed."[36]

A day later a newspaper account explained that Terry had been on trial just a few weeks earlier on a charge of using his pistol while in pursuit of a black man, charged with a misdemeanor. Judge Miller held Terry guilty of the charge. In dealing with that case the judge laid down the law concerning the use of the pistol by policemen and commented on the case in question. He gave the officer a warning and said he hoped others would profit by what he said. When a man named Dye had been Washington police chief he issued an order to members of the force calling their attention to the use of their pistols. The order was intended to serve as a warning against the improper use of the weapons and not many months earlier police major Moore had issued his own order calling the attention of the officers to the order issued by Dye.[37]

Terry had been suspended from duty at the time of the shooting and had been held in custody. On December 18, 1893, he posted bail in the amount of $3,000 and was released. He had been suspended without pay from December 1 and would continue to be so suspended until further notice.[38]

Terry came to trial in May 1894. At the time of the shooting Terry had arrested Washington on the street and, said the cop, Washington became frightened and started to run away. At that point Terry fired at him, wounding him in the back. Terry was held in custody for as long as he was as the authorities awaited the outcome of the victim's injuries. When it seemed apparent that Washington would survive those injuries Terry was subsequently released on bail to answer a charge of assault with intent to kill.[39]

When the trial began on May 22, 1894, Washington had to be brought into court on a stretcher in order to testify. He had been hospitalized for the entire time from the shooting and had been in chronic and intense pain. Policeman William Steurman, who was with Terry at the time of the shooting (he was the other officer in civilian clothes), said that they opened their coats to show Washington their badges and also ordered him to stop. Washington, Steurman said, started off on a run. He and Terry ran after him with Terry being in front. The latter fired his gun twice, with Washington falling at the second shot. A police official testified he had ordered his men to be diligent during the "Jack the Slasher" scare. Terry also took the stand and testified that he and his partner regarded Washington's appearance and actions as suspicious at that early time of the morning and they showed him their badges. Washington was told to halt, but he ran. Terry explained that his shot had been not at the man but into the air, as a warning. He added that after that he fell and that in falling his pistol was accidentally discharged. It was that shot, he claimed, that hit Washington. (In all the early accounts of the shooting no mention had ever been made of Terry "falling" and his pistol accidentally discharging.) In his charge to the jury Judge McComas declared peace officers must be supported by the courts in the discharge of their duty, "but officers of the peace should understand that it is not their duty to shoot a person they seek to arrest if he only fails to halt when commanded. It is their duty to use such means to secure a prisoner as will enable officers to take a prisoner into custody without resorting to the use of firearms, and officers will not be excused for using dangerous weapons in any case where, with diligence, discretion and caution, the prisoner could otherwise be taken." The judge went on to add; "The officer has the right to arrest, without warrant, any one he suspects to be guilty of a felony; if, however, he uses more force than is necessary, he is guilty of an assault. An arrest, not unlawful in itself, may be performed in a manner so criminal and improper as to make the officer who, in the prosecution of his purpose, causes the death of another person, guilty of murder, or, if without malice, of manslaughter only." The jury in the Terry trial deliberated for just 30 minutes before returning a verdict of guilty as charged. The penalty for the offense was not less than two years in prison and not more than eight years. Bail was not allowed and Terry was remanded to custody.[40]

On June 9, 1894, Judge McComas sentenced Terry to three years in the penitentiary at hard labor. A motion for a new trial was denied. An appeal was filed that would not be heard for at least six months and in the meantime the cop would remain in custody. That three-year sentence was to run from the day of imposition, instead of the more usual day of arrival at the penitentiary. Thus the number of months Terry spent in the local lockup waiting for his appeal would count as part of his three years; usually it did not. With added time off for good behavior it could mean only two years to serve in the penitentiary.[41]

On October 8, 1894, Willis Washington died from the effects of the bullet wound he had received close to a year earlier. His spinal cord had been damaged and for a while doctors initially thought the wound would be fatal. But Washington recovered enough to go home; however, he was paralyzed for life and it was felt to be not improbable that death would ensue as a result of the injury in a relatively short period of time. Meanwhile, before the death of Washington the Court of Appeals had dismissed Terry's appeal. Because the law did not preclude Terry from being charged with homicide or manslaughter in this case, since the victim of his assault had finally died, there was speculation Terry would be called to the bar to answer new charges. Terry then appeared before a coroner's jury in October, where the jury ruled that Washington's death was not a result of the pistol shot but from edema of the lungs. So there would be no second trial and Terry was returned to jail. In February 1897 it was reported that U.S. president Grover Cleveland had granted a pardon to by then ex-cop Charles Terry, who had "recently served" a term for killing Washington.[42]

1893 December 9 *[55] Crookston, Minnesota, death.*

On the evening of December 8, 1893, Andrew Thompson was arrested in Crookston, Minnesota, for drunkenness and lodged in the police station. Later that evening he managed to escape from jail and policeman Tweeton found him at the train station at 2:00 a.m. The officer tried to arrest Thompson and scuffled with him. Reportedly, the cop was overpowered and when he was underneath the man pulled out his gun and shot Thompson in the left temple. He died almost immediately. Tweeton gave himself up. Several witnesses were in the area of the train station and their stories were said not to have differed materially from the events related by Tweeton. At the inquest into the death, which took place on the afternoon of December 9, the coroner's jury returned a verdict that Thompson was resisting arrest and that the shooting was done in self-defense. The officer was released from jail on habeas corpus proceedings. However, when the case went to the grand jury on December 12 that body indicted the officer for manslaughter in the first degree. Tweeton was at once arrested but almost immediately thereafter released on bonds.[43]

1893 December 25 *[56] Chicago, death.*

Two Chicago policemen spent Christmas of 1893 locked up in a cell. Inspector Laughlin ordered the arrest of Thomas J. Moran and Michael J. Healy pending an investigation into the killing of Samuel Nelson. At about 3:00 a.m. on December 25 the two officers were standing in front of a saloon when Nelson invited them inside and they accepted a cigar each, for which Nelson paid. The pair then went outside to make their hourly report and when they were finished they returned to the saloon. Once inside they learned that the proprietor had thrown Nelson out of the place. All four of those men then got into a dispute. Nelson struck Healy, knocking him down. Moran arrested Nelson and by that time Healy was on his feet and the three headed outside toward the police call box. Nelson dropped to the ground and refused to go any farther. The arrival of the patrol wagon was heard and Nelson then suddenly jumped to his feet and ran off. Healy order him to halt, but he refused to obey the command. Healy then fired four shots at the man, with one of them hitting him in the back. Nelson died at the hospital according to the New York *Sun*.[44]

On February 9, 1895, Thomas J. Moran and Michael J. Healy were found guilty of manslaughter and each was sentenced to a term of 14 years in the penitentiary. At that trial it was related that Nelson had been celebrating Christmas most of the night, starting on December 24, and when he started off for his house he met the two cops and with them entered a saloon for the purpose of getting a drink. The three men had several drinks and one of the officers insisted

Nelson buy more. When he refused to buy more drinks he was placed under arrest by one of the officers, both of whom were under the influence of liquor by then. Nelson broke away and ran toward his house, followed by both cops, who were firing their weapons at him. One of the shots struck him and wounded him fatally, but not before he managed to take shelter under a house. Healy dragged him out from his hiding place and Nelson died in the patrol wagon while being conveyed to the county hospital according to the *St. Paul Globe*. The case was brought before the Chicago grand jury of January 1894, but no bill was returned. That outcome so angered the Scandinavian community in the area that a determined effort was made to bring the case to trial. On the second time before the grand jury an indictment was returned and the Scandinavian societies spent much time and money in working up evidence against the two officers, who had, the Scandinavians believed, murdered Nelson.[45]

1894 August 8 *[57] New York City, assault.*

In September 1894, New York City waiter Thomas J. Stanton, through his lawyer Cornelius O'Connor, brought suit against city policeman Conrad Schellenburger attached to the Eldridge Street station for $10,000 in damages for an alleged assault. Stanton alleged that Schellenburger attacked him on the night of August 8 on the Bowery. The beating he received was so brutal, he alleged, that he was in a hospital for three weeks before he recovered. Lawyer O'Connor stated that he would not be content with the civil suit but would endeavor to have the cop criminally indicted for assault.[46]

1894 October *[58] New York City, assault.*

Much of the internal workings of the New York City Police Department and its internal affairs structure (trial before the Board of Police Commissioners) was revealed at the beginning of October 1894 during an investigation into the corruption and malfeasance in that department. The Lexow Committee had as its chief counsel Recorder-elect John W. Goff. He had subpoenaed all the members of the force who had been convicted of clubbing citizens in the previous three years and who still retained their places on the "Finest." Lawyer Frank Moss was a colleague of Goff and another member of the Lexow Committee. Moss said there were 90 or more such men on the NYPD and they were all sitting in the courtroom that morning. Said Moss, "We think we have every clubber on the force here this morning and we propose to have some fun with them. At least, we shall try to find out how it is they have managed to keep their places on the force after they have been convicted, some of them several times, of outrageous brutality towards helpless citizens." He continued, "The police records show that during the last three years only four men have been dismissed for clubbing, although, as I say, more than ninety have been convicted of this offense before the Police Commissioners and of these four, three were charged with clubbing other policemen." A journalist remarked: "The 'fanning' brigade, as it may properly be called for the New York policeman never clubs a citizen, he simple 'fans' him, represented every precinct in the city." So many were present in the courtroom on that October morning that there were not enough seats and the overflow had to be accommodated in the corridor. That reporter thought they looked no different from other policemen. Before committee chairman Lexow called the committee to order at 11:00 a.m. the few spectators who had found their way earlier in the morning into the courtroom had been put out of the room to "make room for the clubbers, and the brigade of bluecoats and brass buttons had every seat in the place to itself."[47]

The journalist also remarked that Goff said he wanted to show the attitude of the police to the citizens of New York City "as disturbers and breakers of the peace and as dangerous to the lives and safety of the citizens. To do this he would show the number of accusations of assault upon citizens by the police and the number of convictions under such charges." He also planned to show by evidence of witnesses and records of the police department that "to all intents and purposes the police force of New York was exempted from the operation of the law of the land." Goff declared, "These men can commit felonies and misdemeanors, and have done so for years and have gone unpunished. If a civilian

Sketch of a "band of clubbers" as all of the NYPD officers who had clubbed unarmed citizens were called to a hearing on the same day. There were enough of them to fill a courtroom.

had committed these crimes his punishment would have been State prison." He continued, "In other words, the operation of the law which applies to ordinary citizens stops short when it comes to the police force. A police officer can brain a citizen, and all that he has to fear is a trial before the Police Commissioners, and possibly the payment of the sum of $30." Goff declared, in addition, "We propose to show that in the trials of the police before the Police Commissioners, the perjury committed by members of the force and their witnesses, is unmeasurable and unparalleled. The air of the trial-room at Police Headquarters is blue with perjury, whenever these so-called trials are going on there." At that point Goff called Moss to the stand and went into the history of the early efforts of the Society for the Prevention of Crime and the Business Men's Organization, of which he had been a member, to purify the Tenderloin Precinct of New York in the days of Captain Williams (then Inspector)—a notoriously corrupt cop. That step was reportedly recognized as the beginning of the campaign that the committee had long threatened to inaugurate against the higher officials of the New York City Police Department.[48]

Leading the charge on the NYPD clubbers was a lawyer named Frank Moss. Of course, this hearing was mostly political theater with politicians trying to score political points. Nothing happened that would actually reduce the number of clubbing cops.

That New York State Senate investigating committee (the Lexow Committee) continued its work of probing corruption in the NYPD on the following day. In attendance in the courtroom were again close to 100 policemen from the force, including one or two captains and several sergeants. One officer called to the stand was Thomas Coleman. Goff then proceeded to read out his record of the 16 trials he had been subjected to by the Police Commissions and the 15 convictions registered at those trials. They were trials for drunkenness "and for smashing a man over the head with a beer pitcher." Much of the hearings was devoted to other corruption that the force engaged in, mainly involving brothels and gambling houses and the tendency of cops to lie for one another in "large conspiracies and collusions." Goff then read out the records of two specific cases that involved Coleman; the cases of John Casey and Henry Ott. In the one case Coleman was fined 20 days' pay and in the other he was fined seven days' pay. Those convictions before the police trial board were both for clubbing those citizens. Ott was the citizen hit by Coleman with the beer pitcher. "And poor Casey you knocked down and felled like an ox?" asked Goff. Said Coleman, "No, he was down when I struck him." In addition to those two cases of assault (he was convicted in both instances) there were other assault charges against Coleman. On January 12, 1892, there were two. One was an assault on John Kiely and the other on Mamie Cox. When the 15-year-old girl was walking with her father Coleman knocked her down and blood flowed from her head. "And you were fined thirty days' pay for that?" asked Goff. "No, I was only fined for drunkenness," replied Coleman. When Goff was finished questioning Coleman he said to the man, "We will excuse you now, Officer, in order that you may go back and resume your brilliant and meritorious career on the police force of this great city." A reporter concluded that as soon as Coleman left the stand he took on the same arrogance as his peers in the courtroom: "No sooner had he left the stand than the frightened look left his face, and he became at once the same fellow who knocked down little Mamie Cox and smashed the pitcher over Henry Ott's head. The scathing exposure of the manner of man he is which Mr. Goff so skillfully brought out seemed to have no more effect on this peculiar product of American political conditions than water upon the back of a duck."[49]

Moss took the stand himself to tell of the discoveries he made when he conducted an examination of police trials that had taken place at headquarters. He investigated trials that had taken place since January 1, 1891, a period of slightly less than four years. Of the officers on trial before the commissioners 109 had been accused of criminal offenses and 92 of those policemen were still on the force. A few had resigned or retired. Only four were dismissed from the force. Among the offenses charged were 56 assaults in the third degree and 45 assaults in the second degree. No fewer than 66 of the accused policemen had been found guilty and fined by the commissioners, with the fines ranging from two days' pay to 30 days' pay. In nearly all the cases the accused officers had denied their guilt under oath, but there was no record to show that any of them had been prosecuted for perjury. One of the cases involved Officer John J. Barnes, who had been charged with handling his revolver carelessly and causing the death of a citizen. Barnes had been examined by a coroner who had decided that the shooting was accidental, but the commissioners had fined Barnes ten days' pay. Moss then read from the official record of Police Inspector Alexander S. Williams. On August 3, 1866, he was appointed as a patrolman. On February 29, 1867, he was absent from his post and reprimanded. On June 29, 1870, he was absent from the roll call and fined two days' pay. On September 15, 1870, he was absent from his post, but the complaint was dismissed. On July 10, 1871, he was promoted to the position of roundsman. On September 23, 1871, he was promoted to the position of sergeant. On May 21, 1873, he was promoted to captain. On March 25, 1872, he assaulted a citizen and used "vile language," but that complaint was also dismissed. On March 26, 1876, he insulted, abused and assaulted a citizen; that complaint was dismissed. On March 2, 1879,

Sketch of Officer Thomas Coleman, one of the clubbers who was singled out and exposed by an airing of his long record of abuse.

he assaulted a man, but that complaint was also dismissed. The next five charges against him each involved failure to close a gambling house after complaints were received from citizens—all five of those charges were dismissed. In 1879 Williams assaulted a clerk in the police department and was fined 10 days' pay. On August 21, 1879, Williams refused to give information to a reporter; that complaint was dismissed. On August 10, 1887, Williams was promoted to the rank of inspector.[50]

The next witness called to the stand was a trucker named Thomas Lucas. The upper part of his head was covered with a bandage and he had a black eye, a swollen lip and other bruises and contusions. He said his injuries had been inflicted by a club wielded by policeman Bernard Dunn just three days earlier. When Moss called Dunn's name in order to bring him to the stand to question him there was no response. No one in the courtroom was able to explain why Dunn had not complied with a subpoena to attend. Lucas was then being held in the lockup on a charge of interfering with an arrest. Lucas had been coming home from a picnic about a month earlier and had lain down in a doorway.

Dunn's partner shook him awake and Lucas then discovered the $4 he had in his pocket was gone. But when he asked the cop about it he just laughed and walked away. Then, three days earlier, Lucas bumped into that cop with Dunn—the pair were on duty. Lucas got in front of the policemen and again asked about his $4. Then Dunn suddenly began to club him about the face and head.

When policeman Richard S. Meaney was called to the stand he was asked questions about his record as a clubber. He testified he had been a policeman for three years but had been compelled to answer about 20 complaints before the police trial board, not all of those complaints were for assaults.[51]

Thomas Lucas was a citizen who testified at that hearing. His wounds were so fresh that he appeared to testify with his head bandaged and his face obviously and severely bruised.

Other examples cited at the hearing included Edwin V. Luhman, who had two convictions for assaulting citizens; he had been fined three days' pay by the police board for assaulting E. C. Murtha and 15 days' pay for assaulting John McGlone. William McHugh was fined 15 days' pay for assaulting a woman and her husband, while John O'Connor was fined ten days' pay for dragging a woman along the street, beating and otherwise abusing her. Policeman John H. Hurley was fined ten days' pay for striking Patrolman Henry C. Bishop with his fist in the police station. George Lair had received 24 trials before the police board at headquarters and, in one of those cases, had been fined 20 days' pay on charges of assaulting a woman in a liquor store. Among other abuses, he threw her down on the floor, tried to tear out her teeth and pointed a pistol at her head while threatening to shoot her. In response to a question from one of the committee members Lair testified that policemen who were tried by the police commissioners thought they were all right if they had a "pull." Owen Sullivan was fined ten days' pay for assaulting Thomas Dally. William Roerhig was fined one month's pay for throwing his club at a boy in the street. As a result of that action the boy fell and broke his jaw. Michael J. Rein was fined three days' pay for arresting William Henderson, dragging him to the police station and torturing him by twisting his arm on the way, all because Henderson had asked him to pay a poor newsboy for papers that Rein had taken from the boy without paying the lad. Lawrence J. Hogan had been before the police board for 14 trials; he was fined three days' pay for using "vile language" to a citizen, striking him and threatening to shoot him. Martin Hanify was fined two days' pay for insulting, striking and kicking a citizen. Henry Herrlich was fined three days' pay for clubbing Thomas Jordan and threatening to drive all his teeth down his throat. John McGrath had appeared before the police trial board 22 times on various charges; he was fined 10 days' pay for assaulting a prisoner at the police station. Thomas O'Neill was fined two days' pay for assaulting a citizen. Moss then ended his presentation. He said he would like to have presented about 50 more cases, but he decided he would not take up all that committee time.[52]

1894 October 21 [59] *New York City, assault.*

Late in October 1894 charges were preferred by 18-year-old Teresa Flynn against New York City policeman Bernard Murphy. She alleged he struck her in the face in the afternoon of October 21 while she was trying to prevent him from assaulting her brother. It was also claimed that the policeman, in civilian clothes, was drunk and assaulted several young men that afternoon for no reason whatever.[53]

On November 2, 1894, Bernard Murphy was indicted by the grand jury and arraigned before Judge Cowing on the charge of assault in the third degree upon Teresa Flynn. Murphy declared that at the time in question he was pursuing a "loafer" who had assaulted him and the man ran through the open doorway of a building in front of which the complainant was standing. Said Murphy, "I don't remember that I even brushed against her. I could not make the arrest and went away. I forgot all about it till I was told I had been indicted, and came here to surrender myself." Almost one year later, on October 31, 1895, Judge Allison dismissed the indictment against the policeman. Bernard Murphy had been under suspension from the force since November 1, 1894.[54]

1895 March 4 [60] *Washington, D.C., death.*

At about 1:30 a.m. on March 4, 1895, in Washington, D.C., city policeman Alvin W. Green shot and instantly killed Reuben Foster, a black man who was, reportedly, trying to escape arrest. On the night of March 3 it was said that Foster was involved in a cutting affray with a number of other black men in which he received several serious cuts. He was attended to by a physician who reported the case to the police. Green was sent out to arrest Foster. He did so and started escorting Foster on foot to the police station. On the way a stop was made at the house occupied by Foster's mother in order to inform the woman of her son's arrest. Another stop was made to allow the prisoner to buy cigarettes. It was there that he make a run for it by racing out of the back door of the store, with Green in pursuit. When the cop overtook the man a scuffle ensued, after which Foster broke away and again ran off. Green then drew his revolver and shot Foster in the back of the head. The man died instantly and Green was taken into custody. Foster was about 21 years old and had been arrested several times. As news spread of the death of a black man at the hands of the police crowds of blacks gathered around the police station.[55]

In this case the character assassination of Foster began in an article printed the day after his death. The account observed that Foster had gained a very bad reputation for himself, "which was well known to the citizens and police alike, and many of the former were afraid of him, as he had figured in so many fights and had been known to go armed. During the past two years he had been arrested nearly twenty times, and he had served a number of terms in the jail and on the farm." At the coroner's inquest into the death policemen were called as witnesses, who continued to bad-mouth Foster's character. One cop declared that Foster "was regarded as the worst man on that side of the river." Others reiterated that he had spent most of his time in the jail or the workhouse and had been arrested 20 or more times in the previous three or four years. Officer Anderson told of a difficulty he had with Foster one day in the previous summer. Anderson said he had arrested Foster so often that he was "ashamed" to arrest him at that time and so he let him go. He added that Foster had gone around armed during the past few years and that he had been on the force for 16 years and regarded Foster as the "worst man out there." Anderson further helped out his fellow officer's cause by stating that he had heard of threats Foster had made and Foster was fast on his feet and that it was hard for a man on foot to arrest him. It was also said that Foster had never been known to work. The coroner's jury returned a verdict of accidental shooting, exonerating Green. The jury decided "the evidence showed no desire to inflict injury."[56]

So outrageous was this verdict and the whole coroner's hearing that a Washington newspaper was moved to editorialize. Declared the editor: "The shooting of Reuben Foster by Officer Green at Anacostia was cruel and unnecessary. Foster was escaping arrest; his offense was trivial, and he had offered no resistance. His death was an unprovoked and inexcusable murder." The editor noted that officers seldom used deadly weapons except in self-defense and that prisoners were frequently allowed to escape because of the refusal of their captors to shoot them down without provocation. "It is the natural regard for human life that prevents good officers from acting on impulse, and it is to be regretted that Officer Green was ever clothed with police authority," fumed the editor. But Green's stature as a policeman should not protect him from punishment nor should the alleged bad behavior of his victim palliate the crime; "Life is too valuable to be sacrificed in such a manner and the shooting too cruel to justify any excuse." Then the editor mentioned ex-cop Terry, who was then serving three years in the penitentiary for shooting and killing Willis Washington, an inoffensive black man, "under circumstances almost similar to the present one. A few more sentences for longer terms, will have a wholesome effect upon the few policemen in Washington who would rather shoot than capture, by chase, a prisoner"[57]

On the afternoon of March 6 a meeting of "leading" black men in the community was held to discuss the killing of Foster. At that meeting a committee was appointed to exert pressure to try to bring the matter to the courts. Another meeting was scheduled for a few days later and a fund was started to pay legal expenses in prosecuting Green. Resolutions were passed at that meeting denouncing the killing of Foster and the action of the coroner's jury in pronouncing the shooting to have been accidental.[58]

One day after the first editorial on the murder that Washington newspaper returned with a second editorial on the subject. For the first time the editor mentioned racism. "The verdict of the coroner's jury on the killing of Reuben Foster is either the result of rank stupidity or the offspring of prejudice because the victim was a negro. The evidence shows that Officer Green deliberately pointed his pistol at the fleeing man and shot him dead in his tracks. And no intelligent, unprejudiced jury could render a verdict of accidental killing," stated the editor. Also decried by the editor was the immediate return to duty of policeman Green.[59]

Vermont Avenue Colored Baptist Church in Washington, D.C., was filled on the night of March 12, 1895, with people attending a meeting being held by the Equal Rights Council to discuss the shooting of Reuben Foster. President of the Equal Rights Council Mr. Lawson presided over the meeting, and he said that people of all races had been invited to the meeting with the question being whether a policeman could be at once judge, jury and executioner. The black people of the District of Columbia, Lawson added, were desiring fair play and equal rights. The law had been violated and the meeting had been called to express indignation and to ask the authorities to prosecute the guilty man. One speaker was E. M. Hewlett, a black attorney who was described as being in the forefront of the people in bringing the matter to the attention of the authorities. Hewlett said he was glad there were no "fiery" speeches and there was only "calm, dispassionate discussion." He said he did not think the large attendance was due to the fact that a white cop killed a black man but would have been just as large if the colors had been reversed. Hewlett asserted that a great crime had been committed and all the community agreed that it was not a mere accident: "A policeman, in attempting to make or maintain an unlawful arrest, had wantonly shot down a fleeing, unarmed man, one, too, who was not by any means as bad a character as some desire to make him."[60]

The case had been laid before the grand jury by District Attorney Birney. According to Hewlett, Green had said, "Damn the nigger. I'll stop him." The officer was without the least excuse, Hewlett added, for Judge Miller in the police court had year in and year out lectured policemen on the reckless use of the pistol and had remarked that unless it stopped it would become necessary to take their pistols away from them. Hewlett went on to mention the case of policeman Terry, noting the similarities to the Foster case, and then declared that he would aid in the prosecution of Green despite the fact that Green's friends, he said, had offered him $100 to remain silent and out of the case. Another speaker at the meeting was the Rev. George W. Lee, who said the so-called verdict of the coroner's jury "was an insult to common sense and reason." Thomas C. Jones, an official of the Equal Rights Council, referred to a speech he made several weeks earlier in which he stated "that while negroes were not lynched in the District, they were subjected to harshness, cruelty and disgrace by the police here." On the same night another mass meeting was held at a church wherein money was collected to fund a lawyer to aid the prosecution. With respect to the coroner's verdict, the Reverend Matthews declared, "Did they expect us to swallow that verdict? We are not that ignorant."[61]

All the pressure that was placed on the system by those fighting for justice for Foster was responsible for the case being presented to the grand jury in the middle of March, However, that body attached no blame to Green. With respect to that decision an editor declared that report "is one of the most extraordinary specimens of stupidity known to judicial annals. Either Foster was not shot or the jury has erred, for no sane set of men could have acted rightly and have ignored such a deliberate killing."[62]

That grand jury that refused to act had its term expire on April 1, 1895. The new grand jury that replaced it had the same Foster case placed before it. It also voted to ignore the murder. District Attorney Birney stated he had done all he thought proper and right in the case and while he believed the officer should have been held responsible two different grand juries had held otherwise and therefore he felt he should abide by their decision and that he would take no further action.[63]

Despite those legal setbacks, the protest movement over the murder of Foster did not stop. Early in May some 300 to 400 black people assembled at the Metropolitan Baptist Church in Washington, D.C., and agitated again for the removal of Green from the police force. All of the speakers at that meeting denounced the shooting of Foster as a "cowardly, inexcusable crime" and demanded the Police Commission immediately remove Green. Two grand juries had, by then, passed upon the case of Green and refused to indict him. The Reverend Brooks said that that juries (with respect to those two grand juries) did not always tell the truth. He declared the shooting of Foster was a "cruel murder" and ridiculed the idea the shooting was an accident. He said that he, for one, was in favor of suing the District of Columbia on behalf of the mother of Foster and compelling it to pay for having such men as Green on the force. (The idea of launching lawsuits against police forces in such circumstances as egregious abuse was an uncommon one in the period covered by this book. Such lawsuits were very rare.) Brooks added that if the reckless shooting of black men went unchecked it would someday react on the white people and the exoneration of Green would be referred to as a precedent when, someday, a white man was shot down. He said he felt one reason for no indictment in the case was the fact that Foster was black—if he had been white it would have been different. Hewlett declared the black people would wait a very long time if they waited for the white people to hold an indignation meeting because of the killing of a black man.[64]

As a result of the action of the members of the Colored Baptists Preachers Union in filing charges against Green with the Washington Police Commission the case of Green was set to come before the police board. Those ministers had filed paperwork relating to the provisions of the police manual for violating the rules of that manual with respect to the irresponsible use of his revolver. That "trial" was held—as they all were—behind closed doors. Only the final outcome was made available to the public, none of the details. Late in May 1895 Green came before that board on the charge of careless use of a revolver. It was learned on May 28 that the police trial board recommendation was that the charges against Green be dismissed. All that was then needed was the official approval of the police commissioners (of which the police trial board was a subset) and the case would be over.[65]

1895 September 2 *[61] Topeka, Kansas, death.*

On Monday night, September 2, 1895, in Topeka, Kansas, Patrolman H. E. Gaines shot and killed Albert Cruger. Gaines, accompanied by a civilian man named Schreiber, had gone to Cruger's home to arrest a man named Robbins who Schreiber alleged had stolen part of a buggy from him. Gaines had no warrant for Rollins, Cruger, or anyone else. It was not alleged that any crime was being committed at the time of the shooting. The cop only went there to arrest Robbins. Gaines was not wearing a uniform, he was in civilian clothes and no badge was visible. Robbins resisted arrest in the sense that he ran when Gaines approached. Gaines caught him, and as he brought him back Cruger's mother, an elderly lady, came up with a piece of hose in her hand. She asked Gaines if he had a warrant for Robbins. Instead of answering her question, the officer grabbed the piece of hose and struck her with it, saying, "To hell with your papers." At that point Cruger intervened, resenting the treatment given to his mother, and struck the cop with a piece of something, perhaps an iron hoop.

Immediately after striking the blow Cruger retreated a few steps and Gaines fired his gun at him, a shot that resulted in Cruger's death. Gaines went home and had his head bandaged and, observed a reporter, "was apparently suffering severe pain. However, at the coroner's inquest an examination of Gaines' wounds showed that the blow received on his head was not by any manner of means a severe one. It appears that Gaines exceeded his authority in the matter." When the coroner's jury returned its verdict it declared that Cruger came to his death by a pistol shot fired by H. E. Gaines while in the discharge of his duties "and while we cannot justify Officer Gaines for his act, yet the fact that he was assaulted is an extenuating circumstance." The reporter felt it was a peculiar verdict in that Cruger was moving away from Gaines when the shot was fired and so the cop was in no immediate danger of a renewal of the assault. Cruger was a painter by trade who had a good name and was considered to be an industrious citizen. The reporter remarked that everyone with whom he talked about the deceased said that "he was a good citizen. It is childish on the part of the police to allege that Mr. Cruger was a tramp, or a man of questionable character." Added the journalist; "This man, who is the same man who hit poor old Mrs. Etzel such a blow as to put her in condition that death would afford her relief, is sustained by the police department and efforts are made to show that he is justified in doing what he did. He should be removed from the force at once."[66]

Gaines came to trial several months later and in February 1896 he was convicted of manslaughter in the third degree. He was sentenced in April to one year in the penitentiary. Just four months after that, at the beginning of August 1896, Kansas governor Morrill pardoned Gaines. Said a journalist: "Gaines deserved severe punishment but as he was a member of a redeemer police force he got off with a few months' imprisonment."[67]

1896 September *[62] Gretna, Louisiana, deaths.*

The slapping of a child's face caused the deaths of three people in Gretna, Louisiana, in September 1896. It all began when a black man named James

Hawkins slapped a five-year-old white child on the street in that city. Officer Miller was in the process of attempting to capture Hawkins around midnight. According to one newspaper article, Miller fired his gun at random into a crowd of black people, killing Alexander and Arthur Green. Hawkins was finally captured and lodged in the Gretna jail, but at two o'clock the next morning a mob broke down the door, took Hawkins to the riverbank and lynched him from a tree, and then threw his body into the river. Another newspaper story gave a somewhat different account. After the slap the parents of the white child complained to Miller and he went after the man. Hawkins resisted arrest and was aided by several other black men. The cop drew his revolver and killed Alexander and Arthur Green, "two of the Negroes who were helping Hawkins." Although he managed to escape then, Hawkins was pursued by a mob and captured by a mob who promptly lynched him from a tree.[68]

1896 November *[63] Ocala, Florida, death.*

According to a very brief report that appeared in a Florida newspaper in November 1896, "Crap shooters and skin players in Ocala don't stand much chance. A policeman killed one man and wounded another for indulging in that kind of sport. Now the people are wondering what to do with that policeman."[69]

1897 July 30 *[64] New York City, death.*

While taking a drunken prisoner to the police station on July 31, 1897, in New York City, policeman Thomas Devine, who was described as "an unpopular policeman," was surrounded by a crowd of about 300 hooting men and boys. Soon the men began to strike him with their hands while those on the outskirts of the crowd began to throw stones and bits of sticks at him. Cornelius O'Keefe, a laborer, was behind Devine and kicked the officer's hat off. While Devine was retrieving his hat the crowd managed to free the prisoner. Devine got his hat, reclaimed his prisoner and set off again for the station. Once again O'Keefe knocked the man's hat off. Devine said he then drew his revolver and fired one shot into the air for help, to attract other officers who happened to be nearby. According to one newspaper, Devine then picked his helmet up again, twisted around face-to-face with O'Keefe and shot him through the heart. O'Keefe died instantly. When O'Keefe fell to the ground the crowd quickly vanished, leaving only Devine and the corpse. The officer was immediately arrested and put under arrest on a charge of homicide.[70]

Another newspaper presented some different details for the incident. In this version Devine had his prisoner and was then jumped by a "gang of ruffians." Then the cop fired into the air. O'Keefe came up behind him and hit him on the back of the head, knocking him down. "He was jumping on the prostrate policeman when the latter shot him in the breast, killing him instantly."[71]

A third account appeared in another New York City paper. This one began by stating: "The officer acted in self-defence." During the early part of the evening, the account stated, a gang of young toughs known as the "Gashouse Gang" had congregated on the street. Several times Devine ordered them to move on, but they would return after he left the area and go back to drinking beer. After he issued his "move on" order to them several times and the gang had returned each time, they were all intoxicated. Then the crowd became riotous. One of the leaders, James Lynch, was placed under arrest by Devine. As they made their way to the station the crowd set upon them and liberated Lynch. By the free use of his nightstick Devine beat them back and reclaimed his prisoner. Again they started for the station and again the mob tried to liberate Lynch. Devine fired one shot into the air and as he did so O'Keefe struck him "a violent blow in the left temple," which knocked the officer to the ground. As the cop "staggered" to his feet O'Keefe tried again to assault him. Devine, "realizing his life was in danger," fired the fatal shot. He hit O'Keefe in the left breast and he fell dead. Instantly the crowd dispersed. "Devine was badly dazed and stunned" but managed to make his way to the station house. The reserve force was immediately ordered out and scoured the area for members of the gang "who had participated in the riot."[72]

Devine was arraigned in Harlem Police Court on August 2 charged with homicide. Several "denizens" of the "Gashouse" neighborhood testified variously as to the affair. All of them, however, said a journalist, "painted the policeman in very dark colors." Their testimony conflicted in many of the details. James Lynch was also arraigned on a charge of assault and resisting arrest. He was held in lieu of $1,000 bail; Devine was paroled in the custody of Capt. Timothy Creedon of his precinct, pending further examination. On August 12 Patrolman Thomas Devine was restored to duty by the police board on the recommendation of Chief Conlin. Devine had been exonerated by the coroner's jury.[73]

1897 September 6 [65] *New York City, death.*

Abe Dorfman of New York City was killed by a pistol shot fired by city policeman William F. Goughran in Brooklyn in the early morning hours of September 6, 1897. Dorfman was said to have been one of four thieves who had robbed a clothing store and were driving away in a wagon loaded with stolen goods. Previous to the robbery the thieves had approached a peddler named Cohen with an offer of $10 for the use of his wagon. Cohen gave them the wagon but immediately notified the police. Three officers surprised the thieves as they were driving away. Dorfman jumped from the wagon and ran off. Upon his refusal to obey the order of Goughran to halt, the officer fired. The bullet struck Dorfman in the head, killing him instantly. The other thieves were captured soon thereafter without incident. On September 10 Coroner Mason of Brooklyn held an inquest into the death. The result of that inquest, said a reporter, was the "complete exoneration" of the officer who was declared to have shot Dorfman in the discharge of his duties.[74]

1898 March 13 *[66] New York City, assault.*

In the morning of March 13, 1897, a group of several people that included four newspapermen and three women, used cabs and horses as they pursued a policeman through the streets of New York City's Tenderloin area. Eventually they caught him and later on that same morning city policeman Jeremiah J. McAuliffe was arraigned in Jefferson Market Police Court on seven charges of assault made by seven complainants. The four men had been walking along the street when they saw two men in civilian clothes who appeared to be arguing with two women. As the four men approached the group they saw McAuliffe slap one of the women heavily on the face and then swing his arm around and strike the other woman with the back of his hand. Two other women ran up to that group and one of them, who said something to McAuliffe, was promptly knocked down by him with a blow to her face. The four men then interfered with two of them, seizing McAuliffe. The officer's companion shouted, "We're both policemen. You'll get into trouble." The two men then released McAuliffe, but then he began to hit out at all within his reach. Three of the men say he struck them. The fourth man had run off to the nearest police station, where he received no help when he explained that a policeman was running amok in the area. He then ran back in time to see McAuliffe and a friend jump into a cab and leave the area. That was when the chase began. Finally the group found a policeman who would arrest McAuliffe. When he was taken into custody McAuliffe denied he was a cop, but a search of his person revealed police items, including a police whistle with his number on it. The newsmen declared they saw him pass his badge to his companion, who by then had disappeared. McAuliffe finally confessed to being a cop and was locked up. He was held in $500 bond for each case of assault, a total of $3,500, and committed to await his trial. He had been on the police force for two years.[75]

On March 25 McAuliffe was indicted by the grand jury on the two specific charges of assault that the panel considered on that day. The other five charges remained pending. McAuliffe had been suspended from duty without pay. By April 19 he had been indicted on all seven charges and was then described as ex-cop McAuliffe. When he was in court on April 19 on trial on one of those charges the jury, after deliberating just ten minutes, acquitted McAuliffe. A journalist reported that "after the verdict was announced Recorder Goff said that the District Attorney's office should give to the prisoner's trial the attention it deserved."[76]

1898 April 6 [67] *La Porte, Indiana, death.*

Fred Wilson of Michigan City, Indiana, was struck on the head by Patrolman Henry Dolan of La Porte on April 6, 1898, and died at around midnight. Wilson was said to have been quarreling and Dolan, in subduing the man, used his club and in striking him on the head caused a concussion. Dolan was then in jail, having surrendered himself into custody.[77]

1898 August 11 [68] *New York City, deaths.*

New York City policeman Henry C. Hawley, attached to the Tenderloin station, while he was in an intoxicated condition on August 11, 1898, shot his wife; his mother, Mary Hawley; and his two daughters age five and seven and then shot himself in the head. Four of the victims of the shooting were all dead within a short period of time. Only his wife was alive a day after the shooting and doctors did not expect her to survive. Hawley had been appointed to the force in 1895 and was said to have been an efficient officer throughout his career. Lately, though, he was said to have been seen with other women, and on the day of the shooting he had been drinking heavily. His mother, Mary, was 58; his wife, Bertha, was 36; his daughters were named Mary and Middie; Hawley was 29. On the day of the shooting he had been on duty between 6:00 a.m. and 8:00 a.m. and then returned to the station at 9:15 a.m. to answer roll call. He then asked for a leave of absence, a request that was granted. At that time he appeared to have been drinking slightly. Hawley arrived home at about 10:30 a.m., much more intoxicated. Soon after that neighbors could hear voices from their apartment raised in an argument. Bertha left the apartment weeping but returned soon thereafter. Then more raised voices in quarrel were heard. Then the sounds of four shots being fired were heard. Policemen on beats in the area were notified and two went to the apartment. Hawley talked to them through the closed door and explained that everything was okay; he was a brother officer and had just been cleaning his revolver. The two officers at the door did not believe him and threatened to break open the door if he did not admit them. He told them to go away. Then two more shots were heard. Those two officers then broke in. They discovered the five bodies, all shot. All were still alive at that time. The last words from Bertha before she lost consciousness were: "Rum and bad women have caused all this." Coroner Hart took an ante-mortem statement from Mary Hawley, the only one who was conscious when he arrived at the hospital. She said her son came home intoxicated and said he was tired of living and was going to kill himself and the children. He then shot his wife, his mother and then his two daughters. Hawley held an honorable discharge from the U.S. Navy. He was supposed to have been in bed at the police station "on reserve" from midnight to 6:00 a.m. on the day of the shooting, but he had snuck out and was visiting Mrs. Verna Breen at her apartment for much of that time. Seven "slight" complaints had been registered against Hawley since he joined the force. The worst was registered on May 21 of that year when he was reported for being absent from his post.[78]

1899 February 10 *[69] Chicago, death.*

Chicago policeman Edward Leach was shot and fatally wounded in that city on February 10, 1899, by Patrick Furlong, a fellow officer, during a quarrel over Irish and English politics. Furlong was charged with the murder of Leach and on May 17, 1899, in Chicago he was found guilty of manslaughter and was sentenced to 14 years in the penitentiary.[79]

1899 June 6 *[70] Wilmington, North Carolina, assault.*

Officer S. C. Winner of Wilmington, North Carolina, was indicted in Justice Fowler's court on June 8, 1899, on two charges of assault and battery that arose out of an incident that took place in the afternoon of June 6. It was alleged the policeman assaulted S. Seigler, who ran a grocery store, and that he also assaulted Harry Smith, the black porter who worked in the store. The incident was said to have started with a row between Smith and a black girl in the store during which Smith slapped the woman. She went outside, found Officer Winner and called upon him to arrest Smith. Without a warrant, Winner went to the store to arrest Smith. The cop and Seigler got into an argument over whether or not a warrant was needed. The result was that Seigler interfered with the policeman as he tried to arrest Smith. Both Seigler and Smith swore out warrants against Winner, with the result that he appeared In Fowler's police court two days later. When the case was called, counsel for Winner had the case transferred to Judge Bornemann, who, upon investigation, adjudged the policeman to be guilty but suspended that judgment on the condition Winner pay the court costs.[80]

1899 August? *[71] Minneapolis, death.*

A brief report that appeared in a Minnesota newspaper on September 1, 1899, declared; "A Minneapolis policeman killed a citizen this week when he refused to halt. He was not under arrest, and had been charged with no crime."[81]

FOUR

1900–1909

1900 June 16 *[72] New York City, death.*

Patrolman Irwin B. Cornelius of the Brooklyn, New York, police force shot and killed Patrick Farley on the morning of June 16, 1900. It was reported that Farley had been arrested by the officer and was trying to escape when he was killed. Just before daylight Farley, described as a "pugilist," came home drunk. He dragged his wife out of bed and beat her, but she managed to escape to the street. Officers Cornelius, Murphy and McLaughlin attempted to capture Farley and after a struggle they did so. The three policeman got Farley to the door of the station house and then McLaughlin went back toward his post. As soon as he had gone, Farley, it was said, sprang at Cornelius, battered him and ran away. After he got to his feet Cornelius gave chase. When Farley would not stop when commanded to do so the officer fired at him three times, with one of the shots striking the fleeing man in the back, killing him instantly.[1]

1900 August 2 *[73] Alexandria, Virginia, death.*

While he was attempting to arrest the participants in a street fight in Alexandria, Virginia, at about 6:30 p.m. on August 2, 1900, Officer Weston Atkinson was set upon by Robert and Walter Posey. Reportedly, in the melee that followed the policeman shot and killed Robert and seriously wounded his brother Walter. The trouble began with a fight between the Posey boys and George Beard in a saloon. In response to a call to the police Atkinson was sent to the scene. As he approached, the men ceased fighting and made common cause against the policeman. The cop was knocked down, kicked and beaten and his nightstick taken. Atkinson reportedly called for help from the crowd but received no response. He then warned the Posey brothers that he would shoot. They did not heed that warning and Atkinson started firing. Walter was hit first and then, wrote a reporter, "Bob rushed up, and while on his knees Officer Atkinson shot him through the heart." The coroner was called in to investigate and Atkinson was confined to his home. It was also said that "Walter was well-known to the police."[2]

An account in a different newspaper noted that Robert was 33 and Walter was 28. The fight had started in a saloon when the Posey brothers jumped Beard and beat him up, "without provocation." All three were ejected from the bar but resumed their fight on the sidewalk. When Atkinson arrived the fight was over, but he located the brothers. Atkinson then grabbed Walter and placed him under arrest, whereupon Robert interfered. Both proceeded to beat the cop "badly." They took his club from him and, seeing he was at their mercy, he called for help, but none of the estimated 50 spectators came forward. After a struggle he succeeded in getting his pistol out and then he warned the brothers. But they continued to attack him, "stating they intended to kill him." He then fired, hitting Walter in the lung, but Robert continued his fight and while he lay on the ground Atkinson fired again, shooting Robert through the heart and killing him almost instantly.[3]

A coroner's jury summoned by Alexandria city coroner William R. Purvis met on August 4 to investigate the circumstances of the shooting of the Posey brothers. A large number of eyewitnesses testified and, wrote a journalist, "their evidence showed conclusively that the officer had used his pistol in self-defence." After more than two hours of investigation the jury reached a verdict, finding that Robert Posey was shot and killed by Atkinson "in the fearless and faithful performance of his duty."[4]

Later on August 4 a special session of the police court was held to investigate the shooting. The same witnesses who testified earlier in the day at the coroner's inquest were present in the police court session. Nothing new was presented at the police court hearing and Alexandria mayor Simpson, in disposing of the case, dismissed the officer from custody and complimented him for "faithful performance of duty." The mayor also commented upon the rashness of resisting an officer of the law.[5]

On the morning of March 11, 1902, a train wreck occurred in Alexandria in which Weston Atkinson was killed. Atkinson was employed on that train as a fireman. He was about 38 years old, a former cop, and had worked for the railroad for about one year.[6]

1900 October *[74], Suffolk, Virginia, assault.*

On March 21, 1901, a court magistrate heard the case of Suffolk, Virginia, policeman Edward Dennis, who was accused of assaulting Z. T. Langston, a prominent farmer, whom he clubbed when the farmer resisted arrest in a circus tent in October 1900. That magistrate sent the officer on for indictment under a warrant that alleged a felony. Dennis had stated in advance of the hearing that he did not expect justice. On May 15 a jury found Dennis guilty of assault in the clubbing of Langston and fined the policeman $50. The case was strongly contested and in the street after the trial one of the defense attorneys and a deputy sheriff who had been a witness for the prosecution almost came to blows but were separated before any harm could be done.[7]

1900 November 12 *[75] St. Joseph, Missouri, death.*

In the early-morning hours of November 12, 1900, in St. Joseph, Missouri, city policeman Charles S. Scott shot and killed a gambler by the name of Thomas Smith. The shooting took place in the barroom of the Commercial Club. It was alleged that Smith accused Scott of having an article published that reflected badly upon him. Scott denied the charge when, it was said, Smith tried to assault the cop, and the shooting took place shortly thereafter. An account in another newspaper printed the same details but added that Smith had wrested the cop's club from him and had Scott almost to the floor when he was shot. Smith had accused Scott of giving the newspapers stories about his disreputable conduct in a gaming house. According to this account, "The coroner's jury exonerated Scott."[8]

1901 March *[76] New York City, assault.*

An editorial in a New York City newspaper discussed an assault case that had been decided in a police court in that city on March 13, 1901. The logic of that decision was, declared the editor, not so convincing and reassuring as might be wished. The case was one in which a New York City policeman had violently clubbed a citizen who was one of a crowd surrounding a drunken woman on the street. On the one hand, the cop said he had tried to arrest the woman when the man interfered to prevent him from doing his duty, whereupon he struck the man and arrested him. The policeman's story was corroborated by other cops. On the other hand, the citizen who had been clubbed declared that he had not interfered and that he was clubbed merely because he and other bystanders did not "move on" as quickly as the cop thought they should. That story was corroborated by other citizens who witnessed the incident. The judge in his decision said he did not believe the officer's story about the man attempting to interfere with his discharge of duty, but at the same time he believed the cop had, in accordance with his duty, endeavored to disperse the crowd. He then discharged the man who had been clubbed, and thus ended the case, the cop going out of the court "vindicated." It would be most unfortunate, thought the editor, for such a decision to be regarded as a vindication of the club-wielding cop or as sanctioning the precedent for future action in similar cases. "Upon the face of the judge's decision, on the contrary, the policeman was guilty of a brutal crime, for which he should be severely punished. For if the man did not interfere with the policeman in the discharge of his duty, the policeman had no right to club him. Indeed he would have had no right to do so had the man thus interfered unless the man had caused extreme violence. For a policeman to club a man for not 'moving on,' or for not doing so as quickly as he thinks he should, or to club the members of a crowd for not dispersing at his word, is nothing less than assault and battery, for which the policeman should be punished just as anyone else would be who went upon the street and clubbed passersby without cause," declared the editor. He went on to add: "It is unquestionable that many policemen in this city are entirely too free in their use of the club. With them it is 'a word and a blow.' If a man does not move on, or a crowd does not disperse, the instant the word is given, out comes the club for brutal use. If a person on being arrested hesitates or demurs in the slightest, he is promptly clubbed into a state of helplessness." The editor fumed: "It is an abominable bit of brutal tyranny, and every policeman guilty of it should be promptly transferred from 'the force' to the penitentiary." Admitting the use of the club was sometimes necessary, the editor concluded that such instances were infrequent: "As a rule, the club should be used only as a last resource and not—as is now often the case—as a first resource and on the slightest provocation."[9]

1901 April 26 *[77] Topeka, Kansas, death.*

While resisting arrest on the night of April 26, 1901, in Topeka, Kansas, George Head was struck on the head by Patrolman S. M. Hall. That blow fractured the man's skull and led to his death six hours later. Reportedly, Head had been drinking and was disturbing a religious meeting on the street. When the cop tried to arrest Head the man was said to have "showed fight" and in trying to subdue him Hall struck him on the head with his club. Hall was lodged in the county jail and in that first night of incarceration he was thought to be in danger of mob violence. It was reported that saloon owners and their friends had been trying to organize a mob to lynch Hall but that a sufficient number of people could not be recruited and the attempt to lynch the officer was abandoned. Head had been a saloon keeper. Hall claimed his actions in "quieting" the prisoner were necessary but that he did not intend to hurt him severely.[10]

According to one story, Head had been a police court character for some time; he had been arrested for selling liquor, being drunk, disturbing the peace and ill-treating his wife. At one time he had been mayor of Sabetha, Kansas, and was financially well off. Hall had been on the Topeka police force for three years. A year earlier in the winter he had shot a tramp. While he was attempting to arrest the man on a charge of vagrancy the man ran off and Hall shot him in the back; it was reported to have been a minor wound and the man survived.[11]

Hall was arrested at noon on April 28 in the wake of the coroner's inquest. At that inquest about six witnesses testified that Head had been drinking and was boisterous but that he offered no resistance to Hall before the officer struck him. A reporter declared: "It is plain from the evidence brought out before the coroner's jury that Hall was not justified in striking Head. Head was an old man who was feeble and he could not have made but slight resistance if he had tried. He had no weapon of any kind, so that Hall had no reason to fear bodily violence. The offense for which the arrest was made was trivial."[12]

Hall was soon out on $5,000 bail and he continued to work as a Topeka police officer. On June 27, 1901, he assaulted a citizen by the name of A. Rabinowitz. On July 6 Hall stood trial for assault in city court and pled guilty. The judge sentenced Hall to pay a fine of $1 plus costs; those costs totaled $14, making the total cost to Hall $15. After he paid that fine Hall went back out onto the streets and back to work as a peace officer.[13]

On July 23 by a vote of seven to five the city council of Topeka instructed Police Chief Stahl to dispense with the services of Hall as

Top: Officer S. M. Hall in Topeka arrested George Head for resisting arrest. Hall beat Head with his club so hard that he died. Also immediately Hall was bailed out and back on the street as a cop. While awaiting a legal action for beating Head to death Hall assaulted another citizen. Finally, the City of Topeka had enough and dismissed him from the force. *Bottom:* George Head was the victim of Officer Hall. Like so many others portrayed in this book, Head was beaten while "resisting arrest." Although his assailant, Officer Hall, was a serial thug, nothing published indicated he was ever punished, except for dismissal from the Topeka Police Department.

a policeman. On July 29 Stahl dismissed Hall. In December Hall stood trial for manslaughter and on December 7, 1901, Hall was acquitted on those charges and received many congratulations at the police station that day. On December 23, 1901, by a vote of 6–4 the city council refused to adopt the report of the committee on police. That report recommended favorably the petition received by the city, in September, asking for the reinstatement of Hall to the police force. Thus Hall was finally finished as a Topeka peace officer.[14]

1901 August *[78] Chicago, death.*

When he was within 50 feet of his father's rectory David Lindskog, son of the Rev. Herman Lindskog, was shot and fatally wounded by Chicago policeman James P. Wiley. Upon hearing the shooting Herman ran out of the rectory and helped the police lift his dying son into the ambulance; he was pronounced dead at the hospital. Wiley declared he acted in self-defense in that August 1901 shooting, and, said a reporter, "his cut and swollen face bears out his story." Wiley declared he fired while defending himself against an attack by a band of young men who had been in the habit of congregating at a particular street corner—the spot where the shooting took place. While the gang had reportedly beset Wiley the officer decided he was unable to cope with the gang and he drew his revolver and fired. Later, three young men said to have been companions of Lindskog in the fight were arrested. Herman Lindskog was pastor of the Ansgarius Swedish Episcopal Church.[15]

1901 August 29 *[79] Guthrie, Oklahoma, death.*

Guthrie, Oklahoma, policeman Frank Ellis shot and killed Farris Clayton in that city in the Santa Fe saloon on the night of August 29, 1901. Clayton was shot in the right lung and died almost instantly. After the shooting Ellis fled from the saloon by the rear door and was still on the loose after this article went to press. A horse that was missing from a barn was thought to have been stolen by Ellis and used in his escape. The 24-year-old Farris Clayton, accompanied by his younger brother Lynn Clayton, was riding the rails to make his way home to see their sick father. On the evening of August 29 the brothers reached Guthrie on the top of a train where they were discovered by Ellis and ordered to get down. They obeyed the order. At first Ellis threatened to put them in jail, but he finally agreed to let them go if they would give him a dollar and a half; the brothers did so. Then Ellis invited them across the railroad yard to the Santa Fe saloon, where he insisted on treating them to several rounds of drinks, after which the shooting took place. While the three men were drinking, said Lynn, "not a cross word was spoken. He was telling of his strength and about how well he could shoot." At one point Ellis walked away, apparently to leave the saloon, but then he turned and walked in the direction of the brothers and without saying a word he got in front of Farris and shot him. "I don't know why he did it. I know of no reason in the world," explained Lynn. A witness named Arthur Boring confirmed the shooting as described by Lynn, as being unprovoked and that no arguments had taken place between the men. There was at the time conflicting evidence as to whether Ellis had been drinking earlier that evening.[16]

At about 11:00 p.m. on August 30 Frank Ellis was lodged behind bars at the county jail. He had been taken into custody about 6:30 p.m. at the community of Goodnight, 22 miles northeast of Guthrie. He was found walking along the railroad tracks. When he was questioned Ellis claimed he had a complete loss of memory. He also declared he had been in Chandler, Oklahoma, for the past several weeks working in a butcher shop. Said a reporter after speaking to Ellis: "The prisoner undoubtedly has lost his mind or else is putting up a decidedly clever bit of acting."[17]

On February 17, 1902, Ellis appeared in court for a sanity hearing. A jury in a district court declared that the prisoner was sane. The first ballot was 9–3 in favor of declaring him sane and the seventh and final ballot was 12–0 for that verdict. As a result Frank Ellis had to stand trial for murder. On the morning of March 21, 1902, the jury in the Ellis murder trial returned a verdict of guilty of murder in the first degree. Deliberations lasted about five hours. He was sentenced to a life term of imprisonment.[18]

Shortly after Ellis was sent off to prison Mrs. Ellis moved away to Anadarko, where she died from consumption in May 1903. According to the reporter, "Policeman Frank Ellis was mentally deranged when he committed his crime. Sentiment in Guthrie has changed in Ellis' favor and there now seems to be a general desire to see Ellis released from Lansing prison and placed in the sanitarium at Norman for treatment."[19]

On the evening of January 27, 1908, Oklahoma governor Haskell signed a pardon for Frank Ellis. After being sentenced to life at his first trial he secured a new trial and at the second trial he was sentenced to ten years in the penitentiary. However, the warden of the penitentiary refused to house the prisoner on the ground that he was insane. Ellis was brought back to Guthrie and again tried for the crime. At that third trial Ellis was found guilty of manslaughter in the second degree and sentenced to four years in the penitentiary. Once again the warden refused him admittance to the penitentiary, as the warden still insisted the man was insane. When he was then taken to the asylum at Norman, Oklahoma, Ellis was denied admittance there on the ground that he was not insane.

Ever since that denial Ellis had been lodged at the county jail, at the expense of the county. Ellis was sentenced to the four years in December 1904 and that term was due to expire on February 18, 1908. The last two years of his confinement Ellis had been a "trustee" at the county jail. On the evening of January 27 when Haskell signed the pardon Frank Ellis was in the room with him.[20]

1901 September 5 [80] New York City, assault.

New York City policeman William Laubersheimer of the Mercer Street station was convicted of assault in the third degree in the Court of General Sessions on April 18, 1902. Nicholas Schery, a metalworker, was riding in a transit car on September 5, 1901, carrying a charcoal stove and some tools. Laubersheimer got into the car, took off his helmet and placed it on the seat beside him. He told Schery to keep the stove away from the helmet. Schery said something in reply that angered the cop and the officer struck him twice. One blow broke the drum of one of Schery's ears. The victim got off the car and went to police headquarters to lodge a complaint. Laubersheimer was tried by the police board, but Police Commissioner Devery dismissed the complaint. Then Schery went before a magistrate, who held the cop for trial in the criminal court. After his conviction Laubersheimer was lodged in the Tombs lockup. He was to be sentenced at a later date. It was said that his conviction would put him off the force. The jury in the officer's assault trial deliberated for only ten minutes.[21]

1901 October [81] Missouri, death.

With no specific detail a short newspaper report observed that a Missouri policeman convicted of having killed a young man was sentenced to two years in prison. The officer had declared that the killing was the result of an accident.[22]

1901 November 11 [82] Wilmington, Ohio, death.

While he was under arrest in Wilmington, Ohio, on a charge of larceny, John Pennington attempted to escape. It was reported that Marshal Sliker fired at the ground to frighten Pennington, but the bullet ricocheted and struck the man in the head, killing him instantly.[23]

1901 December 28 [83] Ceredo, West Virginia, death.

Michael West, an engineer on the Norfolk & Western railroad, was shot to death by policeman W. Freeman near the town of Ceredo, West Virginia, on December 28, 1901. It was said that West was resisting arrest.[24]

1902 January 13 *[84] Knoxville, Tennessee, death.*

Early on the morning of January 13, 1902, Knoxville, Tennessee, policeman Joe Cruse (perhaps Cruz or Cruze) was on his way home when he was fired upon, he alleged. Upon his investigation he found Lon and Alexander Nelson (brothers) standing on a corner with some other men. A "difficulty" ensued in which Cruse shot the two brothers. It was alleged that an attempt had been made several months earlier to assassinate the officer. A different account declared that five shots had been fired at Cruz. At the corner there were three men standing around, the third being Oz Ingle. Cruz accused them of doing the shooting, but they denied it. He placed Lon under arrest and the other two men interceded. Cruz drew his pistol and shot both Nelson brothers and fired at Ingle. Alexander died that afternoon, while Lon died in the evening of that day. A day later Cruz was arrested on a murder charge and was lodged in the police lockup. Both Nelson brothers and Ingle were unarmed.[25]

1902 January 14 *[85] New York City, death.*

Policeman William H. Ennis of the Adams Street station of the New York City Police Department shot and killed his young wife and seriously wounded his mother-in-law, Mrs. Alice Gorman, on January 14, 1902. The shooting took place at the home of Mrs. Gorman after Ennis, according to a reporter, "crazed with drink and brooding over his fancied troubles," had broken in the house through a rear door and surprised Mrs. Gorman and his wife, who were both in bed at the time. After shooting the women Ennis ran away, but he was captured at a hotel where he had rented a room and was unsuccessfully trying to sleep. Mrs. Gorman was 52 years old and her daughter Mary Agnes Ennis was 21. The latter had been separated from her husband for some time and had been trying to secure "a limited divorce from him on the ground of inhuman treatment." Ennis had recently proclaimed that he loved his wife and blamed his domestic troubles on his mother-in-law. The latter had recently secured a warrant for his arrest, charging him with failure to support his wife. Reportedly, Ennis had been brooding over his troubles a great deal. On January 11 he was drinking in Manhattan and was arrested on a charge of disorderly conduct. When he showed his shield at the station where he was taken upon that arrest he was allowed to go home, but the charges were preferred against him. When he was due at the Adams Street station on January 12 he reported in sick, and he had not been there since. He was said to have been drinking heavily for some days. That his act was premeditated was said to be shown by a letter postmarked 7:00 p.m., January 13. That letter was sent to a friend who turned it over to the police. In the letter Ennis wrote: "You must pardon me for what I have done but I was driven to it by the mother." Mrs. Gorman said she was in one bed with the couple's four-month-old boy when Ennis ran into the room and shouted he was going to kill her. Then he shot her. He then ran into an adjoining bedroom from which his wife was trying to escape. He shot her through the head. Mrs. Gorman ran to a neighbor's house for help while Ennis fled the scene after he had finished shooting. Ennis, 31, confessed at police headquarters. He had been on the force for nine years and "had a good record."[26]

A different account related that Ennis had a physical fight with another officer in 1894. Both men pled guilty before the police trial board to fighting and each was fined 30 days' pay. A reporter stated, of Ennis, that "his record is a bad one" and he was "known as a bad-tempered policeman."[27]

Ennis was tried for the killing and on the afternoon of May 23, 1902, William Ennis, by then an ex-cop, was found guilty of murder in the first degree by a jury. His defense was that he was insane at the time. Said a reporter: "His behavior during the trial was such as to support that contention. The preponderance of expert testimony, however, was to the effect that the accused man was shamming." On May 26 Justice Aspinall sentenced Ennis to be executed at Sing Sing prison in the week beginning July 7, 1902.[28]

POLICEMAN KILLS WIFE; PLANNED A TRIPLE CRIME

A sketch of William Ennis, the wife he killed and the scene of the crime.

A little over a week later a report appeared that stated Ennis was a mental and physical wreck and had gone "daft" over what he had done, even though the plea made at court that he was hopelessly insane had not worked. Ever since the shooting Ennis had been in solitary confinement, a period of over four months. A journalist declared: "The murderer has been haunted day and night with visions of his slain wife, and the ever repeating scene in the man's mind seems finally to have driven him into hopeless

Sketch of Ennis in his cell being examined by "alienists" to see if he was sane. It was widely believed that he was faking insanity to avoid a trip to the death house.

William Ennis in his cell, supposedly haunted by the wife he murdered. Ennis was executed in the electric chair at Sing Sing prison.

insanity." In November 1903, Dr. Irvine, the attending physician at Sing Sing prison, said that he had sent to the superintendent of prisons at Albany, New York, a report on the mental condition of Ennis. Irvine declined to discuss that report with journalists.[29]

Reportedly, the mental condition of Ennis resulted in a "commission of alienists" (psychiatrists or psychologists) examining the prisoner. They conducted an experiment on him in while he was placed on a table and had an ether mask applied to his face and ether administered just to the point where his mind was "cloudy." At that point he was "thrown from the table to the floor," and then he was "cured." Said Ennis to an alienist, "You have caught me and I am glad of it. No man can realize what my sufferings have been during the past 78 weeks. Pretending madness, I have often approached so near the border line that it has not been wholly pretense." On the morning of December 14, 1903, William Ennis was executed in the electric chair at Sing Sing prison.[30]

1902 February 14 [86] Fulton, Kentucky, death.

When Bill Dooley, black, was murdered in Fulton, Kentucky, on February 14, 1902, two men were arrested in connection with that crime. One was Hardee Beasley and the other was Fulton policeman R. M. Potts. One day later, on February 15, Potts was suspended from the police force pending an investigation.

The examining trial for Potts was held on February 25 and 26 and resulted in Potts being held for trial by the circuit court. Bail was fixed for the officer at $5,000. On the night in question some persons took Dooley from his home at night and killed him. Dooley, wrote a journalist, was said "to have been a peaceable, inoffensive man, and against whom there was no charge." At an earlier hour on the night of the killing Potts was with a posse that visited the Dooley home in quest of a black offender and the men in the posse had words with Dooley. That much was admitted by Potts. Later that same night some men took Dooley from his house and shot him to death. Four black witnesses testified that Potts was in that last group and participated in the killing. One of those witnesses swore he saw Potts fire the fatal shot. The defense provided an alibi that Potts was elsewhere in Fulton at the time of the shooting and thus could not have done the shooting or have been present in that second group of men. Those witnesses were all white men.[31]

The grand jury at Hickman, Kentucky, indicted the by then "former cop" R. M. Potts for the murder of Dooley. Potts was indicted in May 1902. Beasley, who had been arrested with the policeman, was acquitted. That mob involved in the murder was said herein to have contained four or five men. The case against Potts came to court on September 6 but was suddenly continued until December, allegedly because the defendant, Potts, had not been paying his lawyer's fees.[32]

1902 April 2 *[87] New York City, death.*

Brooklyn, New York, policeman John O'Brien shot and instantly killed his young wife, Minnie, on April 3, 1902. The shooting was done in the presence of his three young children and his wife's mother. O'Brien had been drinking heavily and it was reported that he "was on the verge of delirium tremens." O'Brien was reported to have admitted there was no reason for his deed. The couple had been married for eight years and apparently had been happy. On April 2 O'Brien arrived home at 3:00 p.m. and laid his gun and club on the mantelpiece. He ate dinner and appeared to be in a good frame of mind. When he finished eating he rose from the table and said, "Well, I am through for the day." Replied Minnie, "Why, no, you're not, John; you must go back to work." Without replying O'Brien quietly put on his coat and helmet and reached for his revolver. He pointed it at his wife and without the least warning or word he fired at her. She was hit in the heart and fell to the floor dead. The officer then ran out into the street followed by his mother-in-law. The three children were left in the house screaming with terror. Policeman Furey arrived on the scene, drawn by the noise, and after a struggle he subdued O'Brien and got his revolver away from him. It was also reported that O'Brien had always been known as a heavy drinker.[33]

In Kings County Court in June 1902, O'Brien was found guilty of manslaughter in the second degree. During the trial the defense tried to argue that the shooting was accidental, that his revolver discharged accidentally. On June 21, Judge Aspinall sentenced John O'Brien to a term of three years of imprisonment in Sing Sing prison. On the day of the shooting he was on reserve duty and went to his home for the dinner break but not before taking several drinks of whisky on the way home. In passing sentence Aspinall said, "Policemen who are trusted with arms by the public should not drink. When they do, it generally ends with their appearance in this court."[34]

1902 April 17 [88] *St. Louis, death.*

St. Louis policeman Walter Brown was off duty and in civilian clothes on a night in April 1902. He said that Daniel Thomas was one of two black men who tried to hold him up and he resisted. Brown said he found it necessary to shoot in order to defend himself. He shot Thomas, who died at a city hospital on April 20. The officer was suspended pending an investigation. A second account declared that Thomas tried to hold Brown up, but it made no mention of there being two muggers.[35]

At the end of April Assistant Prosecuting Attorney Johnson issued a warrant charging Brown with murder in the second degree. Several witnesses testified at the inquest that Brown was under the influence of alcohol at the time of the shooting and that there was no necessity for the shooting. At his preliminary hearing on June 12, Walter Brown was exonerated. He was discharged in the Court of Criminal Correction. On June 20, 1902, Brown appeared before the police commissioners' trial board on a charge of intoxication. That charge was sustained and Brown was dismissed from the force. That charge had been preferred against him immediately after the shooting of Thomas.[36]

1902 May 1 [89] *Roseburg, Oregon, death.*

Roseburg, Oregon, policeman Frank Reed shot and killed Thomas Owens, a 23-year-old teacher, in that city on May 1, 1902. Reportedly, Owens was suspected of stealing an overcoat and refused to halt when commanded to do so. Reed supposedly fired at the ground to frighten Owens, but the bullet ricocheted upward, striking Owens in the back of the head, killing him. In another news account one subhead declared: "Policeman Was Too Quick with His Gun," while a second subhead stated: "Innocent Man Lies Dead as a Result." According to this account, Owens was mistaken by Reed for a man who had stolen an overcoat in Eugene, Oregon. Owens died within five hours of being shot. After the shooting Reed surrendered himself.[37]

Earlier on the day of the shooting the Roseburg marshal was notified that a man was wanted in Eugene for the theft of an overcoat and Reed was at the train depot when the 4:25 a.m. southbound train pulled into Roseburg. Brakeman Bob Medley called the officer's attention to a man who had just stepped off the train. That stranger wore an overcoat. Reed immediately pursued him and called for him to stop, but the stranger paid no attention to the demand. Reed then fired. It was reported that it was immediately determined Owens was innocent of any wrongdoing and was on his way home. After two hours of deliberation the coroner's jury returned a verdict, on May 8, that Reed was guilty of manslaughter. The officer was placed under a $2,000 bond and released.[38]

1902 September 2 *[90]* St. Louis, death.

In St. Louis on September 2, 1902, ward politician Larry Manion was shot and killed by policeman Thomas O'Hearn, supposedly while resisting arrest. Manion and "several old men" were creating a disturbance in a saloon and a peace officer was called in to quell the disturbance. Manion reportedly attacked O'Hearn and the shooting followed.[39]

Initially O'Hearn was held on the charge of causing Manion's death. Under orders from Police Chief Kiely, Inspector of Police Edward Lally investigated the death of Manion later on September 2 and as a result of that probe Lally reinstated O'Hearn to duty. To Lally, O'Hearn explained that he was standing on the corner when he heard someone calling, "Police," whereupon he ran to the sound and came across John O'Neil, the saloon bartender. He told the officer that Manion and several other men were in the saloon causing a disturbance and requested that the cop come in and end the disturbance. O'Hearn went on to say he entered the saloon and took no more than three or four steps when Manion rushed at him and struck him in the face The blow knocked him down and Manion then fell upon him. Both men went for the officer's gun and jointly pulled it from the holster. Then there was a scuffle for the gun and during that scuffle the gun discharged. They struggled some more and the gun discharged again, at which point Manion released his hold on the gun and got up and ran off. O'Hearn went after him outside but at first could not find him. He said he did not know that Manion had been shot until an hour later when a sergeant informed him of that fact. Manion and a companion were reported to have been met on the street by policeman Mantowski, who conveyed Manion to the hospital where he died one hour later. He was repeatedly questioned by Mantowski on the way to the hospital but would say nothing of the circumstances surrounding how he came to be shot. O'Hearn also declared that he was aware that Manion did not like him.[40]

On September 4 the coroner's jury returned a verdict of homicide in the death of Lawrence Manning (as he was now called). After consultation with Chief Kiely it was decided that O'Hearn, although held responsible for Manning's death by the coroner's verdict, should be permitted to give a bond and continue to serve on the force until he was suspended by the Board of Police Commissioners or indicted by the grand jury. At that inquest John O'Neil contradicted the cop's statement that he had been called to quell a disturbance. Witnesses said that Manning had been in the saloon quite a while when O'Hearn entered. Customer James H. Gallagher corroborated O'Neil. Both witnesses testified that O'Hearn accused Manning of making uncomplimentary remarks about himself and that Manning denied that allegation. They said O'Hearn then drew his pistol and fired two shots. Gallagher said he assisted Manning from the saloon and outside on the street met policeman Mantowski, who summoned a patrol wagon, which conveyed Manning to the hospital. Gallagher further declared that O'Hearn made no effort to arrest Manning after he had shot him. Manning was commonly known as Larry Manion and his name was not correctly placed on the police records until after the coroner's inquest.[41]

On September 6 O'Hearn was charged with murder in the second degree. Two witnesses each testified that O'Hearn was standing several feet away from Manning when the shots were fired, not struggling with him for the gun as the cop had stated. O'Hearn had been remanded in custody since the coroner had returned a verdict of homicide. Nothing more was published about any trial, but a brief news item that appeared some 18 months later, in April 1904, observed that Patrolman Thomas O'Hearn had been charged with intoxication and had appeared before a police trial board where he was fined $25 and reprimanded.[42]

Later in 1904 the World's Fair was under way in St. Louis. During its run, on October 23, Patrolman Thomas O'Hearn was suspended from duty and ordered to go before the police board on a charge of drunkenness. He was said to have become intoxicated at the fair and to have created "a small riot" on a streetcar as it was starting out for town. The failure of the car to start as promptly as O'Hearn desired prompted him to fire a shot in the direction of the motorman. The car was crowded and in the wild rush of the passengers to get outside many windows of the vehicle were broken.[43]

1902 October 25 *[91] Augusta, Georgia, death.*

Despondent over divorce proceedings instituted against him on October 25, 1902, in Augusta, Georgia, Charles H. Walker, a policeman on that city's force, shot and killed his wife at the home of his mother that day and then shot himself dead. After filing the divorce papers Mrs. Walker went to his mother's home. Walker's beat led him past the house and while he was passing he called for his wife. She met him at the door and they had conversed for a few minutes when Walker suddenly drew his revolver and fired four shots at his wife, all hitting her. Then Walker shot himself through the head.[44]

1902 November 12 *[92] Covington, Kentucky, death.*

During a fight in a saloon in Covington, Kentucky, on November 12, 1902, Deputy Sheriffs Nicholas Bodkin and John McInerney were shot by policeman Robert Brown. Bodkin was dead, but McInerney would recover. The shooting was said to be an outgrowth of a political feud between Brown and McInerney. Bodkin interceded when the other two men were fighting and thus came to his death. Bodkin was reported to have been "an exceedingly popular official." On April 18, 1904, Brown was convicted by a jury of voluntary manslaughter in the death of Nicholas Bodkin. In the circuit court in Covington on April 21, 1904, Judge Shaw sentenced Robert Brown to a prison term of two years at hard labor.[45]

1903 February 4 *[93] Plymouth, New Hampshire, death.*

At about 11:00 p.m. on February 4, the train station in Plymouth, New Hampshire, was entered by two masked men who held up Thomas McCough, the employee in charge. The thieves ransacked the money drawer and made their escape. Train station agent George H. Colby was notified and he set off in pursuit of the thieves. Meanwhile, city policeman Lewis C. Mills was also chasing the bandits. At some point the two pursuers came upon each other and each thought the other was one of the bandits. Mills drew his revolver and fired two bullets into Colby, who died shortly thereafter.[46]

1903 February 8 *[94] Bristol, Tennessee, death.*

On February 8, 1903, policeman G. W. Walk of Bristol, Virginia, crossed State Street into the Tennessee side of the city of Bristol and shot and almost instantly killed policeman Houston Childress of Bristol, Tennessee, who had been his friend. Walk then fled the scene. The shooting took place on a Sunday morning. Officers Porch and Childress were together when Walk approached them. Walk invited Childress to go with him to assist in doing some police duty. Childress refused on the ground that he had been insulted by Walk a few days earlier. Unpleasant words then had followed between the pair when suddenly Walk pulled out his pistol and fired twice at Childress, with the second shot entering his brain. Officer Porch allowed Walk to escape without making any effort to stop him. Walk was traced to his room where he had changed out of his uniform and into civilian clothes. A day and a half later, on the evening of February 9, Walk surrendered himself, claiming he shot Childress in self-defense. Walk was denied bail and remanded to jail. He never came to trial, at least not for a long time, because he managed to escape from custody, reportedly by gaining the confidence of the guard.[47]

Walk was on the run for many years before being captured in Idaho in the late summer of 1910. He was finally tried for the murder of Childress and on September 29, 1910, he was convicted and sentenced to 20 years in prison. For at least part of the time he was on the run he served as a member of the merchant police of Spokane, Washington, under the name of J. W. Howard. In November 1910 the Supreme Court of Tennessee denied Walk's request for a new trial.[48]

1903 February 25 [95] New York City, assault.

In General Sessions Court in New York City, on February 25, 1903, before Judge McMahon, city policeman John J. Dawson was convicted of assault in the second degree, an attack that had been committed by the officer five years earlier. District Attorney Jerome explained the five-year delay in bringing Dawson to trial by saying that he had been defending a civil suit growing out of the assault. Witnesses testified that Dawson quarreled with a neighbor named Harry McManus and then struck him on the head with his nightstick. It was said the assault was entirely unwarranted. The jury took only 20 minutes to reach a verdict. Records from the New York City Police Department did not show that Dawson had ever been internally disciplined for that incident.[49] Another account stated the assault took place on October 3, 1898, and that Dawson beat McManus "into insensibility" with his club. This article also stated the reason for the delay was on the basis on Dawson's lawyer declaring that a civil suit was pending against his client as a result of the attack. However, said a reporter, "an investigation by the D.A.'s office indicated there was no record in existence of any such proceeding."[50]

On February 27, 1903, Judge McMahon sentenced John J. Dawson to eight months in the penitentiary. Said McMahon, "I ought to send you to State prison but you have lost your place in the department as a result of your conviction, and I will take that into consideration. The club of a policeman, I want you to understand, is furnished him for the protection of citizens, not to assault them with."51

1903 March 25 [96] Washington, D.C., death.

While prisoners were being loaded into a police wagon on the morning of March 25, 1903, in Washington, D.C., to be taken to police court William Wheeler, a 42-year-old black man who had been charged with indecent exposure, tried to escape. City policeman John L. H. Sawyer chased the prisoner on foot for a couple of blocks, whereupon he drew his weapon and fired at Wheeler, killing him almost instantly. Sawyer returned to the station house and reported the matter. Shortly thereafter he was, reportedly, seized by convulsions and suddenly became very violent. Several officers were required to subdue him, whereupon he was removed to a hospital. One reporter observed that "the doctors pronounce him to be suffering from temporary insanity."52

That shooting took place at about 7:30 a.m. Sawyer had been detailed for duty with the police transfer wagon for about two years and had also acted as bailiff in the police court. That morning he was on his regular duty of transporting prisoners from various police station lockups to the police court. "I didn't intend to shoot him," said Sawyer, in the station for only a few minutes before going into convulsions. With respect to those convulsions a journalist wrote: "He has been subject to such attacks for several years, but today's attack was the most serious one he had ever experienced." Wheeler was reported to have been under the influence of alcohol at the time of his arrest and a charge of indecency was preferred against him. He was locked up overnight only because he had no money to deposit as collateral. (While details of the charge against Wheeler were not mentioned it was likely a trivial question of urinating in public.) It was also related that Wheeler came close to being killed by a cop several years earlier. While under arrest at that time he resisted in such a manner that the officer involved used his club on him: "The club disfigured him to some extent, but he was able to stand trial in Police Court, and was sent to jail." After he had been in jail several days his condition became serious and symptoms of a fracture of the skull appeared. He was transferred to a hospital and recovered. However, he had been arrested several times since.53

On April 1, 1903, an inquest was held into the death of Wheeler by Sawyer for the grand jury. The jurors deliberated only a few minutes before they reached a verdict: "We hold J. L. H. Sawyer for the action of the grand jury." One policeman who testified at that inquest was Captain Bingham. At the suggestion of the coroner he read from the police manual about the use of firearms by an officer. He said it was a general proposition of the law that an officer was not justified in taking life except to prevent an "atrocious" crime or to prevent the escape of a person where an atrocious crime had been committed. But nothing further happened. A small report appeared in the paper on May 9, 1903, that noted policeman Sawyer had been restored to full duty in the Washington police department.[54]

1903 March 28 *[97] New York City, assault.*

Policeman Patrick J. McAuliffe of the New York City police force was shot in his right side early in the morning of March 28, 1903, by fellow officer Daniel E. Hanrahan, who was then placed under arrest. The wound was said to be slight. That shooting was preceded by a quarrel, although the subject matter of the dispute was not known. It was said the two men had been on unfriendly terms for several months and had frequently threatened each other. McAuliffe was on his beat around 4:00 a.m. when he met Officer Gallagher, who had arrested Thomas Sheridan for intoxication. He called for a police wagon and when it came Hanrahan was driving it, with policeman Fenton on the seat beside him. The shooting took place while Fenton and Gallagher were loading the prisoner into the back of the wagon. Those two said they did not hear the dispute. McAuliffe stated that Hanrahan called him some names and when McAuliffe asked what he meant Hanrahan drew his revolver and shot him. Hanrahan said that McAuliffe came to the front of the wagon and struck him with his nightstick and that he was forced to use his revolver in self-defense. Hanrahan was at once placed under arrest and put in a cell, held on $1,000 bail. Hanrahan made a countercharge against McAuliffe, for assault. Both men were said to have "good" records on the force; Hanrahan had been a cop for 12 years, while McAuliffe had served for eight years. In May 1903 each of the two men were held for the grand jury, each charged with an assault upon the other.[55]

1903 June 26 *[98] Renovo, Pennsylvania, death.*

Policeman Michael Crowley of the Renovo, Pennsylvania, police department shot and killed a young man named William Ryan on Friday night, June 26, 1903, near midnight. Ryan and a group of young men were told to go home and cease their rowdy behavior by Crowley when Ryan, reportedly, struck the officer, knocking him down. Upon his regaining his feet Ryan again knocked him to the ground, whereupon the cop pulled his gun and fired at him, almost instantly killing him. Crowley was arrested and lodged in a nearby lockup. The prisoner made a statement claiming that he defended himself when repeatedly assaulted by the young men who were intoxicated.[56]

At the trial of Crowley it was revealed that the officer, while walking his beat, came upon Ryan and one other man, Frank McCarthy, sitting on the front step of a house. They were not creating a disturbance, nor were they committing a breach of the peace. Crowley told them it was late and they were to go home. Ryan jumped up and said it was not Crowley's business if they were sitting there. The judge at that trial agreed that Crowley exceeded his authority in telling the two men to go home and in then trying to arrest Ryan, as the young men were not doing anything wrong. There was evidence that Ryan did knock Crowley down twice, from an independent witness. The officer was convicted of manslaughter but was awarded a new trial. Crowley was convicted of manslaughter at the second trial but was still not in custody, as that second conviction was in the appeal process. Early in March 1905, while that second conviction was still under appeal, Crowley complained of not feeling well. A few days later the 62-year-old was found dead from natural causes, as determined by a medical examiner. The official cause of death was listed as "apoplexy" (stroke).[57]

1903 June 27 [99] *Shenandoah, Pennsylvania, death.*

When Patrolman Thomas Dodd was passing along a street in Shenandoah on Saturday night, June 27, 1903, he heard cries for help and, going to the location of the sound, he saw two men engaged in a fight. One was on the ground, while the other, Stinoy Barwick, known to the police as a "dangerous character," was beating him with a club. When Barwick saw the cop he dropped his weapon and he ran off, with the officer in pursuit. Dodd caught up to the man in an alley and the pair started to struggle. Before Dodd knew what happened he received "several hard blows" on the head from a pair of steel knuckles. Realizing his life was in danger, he drew his revolver and shot his assailant in the stomach, or so he claimed. With blood flowing from an "ugly wound" Barwick took off again and was soon lost in the alley. Weak and somewhat dazed, Dodd made his way to the police station and reported the events. When other officers went in search of Barwick they found him lying unconscious in the middle of the street where he had been fighting. Then they took him to the station house and only after that did they transport him to the hospital, where he died. Dodd was locked up on a charge of murder.[58]

1903 July 4 *[100] Philadelphia, death.*

Edward Stinger, 28, was shot and killed by a Philadelphia policeman in that city on July 4, 1903, while attempting to steal a crate of fruit in the produce district of the city. Stinger, with three companions, was discovered by the officer and when they all ran off the pursuing policeman fired his revolver, killing Stinger.[59]

1903 September 28 *[101] Johnson City, Tennessee, death.*

David Britt, who worked as a watchman at the federal soldiers' home, was shot and killed on September 28, 1903, by city policeman George S. Allen in Johnson City, Tennessee. Allen claimed he shot in self-defense and admitted that he had a previous "difficulty" with Britt over the arrest of the latter's son on a trivial charge.[60]

The shooting took place on a main shopping street in front of a store. Allen was placed under arrest by citizens who witnessed the shooting and turned over to Deputy Sheriff Boring. Because of threats made to lynch the officer he was taken to Jonesboro and lodged in a cell there. A reporter observed: "This was one of the most unprovoked murders ever committed in this section. There was neither reason nor excuse for it. Beginning in folly it ended in crime." The story began when a section of garden hose was missed by Mrs. Browder and a neighbor told her she had seen a little boy take the hose away. Mrs. Browder notified the police chief and described the boy as best she could. Police Chief Remine and Allen surmised that a small son of David Britt had taken the hose, and went to the Britt family home and not only accused the six-year-old but also searched the premises without either a warrant for the arrest of anyone or a search warrant. Knowing his boy to be innocent, Britt was incensed at such an insult. On September 28 Britt, along with his wife and two young sons, came to the Recorder's office on business at a time when Allen happened to be present. The two men got into another heated argument over the hose and finally Recorder Pounder told them they must not fight in his office. Britt left the office first and waited outside in the street for Allen. When the officer came out the altercation was renewed. Britt struck Allen with an umbrella, whereupon Allen drew his revolver and fired at his adversary three times. All bullets struck the man and Britt sank to the ground to die at the feet of his wife and sons. It was that incident that prompted rumblings of a lynching. Said a journalist: "This shooting shows that he has no idea where or when an officer should use a gun. He claims to have killed four men with the same weapon and took great delight in showing it to those working under him." Britt was described as hardworking, a man who left behind a wife and four children, with the oldest being a 12-year-old girl. A fund was started for the family to raise the $400 still owed on the family home. A second fund was established to raise the money to employ counsel to assist the prosecution. Britt did not live long enough to see his son officially vindicated, but soon after his funeral it was ascertained the hose had not been stolen. A relative of Mrs. Browder had sent a young boy over to borrow the item, but Browder was not at home. The lad borrowed the hose anyway but left no note to that effect.[61]

When Allen came to trial he was convicted of involuntary manslaughter and sentenced to two years in the penitentiary. However, in October 1905 a court of appeal declared Allen had been given that term in error: "Britt struck Allen on the head with an umbrella staff which caused a wound that bled profusely. Allen then fired to cause Britt to desist. This he did not do and then Allen fired two additional shots, causing death." That court of appeals held the verdict rendered at the trial was "impossible," and the appeals court further held that Allen should have been acquitted of the charge, that his acts were justified. Thus the appeal court remanded the case back to the lower court.[62]

1904 February 23 [102] *Denver, death.*

On the night of February 23, 1904, in Denver, Colorado, Samuel Emrich, a detective on the city police force, shot and killed William Malone, a saloon keeper. Emrich shot and killed Malone in the latter's saloon after a quarrel with Mike Ryan over a game of dice. Malone intervened in the role of peacemaker. Emrich claimed the shooting was in self-defense. When a coroner's jury investigation the death it declared that the killing was felonious and recommended murder charges against the officer. On May 14, 1904, Samuel Emrich was convicted of murder in the second degree.[63]

1904 March 20 [103] *New York City, death.*

Charged with being responsible for the death of Patrick H. Farrell, a bartender who died in the Brooklyn Hospital several days earlier, New York City policeman William H. Bosse of the Classon Avenue police station in Brooklyn was arrested on March 30, 1904. Farrell was found in a dying condition on Sunday night, March 20, in the toilet room of the saloon where he worked. He had been badly beaten about the head. Shortly before he was found, it was alleged, Bosse had been in the saloon and had some kind of row with him. After the death of Farrell, Captain Thomas F. Maude of the Classon station conducted an investigation and professed to have discovered evidence that Farrell was beaten by Bosse and that his death was due to the injuries inflicted by the officer. Bosse denied having a fight with Farrell and declared the deceased fell and struck his head against a pile of beer crates in the saloon.[64]

After Bosse was charged with murder and arraigned in the Myrtle Avenue court on March 30, Magistrate Higginbotham paroled him in the custody of Capt. Thomas F. Maude, the commanding officer of Bosse. On that same day the case was brought before Coroner Michael J. Flaherty and a jury inquiring into the death of Farrell. By its verdict the jury declared that Farrell came to his death on March 24 from a cerebral laceration and hemorrhage due to a fracture of the skull caused by a blow from a blunt instrument "and in our opinion the evidence all points to the presumption that said blow was administered by the officer who was in the saloon with the deceased." The story Bosse told his captain was that early in the morning of March 20 he was passing the saloon and saw three men drinking there. It was then after hours and he entered the place and ordered the bartender to close the establishment. While Bosse was talking to Farrell, he said, "the latter fell to the floor in a fit." Bosse denied he had struck the man and told the other men in the saloon to lock the door of the place and remain there while he went to call an ambulance. Upon his return he said he found Farrell still lying on the floor with the door locked but with the other men gone. Later, Bosse continued, those men returned and two of them carried Farrell to his brother's house. The following night Farrell was taken to the Brooklyn Hospital, where he remained unconscious until he died a few days later. There were no eyewitnesses either to the supposed fall or to the assault. Dr. Harry W. Haskell, who was called in to attend the man at his home, declared it would have been impossible for Farrell to have received his injuries through such a fall as was described by Bosse. Haskell was certain the injuries that fractured Farrell's skull came from a blow. As well, the deceased had two black eyes and injuries to his upper lip.[65]

On May 12, 1904, in the Criminal Branch of the County Court in Brooklyn a jury deliberated for just 25 minutes before returning with a verdict that acquitted Bosse of all charges in the death of Farrell. When the jury brought in its verdict friends of Bosse in the courtroom applauded. That applause was quickly stopped by the judge and when Bosse walked out of the room he was accompanied by a band of sympathizers, most of whom were fellow officers.[66]

1904 April 27 *[104] Rock Hill, South Carolina, death.*

A brief report that was published in May 1904 stated that "in Conway [South Carolina] a police official killed a leading citizen who interfered with the arrest of a negro. In Rock Hill [South Carolina] a policeman shot to death a turbulent white man who resisted arrest." Another brief report that appeared in a different South Carolina paper may have explained one of the preceding items. That second report noted that on April 27, 1904, J. A. Eubanks, a white policeman at Rock Hill, shot and killed Spencer Doster, a black man. As of November 1, 1904, it was reported that a trial was pending in that case and Eubanks was out on bail.[67]

Spencer Doster was shot in the afternoon in front of the city lockup. The cause of the shooting was said to have been that Doster was resisting arrest, having taken Eubanks' club from him, and was beating him "fearfully" with it. The inquest exonerated Eubanks, who, they declared, was simply discharging his duty while the deceased was resisting arrest. Nevertheless, Eubanks was taken to Yorkville and committed to the county jail. In the middle of November 1904 the trial took place and lasted one day. Testimony was reported to have shown Doster was resisting arrest and that in the shooting the policeman used only "so much force as he deemed necessary to protect his own life." The jury returned a verdict of not guilty.[68]

1904 May 8 *[105] New York City, death.*

On May 9, 1904, Arthur J. Mallon, a New York City police officer, was a prisoner on parole charged with having shot Robert Brennan, then in critical condition. The shooting occurred at 6:00 a.m. on May 8 in the Bowery section of the city. Several versions of the story were then in circulation, with Mallon himself being responsible for two of them, one of which he gave to police inspector Schmittberger and the other to police captain Flood. The other versions came from policeman Doogan (attached to the same station as Mallon), who arrested the shooter, and from a young man named Wolfe who worked in the drugstore to which the wounded Brennan was taken pending the arrival of an ambulance. At police headquarters it was said that Mallon's record "was of the best." Flood said he talked to Mallon two hours after the shooting and that he was sober. Mallon told him, said Flood, that his foster brother Robert Jones was an "indiscreet" young man and he heard that he was on the Bowery early in the morning of May 8 and Mallon decided to go and look him up. Mallon traced him to a saloon and decided to go in and get him. Going to the rear door of the closed saloon, Mallon knocked at the door but was refused admittance. When he explained that he was a cop the man behind the door laughed and said he did not believe he was a cop. Mallon then walked away, but a few minutes later Jones, who, Mallon thought, must have heard him at the closed door, came out onto the street and joined him. They started walking down the street when four or five men came out of the saloon and came up to them from behind, whereupon one of them struck Mallon in the back of the neck with a blackjack. Then there was a struggle, in the course of which Mallon drew his pistol, which was discharged, wounding Brennan. It was said that Brennan had only been released from prison a short time ago after serving a term for larceny. Flood could not explain why it was that in the report of the shooting sent to police headquarters the paperwork stated that Mallon had shot Brennan while the latter was resisting arrest.[69]

According to Inspector Schmittberger, Mallon gave a different account. The story, as told to Schmittberger by Mallon, was that at a little before 6:00 a.m. on May 8 Jones came to Mallon's home and informed him that he had been robbed of a gold watch on the Bowery. He went out with Jones to try to recover the watch. They went into a saloon where Mallon asked Jones if any of the men there had robbed him. Jones could not identify any of the men as the thief and the pair left the place. When they had walked about 50 yards away Mallon said they were attacked from behind by four men, one of whom had a blackjack. He turned around and in the scuffle he pulled out his pistol, which discharged, with the bullet hitting "Brennan's back." All of those men then ran off with Mallon in pursuit. When he caught up with Brennan he saw the man was shot and called for an ambulance. Mallon also declared it was Brennan who had the blackjack. At Mallon's home the statement he made to Schmittberger was said to be the correct version of the affair.[70]

Officer Doogan provided yet another story. According to him, he was on duty in the area at the time of the shooting. When he heard a pistol shot at about 6:00 a.m. he ran to the sound and saw a man staggering and half-running before falling down. After doing what he could for Brennan by way of emergency medical attention Doogan ran back toward the saloon and found Mallon, in civilian clothes, standing there. He had a pistol in his hand and was arguing with a drunken sailor. Doogan arrested Mallon. Brennan was taken into a drugstore where he received further attention while waiting for the ambulance. Late in the afternoon of May 8 Brennan regained consciousness a little and said he had been in various places in the Bowery with a number of friends and that he was walking along the street when he felt a pain in his back. Then he discovered he had been shot, but he did not know who shot him. When Mallon was arraigned in Essex Market Court on May 8 Magistrate Mayo paroled him in the custody of Captain Flood.[71]

As the result of a "secret investigation" by District Attorney Jerome's office Arthur J. Mallon was lodged in the Tombs prison in New York on August 4, 1904, charged with murder in the first degree. The grand jury had indicted him earlier that day. The 21-year-old Brennan had died on May 8, two days after being shot. Reportedly, that indictment was unexpected by the accused man and by his superiors, as he had been discharged by a Coroner Schuler jury that held the shooting to have been accidental. What led the District Attorney to get involved were the "widely varying stories" that Mallon told his superiors and after hearing from Brennan's mother. She went to the District Attorney's office a day after the shooting and said that a young male friend of her son called at her house and said he had seen the cop shoot Robert but that he was afraid to tell the police what he saw. He further told the mother that the cop was drunk when he shot Robert and that the shooting "was entirely unprovoked." Jerome learned the name of the witness from Mrs. Brennan, as well as the names of several other young men who were with her son when he was shot. According to the mother, her son was home all evening and rose at about 5:00 a.m. on May 8 and went out to get a newspaper, or so he told her. A reporter remarked: "A strange feature of the case was the reports of Detectives (2) who said in the hospital Brennan did not identify Mallon as the man who shot him." Jerome's investigation brought out the fact that Mallon had been drinking on the morning of the shooting and on the night before as well and had gotten into a quarrel with some men on the Bowery. It was also learned that Jones was not with Mallon at the time and he could not be found for "some time" after the incident. Mallon had been on the police force for seven years. The reporter then remarked that in two similar cases recently, the shooting of William Dacy by Detective McEvoy and of a young man in Newark by Detective Sergeant Farrell, the same excuse was used as in Mallon's case—that the revolver went off accidentally.[72]

Mallon was out of custody on $10,000 bail and came to trial before Recorder Goff in General Sessions Court in New York on December 6, 1904. William O'Brien took the stand and declared he had been an eyewitness. He said he had been in the saloon when Mallon, Brennan and Jones were there. He left the saloon and later saw Jones and Mallon standing together on a Bowery street. Brennan was about to walk past when Mallon put out his hand. They had some words and a fight broke out. After a few punches were thrown Brennan ran off with Mallon after him. After taking a few strides Mallon shot Brennan in the back. O'Brien added that he went to the spot where Brennan fell and was holding the head of the wounded man. Then Mallon said to the policeman who had just arrived on the scene, referring to O'Brien, "Get that fellow away from here. He knows too much."[73]

When Assistant District Attorney Train summed up the case on December 8 he charged the police with hampering the prosecution and failing to get witnesses against Mallon because he was a cop. On the stand, Mallon reiterated the story that in a struggle with four friends of the deceased the revolver was accidentally discharged. One cop backed that up. Sergeant Sherwood testified that Mallon told him at that time that Brennan had robbed Mallon's relative Jones and he had put him under arrest and that Brennan had then assaulted him and started to escape when the accused officer fired. Mallon insisted he called on Brennan to "halt," but he kept on going and then Mallon shot him.[74]

On December 9 after deliberating for about two hours the jury in the Mallon case returned with a verdict finding him guilty of manslaughter in the first degree. The maximum sentence was a term of 20 years. While the accused had been on the stand one day earlier he made no mention at all of the story he had supposedly told to Sherwood but told a different version. Mallon was 33 years old and by this account had been on the NYPD for 12 years. Recorder Goff sentenced the prisoner on December 16 to a term of 20 years' incarceration at Sing Sing prison. Goff said to the prisoner while he was sentencing him, "It is a spectacle to be regretted that an officer charged with the enforcement of the law and the protection of citizens should stand at the bar convicted of a crime like this." Goff found no mitigating circumstances and thus imposed the maximum sentence.[75]

William K. Smith of the firm Smith and Buchanan, proprietors of the saloon where the murder started, surrendered himself to the police on December 30, 1904. Smith did so because he heard he was wanted in connection with the shooting of William O'Brien, the chief witness in the Mallon case. O'Brien had been shot near Smith's saloon early on the morning of December 29. A witness declared to the police that he saw Smith shoot O'Brien. That witness was Cornelius J. Donlon and he told District Attorney Jerome that he had already told the story to two detectives at a police station, but they had failed to act and failed to investigate and make an arrest. Jerome then interceded and tried to get the police to act, but Smith then surrendered himself. The detectives involved, along with Captain Flood, said they were not guilty of negligence but could not find Smith to arrest him. When Smith was taken to the hospital and brought before O'Brien the wounded man looked at him and declared, "I don't know who shot me—if I did I wouldn't tell."[76]

On March 17, 1905, Mallon was released on bail of $20,000 by Recorder Goff. Because Mallon's appeal was pending he had been granted a "certificate of reasonable doubt" by the court. However, late in December 1906 the Appellate Division affirmed his conviction. He had been suspended without pay by the NYPD since August 1904. On June 14, 1907, the Court of Appeals affirmed the conviction and the police at once arrested Mallon, who was still free at that time.[77]

Early on the morning of April 18, 1907, William O'Brien was shot and killed in the Bowery by a man named Edward Purcano, who was said to have confessed. Within this article the character of O'Brien was blackened much more than in previous stories and articles wherein he was mentioned.[78]

A news report published in January 1916 noted that a few prisoners would be having their sentences commuted by New York State governor Whitman.

It was said that one would be Arthur Mallon, who was to have his sentence commuted. Mallon had made an application for a commutation.[79]

1904 June 4 *[106] Rutherford, New Jersey, death.*

Rutherford, New Jersey, policeman Charles McManus, while on duty early in the morning of June 4, 1904, shot and killed a man named Paul Brickner, 35 years old. The cop took Brickner for a burglar and said he found him trying to gain entry to a home in a fashionable section of Rutherford. For the previous few months several attempts had been made to rob the houses of wealthy residents in that neighborhood, and Police Chief George Holland had cautioned his men to keep a sharp lookout in that area for thieves. On the morning in question McManus and another officer were patrolling that area and saw a man who was apparently trying to force a window. McManus called to the man to surrender and as the burglar, who proved to be Brickner, tried to run off one of the officers fired three shots at him, none of which took effect. Brickner kept running, as did the two cops, and McManus fired one shot, which hit the fleeing man in the back near the heart. He survived about ten minutes more, long enough to tell the police who he was and that his family resided in East Rutherford and that he had seven children. The Rutherford police declared they believed that Brickner was concerned in the other robberies or attempted robberies that had been committed in Rutherford in recent time. No weapon or burglar tools were found on the deceased. McManus was paroled in the custody of Chief Holland.[80]

A day later a different newspaper presented an account of the killing in which the victim was identified as Paul Bitterlich, a widower with six children, the oldest of whom was 16. On the evening of June 4 a coroner's jury exonerated McManus, delivering a verdict that stated the officer was justified in shooting Bitterlich, who was detected in a suspicious manner and refused to halt when called to do so. It was reported that several witnesses testified in favor of the policeman. Friends of the victim said it was a mystery to them. They said Paul left his home to escort a woman to her home, which was near the scene of the shooting. They claimed that Paul was leaving that woman's home when the cop saw him. McManus was the main witness called at that coroner's inquest. He testified that Bitterlich, when discovered, started to run and that McManus fired several shots in the air. When those warning shots did not stop Bitterlich he fired another shot and the victim fell dead with a bullet near the heart. Daniel Burns testified that Bitterlich was attempting to enter the Burns residence when McManus caught him and that his home was a quarter of a mile away from the residence of the woman Bitterlich had escorted home. Other witnesses testified the dead man was a laborer and had always borne a good reputation.[81]

1904 July 27 [107] *New York City, death.*

On the afternoon of August 9, 1904, the coroner's jury was hearing the case that involved NYPD detective Edward McEvoy. The inquest was looking into the death of 18-year-old William Daly, an escaping prisoner who was shot and killed by McEvoy on July 27. Five of the members of that jury held McEvoy responsible for the death of Daly, while the other four panel members issued a verdict exonerating him. His case was due to go on to the grand jury. At that inquest McEvoy gave testimony. He swore he came across Daly in a pawnshop carrying a bundle and that the actions of the young man were so suspicious that McEvoy placed him under arrest. McEvoy added that Daly confessed to him that he had stolen the contents of the bundle. As the pair left the pawnshop and came to a street corner Daly broke away from the cop and ran off. Said McEvoy, "By that time I was played out and he was gaining on me, so I shot at him. I didn't intend to kill him. I wanted to strike his foot or leg." A journalist commented: "Policemen from Harlem testified that Daly's character was bad in that he had been arrested. It was not shown that he had ever been convicted of a crime."[82]

Another article about the coroner's inquest stated that the coroner's report accepted the verdict clearing the officer. It mentioned the 5–4 jury split that favored no exoneration and then said, "By some process known only to the initiated at the coroner's office, only the minority report is entered in full in the big book which contains the record of inquests. A supplementary mention is made of the majority report." This account reported that two other policemen, Detectives Black and Horton, were with McEvoy at the time of the shooting and corroborated everything. Several cops came forward to testify to Daly's bad character. One said the dead boy had been arrested 20 times or more but admitted he had never personally arrested him. He added that he knew a man who said Daly had stolen his pocketbook. The bundle found on Daly contained some clothing and linen, but the police were never able to show that it was stolen.[83]

An account of the actual shooting stated that the chase featured "sensational gunplay in the streets of Harlem." That account described Daly as "a self-confessed hotel and flat thief." Three policemen came across him at 5:30 p.m. in the pawnshop and McEvoy followed him out of the store and stopped him on the street after a block. Thinking him to be acting suspiciously, McEvoy started to take him in. The other two policemen followed a little distance back to keep back the crowd that had assembled. Then Daly broke away and was shot. On the way to the hospital, it was said, he told the policemen he had been engaged in robbing flats ever since he left his home 18 months earlier. William Daly died in the hospital at 4:00 a.m. on July 28.[84]

1904 August 3 *[108] Newark, New Jersey, death.*

Thirty-year-old Herbert Earl was shot and killed by Detective Sergeant Joseph Farrell in Newark, New Jersey, on the afternoon of August 3, 1904. Earl had been arrested by the detective and was being taken to police headquarters when he made an attempt to escape. Farrell called for him to halt and when he refused Farrell drew his revolver and fired. Earl died almost instantly. It was reported that Earl had been pointed out to the officer by John Welch, who kept a boathouse, as the man who had given him a forged check for $18. Farrell arrested Earl and the pair were walking along the street when the shooting took place. The officer said he intended to fire into the air but that the revolver discharged while he was taking it out of the holster. Farrell surrendered to the authorities; Earl had 13 cents in his pockets.[85]

One day later, on August 4, Farrell was arraigned on a charge of manslaughter preferred by Police Chief Hopper and was released on $5,000 bail. The police declared they had "secured indubitable proof" that Earl had been forging checks since he was an office boy over 15 years earlier: "He was arraigned at that time, but was allowed to go free on account of his youth." Since then, said the police, he had been in custody twice and spent a term in the penitentiary at Caldwell, New Jersey. Joseph Farrell was suspended by the Newark Police Commissioners on August 6, pending the action of the grand jury. While nothing more was reported on this case, as with so many others, Farrell apparently received no punishment. A brief report published on July 23, 1906, told of a raid conducted by Newark police. One of the participants was Detective Sergeant Farrell.[86]

1904 August *[109] Laurel, Mississippi, death.*

Officer Fred Bounds, who shot and killed Frank Williams of Louisville while he was trying to arrest him for stealing a ride on a passenger train, was convicted in the circuit court in Laurel, Mississippi. A jury returned a verdict of manslaughter and Bounds was sentenced to two years in the penitentiary. It was reported that he did not plan to appeal.[87]

1904 September 29 *[110] Savannah, Georgia, death.*

Savannah, Georgia, policemen E. O. Zipperer and W. C. Goodwin were members of the train station squad. On Thursday, September 29, 1904, they got into an argument about how drummers (traveling salesmen) and the train depot should be treated by the police. A fight ensued between the officers in the course of which Zipperer was shot and killed by Goodwin. When the coroner held an inquest his jury reached a verdict that the killing was murder. Goodwin was locked up pending further legal action. In superior court at Savannah on October 24, 1904, Goodwin stood convicted of the killing and Judge Cann sentenced him to eight years in the penitentiary. Immediately thereafter the prisoner's lawyer made a motion for a new trial and Goodwin was admitted to $2,000 bail.[88]

1904 October 22 *[111] Pittsburgh, death.*

While he was at pistol practice at a police station in Pittsburgh on the morning of October 22, 1904, Lieutenant Walsh was accidentally shot and killed by Capt. Albert H. Teeters. It was reported that Walsh had been the closest friend of Teeters. That shooting took place in the cellar under Number 6 Police Station on Frankstown Avenue.[89]

1904 November 2 *[112] New York City, death.*

On the evening of November 2, 1904, New York City policeman Eugene L. Devanna found himself surrounded by what was described by a reporter as a "crowd of fighting mad boilermakers" and because he feared they meant to beat him the patrolman drew his revolver and shot one of those boilermakers, George Dowrick. The bullet struck the man near his heart and he died within about ten minutes. Devanna surrendered himself and was placed in the lockup at the High Bridge police station, to which he was attached. At the time of the shooting the cop was off duty and in civilian clothes. He was an unmarried 31-year-old of whom it was said that "he has a good record and is liked by his fellow officers." Dowrick was 32 and came to New York City from Chester, Pennsylvania. He was employed by the Gas Engine and Power Company and rented a room and ate his meals at the Morris Dock Hotel, where the shooting occurred. Police officials stated that Devanna was sober before he entered the hotel and that he drank only two glasses of beer in the establishment. Devanna explained that when he was drinking at the bar the bartender, James Costello, was joking with two boilermakers, James Malone and John Roberts, and that Malone was boisterous. Devanna remarked to them that he wanted to be left alone, but the two men became personal and soon the three got angry. Mrs. Patrick Murphy, wife of the hotel proprietor, attempted to quiet the group and induced the cop to go out into the hallway. At that point it was said that Dowrick interceded. Devanna said he warned Dowrick to keep away from him but that Dowrick drew a knife and slashed the officer across the fingers of one hand. The officer, wrote a reporter, had several "badly cut fingers to bear out this assertion." Then the peace officer fired. As a number of angry boilermakers poured from the bar into the hallway in response to the sound of the shot, Devanna ran out through a rear entrance of the hotel and disappeared. When the police were informed of the incident they sent about 12 officers to the saloon and arrested as witnesses all those directly involved in the shooting and in the dispute leading up to it, including Mrs. Murphy. No knife was found on Dowrick's person nor on any of the prisoners. Devanna surrendered himself after the shooting.[90]

An account of the shooting in a different newspaper said the shooting occurred after a heated political argument. Devanna ran off after the shooting and was not seen again until almost two hours later when he surrendered and declared he had acted in self-defense. Several boilermakers were in the saloon that day and after a time Dowrick and Malone began to talk politics. While they were doing so Devanna entered the bar and soon joined in the discussion. The men, it was said, resented the cop's remarks and soon an argument erupted. That angered Devanna and a fight appeared to be imminent. The bartender then interceded and got the men from the barroom into the dining room in the rear. There the quarrel continued. Suddenly a shot rang out. When the bartender ran back he found Dowrick stretched out motionless on the floor and Devanna was nowhere to be seen. Police were informed and when they learned Devanna had disappeared police reserves were called out to conduct a search. Shortly before 8:00 p.m. Devanna, while supposedly on his way to surrender, met some of the cops who were looking for him and surrendered to them. At that time he declared, "I did the shooting but I had to. There was a bunch of men who were trying to do me, and I shot to save my own life. One of the men attacked me with a knife. I was cut all over the hands." Devanna showed the officers his hands, which were said to be gashed in a dozen places. Devanna was locked up. Malone declared that Devanna had "butted in" on the discussion and had caused all the trouble himself. Dowrick, Malone added, was trying to act the role of peacemaker when Devanna drew a revolver and killed him.[91]

A third account of the shooting by a third New York City paper began by announcing that Devanna, who was "a protégé of President Roosevelt who fought through the Spanish War with the Rough Riders and was appointed to the police force at the special request of the President, is lying in a cell in the Tombs orison today" held to answer for the murder of his "best friend," Dowrick. (The preceding "facts" were all complete lies. That was the reverse of demonizing the victim—sanctifying the killer.) The account continued to say that Dowrick was shot down at a moment when he was doing everything he could to save his friend Devanna from the consequences "of his own drunken folly. The policeman was crazed with drink and whipped out his pistol and fired it without the slightest provocation." On that fateful day Devanna had a day off and went to a bar where he drank for a while. By 4:00 p.m. "he was very drunk" and wandered into the Morris Dock Hotel and engaged in more drinking. When the proprietor's wife suggested he had enough he picked a quarrel with a couple of the boilermakers. That quarrel got ugly and Mrs. Murphy got Devanna out into the hallway. She was holding him to restrain him from returning to the barroom when Dowrick came out from the bar and tried to quiet Devanna down. They grappled for a bit and then Devanna drew and fired his revolver.[92]

The coroner's jury investigating the death of Dowrick returned a verdict on the night of November 4 that the shooting was accidental. A reporter described the verdict as a "surprise." Apparently it surprised Coroner Berry, because he ignored that verdict and committed Devanna to the Tombs prison to await the action of the grand jury. The verdict was called a surprise because Berry had charged the jury that there was no excuse for the officer's act. Several witnesses testified to the effect that Devanna was clearly at fault and clearly the instigator. On the other side several policemen testified in Devanna's behalf that the weapon used was practically a hair-trigger instrument that could discharge on the slightest use of the trigger. Such testimony was intended to convince the jury that Devanna, although he drew the weapon from his pocket and pointed it, had no intention of shooting the man who had been his friend.[93]

Devanna was indicted for murder in the first degree by the grand jury on December 23, with a reporter noting that he did the shooting "while intoxicated," a fact that by now seemed to be accepted. On January 21, 1905, the jury convicted Devanna of manslaughter in the first degree. Ten days later Judge Foster sentenced Eugene Devanna to 20 years' imprisonment in the state prison. Arguing for his client, lawyer Hal Bell pled for clemency on the ground that Devanna was under the influence of alcohol at the time the crime was committed. To that plea District Attorney Jerome stated, "If nothing more could be said in extenuation of the crime of shooting an inoffensive citizen than the fact that the police officer was intoxicated I would think it best not to mention it." When he passed sentence Judge Foster found no extenuating circumstances and therefore imposed the maximum penalty. At the time of his sentencing Devanna admitted to the judge that the report linking him to Theodore Roosevelt and his famed Rough Riders was completely untrue.[94]

1904 December 20 *[113] New York City, assault, death.*

At the direction of Police Commissioner William McAdoo, police officials began an investigation, on December 21, 1904, into the brutal clubbing of James P. Robbins, a well-known newspaper reporter, by New York City policeman

Frank McLaughlin. According to Robbins, McLaughlin without the slightest provocation attacked him on a street corner early on the morning of December 20, broke his arm in two places "and gave him a good clubbing generally." The only explanation for the assault at that time was that McLaughlin mistook Robbins for someone else. As a result of the investigation an inspector sent word to McAdoo that the case was a very serious one and recommended the immediate suspension of the cop. McAdoo said he would suspend McLaughlin that very day. Said McAdoo, "The man has had eighteen complaints against him since 1896 and has been fined sixty-eight and one-half days' pay. If all that is told of this case is true, it is an outrage. It is a mystery to me how such brutes as this man can get on the force." That investigation began with both Robbins and the officer in the same room. Robbins told the same story as related earlier. Then McLaughlin was asked to tell his side. He said he was at a street corner early in the morning when Robbins came along and told him that the excise (tax) law was being violated by a man named Kennedy who keep a nearby saloon, at the street corner where the assault took place. McLaughlin accompanied Robbins to that saloon but found nothing amiss. McLaughlin then gave Robbins a good "dressing down" for wasting his time and left him at that corner. Later, McLaughlin said, he saw Robbins fall down and gave it as his opinion that the man sustained his injuries from that supposed fall. After telling that story McLaughlin suddenly remembered that policeman Willis G. Paine was with him though all those events he had described and called Paine in to verify his story and, said a journalist, "Paine solemnly verified it in every detail." Robbins declared he had never seen Paine before in his life and that no cop was with McLaughlin at the time of the assault. While waiting for the police board to take action, based on that investigation, Robbins stated his intention to apply for a warrant for the officer's arrest on a charge of assault, thus bringing the case into the criminal courts. Robbins had left a friend at the street corner of the assault at about 2:40 a.m. on December 20 and was standing there waiting for a streetcar when, without warning, he was almost felled by a blow from a club across his back. As he turned he was in time to catch another blow from the club of a uniformed policeman on his elbow that fractured his wrist and paralyzed the lower part of his arm. He received several more blows and then the cop pulled his revolver, aimed at him and pulled the trigger. The gun failed to fire and while the policeman was examining it Robbins managed to run off. McLaughlin after failing to fire his pistol disappeared. Eventually Robbins made his way to a hospital and got treated and then went to a police station.[95]

A warrant for felonious assault was issued on December 21 by Magistrate Moss. Of the 18 complaints on McLaughlin's record all but about two or three came from citizens. That in itself was unusual. Many officers on the NYPD had ran up 12 or 15 or 18 complaints against themselves, but it was more normal for all but two or three to have come from the police department. That is, complaints lodged by superiors against officers for being absent without leave, intoxicated while on duty, loitering inside instead of walking their beat, and so forth. The police trial board existed mainly to deal with such internal disciplinary issues; it was always reluctant to deal with citizen complaints. With respect to the assault of Robbins a man by the name of John C. Myers was located who had witnessed the assault. He corroborated, said a reporter, "in every detail" Robbins' story.[96]

Regarding the McLaughlin case police captain Cooney said on December 23, "A policeman who attacks a citizen with his club as McLaughlin is alleged to have done is a disgrace to the force and brings decent policemen into disrepute. When such a man is found out the courts should make an example of him. The police should be more anxious to be rid of him than anyone else." Police officials were then going over McLaughlin's entire record carefully. In the West 68th Street station where he had been doing duty since June 9, 1901, "he has earned for himself the reputation of a clubber. He has been a terror alike to white and colored people in the tenement house section." Officials were also looking at charges against him that had been dismissed "because of the excellent defenses which McLaughlin always put in" but were similar to the complaint lodged by Robbins. One of McLaughlin's habitual methods of defense, as shown by the record, was "to assail the character of the complainants and their witnesses."[97]

On December 28 McLaughlin appeared in court to plead to the charge of assault made by Robbins. To his surprise he was instead committed to jail on a charge of murder in the first degree. McLaughlin had been arrested before in connection with the death of John W. Patterson, a black watchman. The coroner's jury in that case declared McLaughlin had shot Patterson in self-defense and he was discharged. When District Attorney Jerome's office was going over the officer's record it said it was not satisfied with the disposition of that case and began its own investigation. That probe led to McLaughlin being indicted for murder.[98]

The Patterson incident occurred on May 27, 1904, and came about, said a report, when police were trying to disperse a crowd of black people who had congregated in front of a dance hall. Passing through the area, policeman Frank McLaughlin came upon that crowd of black people and ordered them to move on. He returned five minutes later to find two of that crowd still there. One of them, who turned out to be John W. Patterson, according to McLaughlin seized him by the waist, pinning both arms, while the other man took the officer's club and hit him. Supposedly, McLaughlin soon found himself on the ground with more black people in the area throwing missiles at him. Patterson was about to hit McLaughlin in the head with a brick he had in his raised hand when McLaughlin shot him, according to the cop.[99]

In January 1905, McLaughlin was prosecuted by District Attorney Nott, who argued he should be found guilty of murder in the first degree and sentenced to death in the electric chair. One witness was Robert Telfair, black, who was walking through the area early in the morning of May 27 when McLaughlin walked up behind him and hit him on the back of the head with his club and knocked him down. After McLaughlin hit him, Telfair said he saw him club Patterson, who said, "What are you hitting me for? I didn't do anything." Then Telfair saw the pair struggle and fall to the ground, at which point he saw the cop pull his revolver and fire. A second black witness corroborated the testimony of Telfair. There was no crowd there at all that night and no riot, as some of the papers had suggested. After the shots were fired then a crowd did assemble. Altogether four or five other witnesses corroborated the story told by Telfair. McLaughlin maintained he was attacked by a crowd of black people and he had to shoot in self-defense. McLaughlin was found guilty of manslaughter.[100]

Recorder Goff granted McLaughlin a new trial on April 1, 1905. Goff said that McLaughlin was on duty that night in a street filled with riotous people and it was while he was trying to quell the riot that he shot Patterson: "The verdict is contradictory to the weight of evidence and justice requires a new trial." McLaughlin was out on bail of $7,500 on that charge and he was also out on bail of $1,500 on the Robbins charge, which was said to be still pending. On March 7, 1908, the indictment for murder in the first degree against McLaughlin was dismissed in court. Because the District Attorney showed no disposition to try McLaughlin again the case failed to meet the standard of a speedy trial and it was thus dismissed. After his conviction for manslaughter Frank McLaughlin was dismissed from the New York City Police Department.[101]

1905 January 16 [114] New York City, death.

New York City policeman Ira B. Kinne was shot and fatally wounded by fellow officer John Clare in the rifle range of the Ninth Regiment Armory on January 16, 1905. The shooting, all agreed, was accidental, but both police surgeon John D. Gorman and the ambulance surgeon who took the wounded man to the hospital signed affidavits to the effect that they found Clare to be under the influence of alcohol. Clare had also violated the rules of the police department in entering the rifle range with a loaded revolver. Clare was standing near the firing line a few feet behind Kinne, who assisted in instructing policemen in revolver practice, waiting his turn to shoot. Just as the man who was before him practicing had taken his last shot Clare started to step forward to take his place. Clare had his loaded revolver clasped in his hands and suddenly it discharged. At the coroner's inquest that was held in February, said a reporter, "there was a lot of technical wrangling about whether Clare was drunk. Coroner Brown and some doctors testified and [Deputy Police Commissioner] Lindsley reserved decision." That is, it was strictly a police board matter and nothing more was reported.[102]

1905 February 27 [115] Chicago, death.

At around the noon hour on February 27, 1905, an actress and substitute teacher by the name of Mary Catherine Mulveil was murdered by Chicago policeman Daniel Herman, a man whose attentions she had refused. The crime was committed in the most fashionable part of Michigan Avenue at a time when the street was filled with pedestrians and carriages. After killing Mulveil, Herman made his escape and on the night of February 27 he committed suicide in a lodging house by shooting himself in the head. Mulveil was walking along Michigan Avenue when she met the cop, who was evidently waiting for her. Suddenly he grabbed the woman's arm and fired three times; one of the bullets pierced her brain. Reportedly, Herman had become infatuated with her through hearing her play as an organist at the church he attended and, said a reporter, "had for a long time annoyed her with his attentions, constantly urging her to marry him." He had been a member of the Chicago police force for several years acting as a "plain clothes" man, but for almost a year he had been on a leave of absence.[103]

Mulveil had always refused Herman's repeated offers of marriage and had recently told some of her friends that he had threatened to kill her unless she married him. At that time she expressed herself as being afraid to walk the streets for fear of meeting him, as he followed her wherever she went. Mulveil was 23 and a wealthy heiress, and the executrix of her father's estate ($150,000) and her uncle's estate ($70,000). Her father had died several years earlier and her uncle passed away a year ago. Herman's infatuation with the woman was said to have increased markedly in the last year of her life, coinciding with the receipt of the second estate and, remarked a journalist, "in the last year of her life he made her life almost unbearable for her, intimates assert." When U.S. president William McKinley last visited Chicago, Herman was selected as one of the Chicago officers detailed to act as bodyguard. However, exclaimed a journalist, "he had been on furlough for the past year and had devoted most of his time to pursuing Miss Mulveil."[104]

1905 March 17 *[116] Hattiesburg, Mississippi, death.*

S. Morris, manager of the Mississippi Club in Hattiesburg, Mississippi, was shot and instantly killed by Police Chief E. O. Bufkin on or about March 17, 1905. The killing was said to have been the result of continued raids for illicit liquor made by the chief on the Mississippi Club. Bufkin was released on $1,000 bail. That club was said to be the exclusive social organization of the city and the police had raided the place on the three successive Sundays before the shooting in an attempt to discover illicit liquor sales, as the sale of that product was banned on Sundays. After that third raid on a day in the following week E. O. Bufkin was standing on a street corner near the club when Morris, the secretary and treasurer of that club, approached him and asked him if he intended to make another raid on the club. Morris said he was tired of having his club raided and, it was said, reached for his pistol. Before he could shoot, Bufkin fired.[105]

1905 March 23 *[117] St. Louis, assault.*

Patrolman Anton Tomasso of the Fourth District in St. Louis was charged with assault to do great bodily harm in an indictment returned with the April grand jury's report. Henry Schmidt of the Helmich Liquor Company was the complaining witness. He alleged that on the night of March 23, 1905, while he and his brother were on their way to a saloon policeman Tomasso and another cop stopped the brothers. Schmidt said Tomasso grabbed him and jerked him around and asked the other cop if he was the man. "No," replied the other officer whereupon, Schmidt said, Tomasso ordered him to go home. Schmidt replied that he had as much right to be on the street as the policeman. That angered Tomasso, who struck Schmidt with his club. Then Schmidt was arrested and he said Tomasso would have attacked him again, in the patrol wagon that transported them all to the station, had not another cop interfered. The incident was brought to the attention of the police board in St. Louis, but that board took no action. As a next step Schmidt took the matter to the grand jury. Tomasso was suspended from duty pending the outcome of the trial.[106]

Tomasso was tried in June and convicted on the assault charge. The jury deliberated a little over two hours before returning with a guilty verdict. On June 23 Judge Bishop sentenced Tomasso to three months in jail and a fine of $100. Thomas Morris was the other cop, the one with Tomasso on the night of the assault.[107]

1905 April 25 *[118] Pittsburgh, death.*

W. De Forrest Lappe, who was 19 and, it was reported, "a member of a prominent and wealthy East End family," was shot and killed early in the morning of April 25, 1905, by Pittsburgh peace officer Rufus Ullom. Two of Lappe's companions were arrested as witnesses and a third escaped. The four young men were reportedly having an argument on the street at about 3:30 a.m. and were ordered to move on by policeman Baker. After moving away a short distance the men stopped and began arguing again. Baker started after them and they ran off. Ullom, who was nearby, joined in the chase, calling on the group to halt. They paid no attention to that order and Ullom drew his revolver and fired three times, with the second shot striking Lappe. He died in the hospital at 5:00 a.m. Ullom was arrested. Reportedly, Lappe was a protégé of famed composer Victor Herbert, while Ullom, before becoming a policeman, was a captain in the Salvation Army.[108]

Thirty months passed before anything else was published about the case. In October 1907 the case was summarized, with the reporter noting that Lappe was shot and killed by Ullom. The brothers were members of a crowd of young men trying to escape arrest. W. De Forrest and his brother Howard fled with the other men, with the cops in pursuit. It was reported herein that Ullom believed a burglary had been committed. In conclusion the reporter said: "Ullom was indicted for murder, but never tried."[109]

1905 May 11 [119] *Phoebus, Virginia, death.*

Artilleryman George A. Dowrey was killed on the night of May 11, 1905, in Phoebus (now Hampton), Virginia, by policeman Robert A. Phillips. According to the officer, he had occasion to reprimand three artillerymen for an infraction of a town ordinance, whereupon Dowrey picked a fight with him. In the melee that followed seven artillerymen participated, handling the cop roughly and beating him with his own club. Citizens interfered and the soldiers tried to escape back to their base. Phillips, however, pursued and cornered Dowrey. Then, continued the cop, the soldier advanced on him and refused to halt, whereupon he shot him. Dowrey died from his injuries shortly thereafter. The town was said to be in an uproar and Phillips was placed under arrest. After the Phillips case was sent on to the grand jury he was admitted to bail in the amount of $1,000. The verdict of the coroner's jury stated that the soldier was killed by the officer while the latter was on duty and endeavoring to retake an escaped prisoner. It was said to have been a verdict that neither condemned nor exonerated the policeman.[110]

At Newport News, Virginia, on May 16, 1905, the grand jury indicted Phillips on the charge of "deliberate murder" in the death of Dowrey. In the circuit court on September 20, 1905, the jury in the Phillips case returned a verdict of not guilty. The officer made a plea of self-defense and, said a reporter; "was completely exonerated."[111]

1905 June 24 [120] Raleigh, North Carolina, assault.

John Dockery, son of Henry C. Dockery, U.S. Marshal for the Eastern District of North Carolina, was shot and seriously wounded on June 24, 1905, in Raleigh, North Carolina, by policeman Isaac Rogers. John had been paying attention to the daughter of Rogers, a behavior that was unacceptable to the policeman. John was a deputy marshal who served under his father. The shooting had taken place in the morning at an office building where Rogers had been apparently waiting for John. The daughter was 19-year-old Lula Rogers, who had been seduced by John, according to the father. The story was that John and Lula along with another couple went to a brothel for the day recently and therein Lula was "dishonored." After the shooting Rogers phoned the sheriff and declared he wanted to surrender. Initially Rogers was committed to jail without bail, but soon he was released on $500 bail. John Dockery was 27 years old. A true bill for assault was returned against Rogers by the grand jury on October 1, 1905.[112]

The case came to trial in January 1906, but by then the parties had reached some type of settlement. The original bill of indictment was amended to "secret assault" back in July 1905. At the trial the plaintiff, Dockery, stated he had no malice toward Rogers and prayed the court not to inflict punishment on Rogers, as he had done what any father would have done under similar circumstances. Judge G. W. Ward agreed to impose a sentence that was more token than anything else. Ward fined Rogers $50 and costs.[113]

1905 July 5 [121] Philadelphia, death.

Philadelphia policeman Albert Landgren was committed to the lockup at that city on July 6, 1905, charged with shooting to death Michael Cleary, a man who was described as a "minor" politician. The shooting took place on July 5 when Landgren attempted to arrest Cleary and a gang of alleged thugs who were acting in a disorderly manner. It was reported they attacked the cop, pinned his arms behind his back, throw a potato basket over his head, and relieved him of his club. Landgren was being "kicked and beaten unmercifully" when he drew his revolver and fired into the crowd. Cleary was struck in the back by a shot and died while entering the hospital. A different account said that Cleary and a friend were celebrating the July 4 holiday when they got into a fight with another man. Landgren stopped the fight and arrested Cleary and his companion. Then a crowd pounced on the officer and was beating him when he shot into the crowd, killing Cleary.[114]

1905 August 3 [122] *South Boston, Virginia, death.*

At South Boston in Halifax County, Virginia, on the evening of August 3, 1905, peace officer Joseph Carter shot and fatally wounded Henry Easley, Jr., son of Col. Henry Easley a member of the staff of the governor of Virginia. He was shot at about 2:00 a.m. and died that morning at 9:00. Easley was said to have been resisting arrest and had the officer down on the ground and was beating him when the fatal shot was fired. The officer was exonerated by the coroner's jury on the afternoon of August 4, with the jury declared the shooting was an act of self-defense. Henry was about 25 years old and evidence supposedly showed that he had been drinking and while under arrest for being disorderly had launched his attack on the policeman.[115]

1905 August 10 [123] *Chicago, death.*

On the afternoon of August 10, 1905, in Chicago, policeman Oscar Benson of that city's force shot and killed his brother-in-law Matthew Mamer, 50. Benson also fatally wounded Nicholas Ketten, 60, a clerk in Mamer's jewelry store, and then committed suicide. All of the shooting took place in the store. For some time, it was reported, Benson and his in-law had not been getting along. On August 10 Mamer complained to the police department about his brother-in-law Benson. The latter heard of the complaint and on the afternoon of that day went to the store, jumped over the counter, placed his revolver against Mamer's head and fired. Ketten had been in another part of the store and was shot in the abdomen as he attempted to flee the store. Benson then shot himself to death.[116]

1906 February 1 [124] *Philadelphia, death.*

A man who gave his name as Patrick Say of Peoria, Illinois, died in a Philadelphia hospital on February 2, 1905, from the effects of a bullet wound received on the evening of February 1 while he was endeavoring to escape from a policeman. Say was reportedly detected in the act of robbing a grocery store, at which point he tried to run off. He was pursued by Officer Kellar, who fired two shots at the fleeing man. The second of those bullets struck Say in the back.[117]

1906 February 9 *[125] Denver, death.*

When he became angry at losing two games of dice in a saloon that were meant to settle who paid for drinks on the morning of February 9, 1906, in Denver, city policeman Charles Secrest shot Thomas Johnson twice, killing him instantly. Johnson was a traveling salesman from Chicago and participated in the dice game at Secrest's request. A reporter noted that "it is the second man Secrest has killed." Johnson traveled for the Monarch Book Company of Chicago and died at around two o'clock that morning. Secrest was in the saloon when Johnson entered. Not long after Johnson arrived in the bar the policeman challenged him to a game of dice for the drinks but was beaten several times by the newcomer. That apparently angered the cop and he shot Johnson twice or maybe three times, with the victim dying as he was being transported to the hospital. Secrest refused to submit to arrest until a detail arrived from headquarters. Wrote a different reporter: "Secrest is considered a dangerous man when drinking and quick to use a gun. Several years ago he killed a man under similar circumstances but escaped punishment."[118]

Another account described Johnson as a steam engineer who arrived in Denver from Duluth, Minnesota, a few weeks earlier. After shaking the dice for drinks and losing and paying the second time Secrest got angry and said several words of abuse at Johnson before shooting him. Johnson told him there was no reason to abuse him, but at that point Secrest drew his gun and fired. According to this account, four years previously Secrest had killed Henry Reed in a Denver saloon "in exactly the same manner as he killed Johnson. Three shots were fired after a quarrel had started over drinks." Secrest claimed that Reed had threatened to whip him, but he told the police when they came to arrest him that he was "trying his new gun." Reed died at the county hospital the next day and Secrest escaped punishment.[119]

At the Secrest trial the man was found guilty of murder in the second degree, in March 1906. On April 16, 1906, Charles Secrest was sentenced to a term of from 14 to 20 years in the penitentiary for killing Thomas Johnson. According to this account, when the shooting of Johnson took place Secrest was a policeman but was under suspension from the force for drunkenness.[120]

1906 April 3 *[126] Spokane, Washington, death.*

On the night of April 3, 1906, in Spokane, Washington, city detective Bob Briley shot and killed Edward Donnelly, who was said to have been found burglarizing a clothing store. A woman in a neighboring building discovered the burglar at work and contacted the police. Briley crawled in the window through which Donnelly had secured an entrance. He found the burglar hiding beneath the safe and upon his refusal to throw up his hands the officer shot Donnelly. The store had been robbed several times of valuable furs in the recent past. When the police received the tip three officers were sent to the scene. One remained at the front door, while the other two, including Briley, went to the back door. One stayed guard there while Briley entered the building. By this account Donnelly refused on two occasions to put his hands up when so ordered and upon the second command Donnelly stood up and, said Briley, reached for his back pocket for something Briley thought was a gun. Briley then fired and "shot him in the back." No weapon was found on the deceased except for a penknife. Nothing more was heard until three months later when a small item appeared that discussed one of Briley's current cases, indicating, of course, that he was obviously on the job and unpunished.[121]

1906 July 11 [127] *Atlantic City, New Jersey, assault.*

William J. Broom, a summer policeman appointed in Atlantic City, New Jersey, early in July 1906, was stripped of his uniform and put in jail on July 12 on a charge of criminally assaulting Mrs. Margaret Crowley, a 17-year-old visitor to the city, on the night of July 11. The woman alleged she was placed under arrest while walking along the boardwalk by Broom, who told her he intended to lock her up. Then she said Broom assaulted her. Broom was said to have admitted the crime to Police Chief Maxwell. Crowley picked out her alleged assailant at a lineup and he was jailed.[122]

1906 July 29 [128] *Washington, D.C., assault.*

Daniel J. Boyle, whose home was on the Conduit Road, was accidentally shot on the afternoon of July 29, 1906, near the intersection of Conduit Road and Little Falls Road, by mounted policeman J. B. Lipscomb. Boyle was at that intersection when he was observed by Lipscomb, who was of the opinion that Boyle was engaged in disorderly conduct and started to pursue him. Boyle ran and the officer drew his revolver thinking he might "intimidate" the man. While the cop was running and flourishing the weapon he stumbled and fell. The pistol struck the ground "with considerable force" and was discharged, the bullet striking Boyle in the knee. At the police station house a charge of disorderly conduct was entered against Boyle.[123]

After receiving the report on the incident wherein the 21-year-old Boyle was shot, Washington police superintendent Sylvester preferred charges against Lipscomb for the wrongful use of his revolver. That rule was covered by section 16, paragraph 10, of the police manual, which read: "Members of the force shall not use their revolver except in the most urgent cases, and then shall not do so in such a manner that the lives of innocent persons will be jeopardized. Wanton disregard of life by an officer in the use of a revolver will subject him to removal from the force." Lipscomb was to appear before the police trial board to answer the charge. The delay in the hearing was due to waiting for the outcome of Boyle's condition—that is, whether he would or would not survive the wounding.[124]

John B. Lipscomb was made a defendant in the police court on October 2, 1906, when a charge of assault with a dangerous weapon was filed against him. The criminal aspect of the case had been under investigation for some time, with the result that prosecuting attorney Ralph Given decided that a warrant against the officer should be filed. Lipscomb posted a bond for $1,000 and was released from custody. The cop's story remained as he had told it before. That case was continued, as Boyle was unable to attend proceedings as he was still in the hospital.[125]

Members of the police trial board went to Boyle's bedside in the hospital on October 18 to take his statement. Boyle declared that on the day in question he was driving along the Conduit Road with two friends and that the hat of one of them blew off his head. Boyle started to run after the hat and he also asked the cop to get it for him. "I'll get the hat, and I'll get you, too," is what Boyle stated that cop said to him. As he was running across the road to retrieve the hat he heard the cop say, "Stop or I'll shoot you." He turned around, he said, and as he did so the cop shot him. Then the officer came to him and asked if he had shot him, saying he had not intended to do so.[126]

At the police trial board hearing near the end of October two of the witnesses were Thomas E. Drake, superintendent of insurance, Washington, D.C., and Thomas P. Kane, deputy controller of the currency, U.S. Treasury, who were passengers on a train returning to Washington. They witnessed the pursuit of Boyle by Lipscomb from that train and they saw the cop draw his revolver and aim it toward the fleeing boy and saw the latter fall. The noise of the train drowned out the sound of the shot. John M. Perry, motorman of a trolley car, testified to the same thing, swearing the cop did not stumble while chasing Boyle and in his opinion the shooting was deliberate. Four other witnesses backed up the first three. One of the young men with Boyle in their buggy was Patrick Kelleher. He declared there was no disorder or fast driving or anything that would have justified the cop in pursuing or arresting any of them.[127]

The police trial board did not release its verdict until the middle of February 1907, when it ruled that the officer had shot Daniel Boyle "without provocation" and the board recommended Lipscomb be dismissed from the force by the Police Commissioners. Boyle remained in the hospital for four months after the shooting and while he was then out of the hospital he was described as "permanently injured."[128]

At an executive board session of the police commissioners on March 12 it was decided to give Lipscomb a chance to resign, in view of his good record and his "consideration" for his victim. Lipscomb had offered to pay his victim's expenses. In this account it was said that Boyle had "fully recovered." On March 16, 1907, John B. Lipscomb resigned from the Washington, D.C., police force.[129]

On May 16, 1907, Lipscomb was arraigned in criminal court on a charge of assaulting Boyle with a dangerous weapon. He was released on a $500 bond. On October 25, 1907, Lipscomb was acquitted by a jury and discharged. This account said that testimony at that trial indicated that Lipscomb took the gun from his pocket to keep it from dropping out while he was running. And, wrote a journalist, "in his defense Lipscomb presented witnesses to prove that the defendant while pursuing Boyle stumbled and accidentally discharged the pistol." It was also declared that "a number of prominent citizens testified to the good character of the defendant." A different report on this trial stated: "From the evidence, it appeared that Boyle was one of a group of boys with whom Lipscomb remonstrated for alleged disorderly conduct, and whom the latter attempted to arrest. The boys ran, and Boyle was accidentally shot by the policeman."[130]

Daniel J. Boyle was the victim of an assault by police and is shown here still on crutches as he recovered. His father J. D. Boyle, Sr., is shown also (top) as well as his attorney Crandall Mackey.

1906 August 2 *[129]*
Houston, death.

Walter Dudley Hightower, a vaudeville actor, was shot and killed on the night of August 2,

1906, by a special policeman, C. A. Lewendowski, who was on duty at Highland Park. Reportedly, the officer had an altercation with an actor named Zebb about sitting on a table in the park. Hightower intervened to the extent of advising his friend. At that point the officer reached for his revolver and Hightower ran off. He had gotten only a few feet when Lewendowski shot him in the back, and he died while being taken to the hospital. The cop declared that Hightower and Zebb threw him to the ground and beat and trampled him and it was then, in self-defense, that he fired his gun. Lewendowski surrendered and was jailed.[131]

1906 August 25 *[130] Pittsburgh, death.*

A squad of about six policemen was out on the streets of Pittsburgh on the night of August 25, 1906, to continue that police force's crusade against street corner loafing. Twenty-year-old Herbert Gowland and his friend Herman McGinnis were standing on a street corner at about 9:15 p.m. when the police squad arrived. Each of the officers had been instructed to take two loafers and hold them until the police wagon arrived to transport them to the station house. One of those officers was David Bowles, who was said to have been on the force for less than a week. Bowles reached for Gowland and McGinnis and the pair ran off with Bowles in pursuit. He fired his gun in the air once, but they continued to run. Soon thereafter he fired two more shots and one of those struck and killed Gowland. McGinnis was caught and jailed, while Bowles was detained at the station pending the arrival of and investigation by the coroner. Despite the tragedy, the raids against loafers in Pittsburgh continued through the night and by one o'clock the next morning over 100 people had been arrested and locked up in the central station. They were all charged with violating a city ordinance that banned loitering in the street.[132]

After being convicted of involuntary manslaughter in court in October 1907, the by then "former" policeman David Bowles was sentenced to one year in jail by Judge Marshall Brown. According to a report, "Judge Brown spoke bitterly from the bench of the careless shooting by policemen generally." In a different newspaper an editor declared that the decision in the Bowles case established a precedent in Pennsylvania to the effect that if a police officer was chasing a fugitive without a warrant he had no right to shoot after calling on the pursued person to halt, even if the latter continued running.[133]

1906 September 18 *[131] New York City, death.*

New York City policeman John McSherry shot and instantly killed Charles Connor, 22, on a street corner in New York on the afternoon of September 18,

1906. A crowd of loungers had for some time been hanging around that street corner and the area and, said a reporter, "have caused passers considerable trouble. Many complaints have been sent to Capt. Baldwin of the Sixth avenue station regarding the obscene language used by the gang." Baldwin had instructed his men to keep a careful watch on the crowd of idlers. As McSherry approached the crowd on September 18 Connor and John McCarran became involved in a quarrel. Then they started a physical fight and McSherry interceded and told "the gang" to disperse. Instead of doing so, he stated, they "abused" him. The officer then grabbed McCarran and started to take him to the station house. Connor and another man by the name of Martin Casey tried to rescue their friend. McSherry warned the two would-be rescuers to desist, but they refused to heed the warning. Connor finally threw a cobblestone at the cop, hitting him in the chest. Again and again McSherry told the pair to go away. McSherry drew his revolver as Connor threw another stone at him and fired. Connor, it was said, had turned to run and the bullet hit him in the back and he fell down dead. McSherry took the two other men to the station house, where they were locked up. The officer was also locked up. He claimed he had no intention of killing Connor, but he believed his life was in danger. He had been on the force for five years and Captain Baldwin and "the other officers" of the Sixth Avenue station "say that he has an excellent record.[134]

1906 September 25 *[132] Concord, New Hampshire, death.*

Because he was jealous Concord, New Hampshire, policeman Whitney D. Barrett entered a streetcar in that city and shot to death Miss Julia Chadwick. Barrett, who was 50 years old and married, then committed suicide. The shooting took place in the vestibule of the streetcar at 7:53 a.m. on September 25, 1906. Barrett had made an earlier attempt to shoot Chadwick when George Jenness intervened and wrested the gun away from the officer. Barrett then went at once to the police station and procured another revolver. Chadwick, in the meantime, had hastened to the elevated car that was to bring her to Concord, where she was employed in the telephone exchange. Barrett ran through the streets in pursuit of Chadwick, who as she boarded the car pleaded with the motorman not to allow Barrett to molest her. But the cop was right after her and shot the young woman in the vestibule of the car. He then shot himself, with both bodies falling to the floor of the car. Chadwick died in about half an hour and Barrett sometime thereafter. Chadwick was thought to be about 35 years old.[135]

A slightly different version of the incident appeared in another newspaper. In this account Chadwick was listed as 30 years old and Barrett was said to be the oldest officer, with respect to service, on the force in Concord. According to this account, a few minutes before the shooting Barrett had confronted the woman in the coal and wood office of Everett Davis and threatened to shot her but was disarmed by Davis, with the revolver being discharged during the struggle. Barrett then seemed to come to his senses, and as he seemed to repent of what he had done Davis gave him back the revolver and left the place. Soon after his departure Chadwick boarded a car but had no sooner seated herself than Barrett again appeared and before he could be prevented had shot the young woman in the chest. Then, an instant later, he shot himself in the head. As of a couple of days after the shooting Barrett had not died, but doctors expected that he would not survive.[136]

1906 September 30 *[133] Minneapolis, death.*

Fighting to gain his freedom from Minneapolis, Minnesota, patrolmen William Munger and Peter Quist, who had arrested him on a charge of drunkenness, a man named Sigwald Brandenborg stumbled and fell against the curb, receiving injuries that caused his death while being taken to the South Side police station in the patrol wagon. The incident took place shortly after midnight. The officers said he was so noisy as he came reeling along the street that they decided to arrest him. The moment they attempted to seize him he showed fight and a fierce struggle ensued before he broke free from his captors and pitched headlong to the curb, his face striking the stone, and he went unconscious. He died in the wagon just before the station was reached. At least that was the story the pair of officers told. It had, however, no relationship to what actually happened.[137]

Within a day or two it was announced that an inquest into the death of Brandenborg would he held and the matter would also be taken to the grand jury. Earl Higgins, a man who had been arrested for drunkenness about the same time as the death, had testified about the incident in police court. He said he came up to the two cops who had Brandenborg on the ground and were beating him. Higgins asked them if the man was dead and was immediately arrested and placed in the police wagon.[138]

When the coroner's jury delivered their verdict on the case on October 6 they held the two cops responsible for Brandenborg's death, declaring he died "as the result of a severe beating at the hands of" the two policemen. Earl Higgins testified that as the cops were beating Brandenborg with clubs the latter was pleading for mercy. Three other men who had been with Higgins told similar stories.[139]

Munger and Quist had remained on duty up to the time of the coroner's jury verdict, at which time they were immediately suspended. The cops tried to argue that the four men who had testified at the coroner's inquest all had it in for themselves, but several other independent witnesses, including area businessmen, confirmed the story of a police beating. One of those men had even stepped forward to ask of the cops if it was necessary to be so severe. Munger turned on him, called him a name, and told him to move on or be arrested. It was said those men would testify before the grand jury.[140]

Earl Higgins was cleared in police court on the charge of drunkenness. He had several witnesses who testified they were with him all night and that he had not taken a drink during that entire time. The only witnesses against Higgins were Munger and Quist. While he was cleared of drunkenness on October 13, Earl Higgins was before the courts again on October 22, at which time he was given a sentence of a $75 fine or 20 days in jail. That police court appearance resulted when the police declared that Higgins and some friends had been making a disturbance in Minneapolis the night before and when pursued by Patrolman Warde he boarded a train and escaped but was later arrested.[141]

On October 19, 1906, William Munger and Peter Quist were indicted by the Hennepin County grand jury for manslaughter in the first degree. However, in March 1907 William Munger, in an apparently severed trial, was found by the jury not guilty on a charge of manslaughter.[142]

1907 January 9 *[134] New York City, assault.*

Patrolman Thomas G. Walsh of the NYPD West 47th Street station was convicted of assault in the Court of Special Sessions in New York on March 1, 1907, and was remanded for sentencing. The complainant against him was Moses Johnston, whose wife ran a rooming house. Johnson said that on the night of January 9, 1907, he was obliged to remonstrate with Walsh, who replied by assaulting him with the butt of his revolver. That blow knocked him down and then the officer struck Walsh with his club. Walsh denied the assault.[143]

After the verdict of the jury was announced one of the justices said he had never heard "so much bare-faced perjury" since he had been on the bench. Testimony showed that a cop named Rinn, who was a friend of Walsh, had engaged a room from Mrs. Marie Johnston for a young woman who Rinn said was his cousin. On the night of January 9, Rinn, Walsh and the young woman (who said her name was May Russell) and another young woman, Miss Margaret Carlin, went to the theater and afterward returned to the rooming house. They entered the room rented for Russell and while there Johnston tried to eject them. Johnston charged that Walsh struck Marie on the breast with his fist and threatened to shoot her. Johnston then went outside to find a policeman while a lodger in the dwelling by the name of Martin went to Marie's assistance. Martin and Walsh engaged in a fight that went through the first room, then into the hall, then into Martin's room. Johnston had, in the meantime, run to the 47th Street station but got no satisfaction and returned alone to his home. He refused to permit Walsh and his companions to leave until they had paid for the furniture that had been destroyed. At that point Walsh struck Johnston with his revolver and knocked him down. While he was lying on the floor Walsh struck him several times with his club. Johnston was finally rescued and taken to the back parlor. Walsh followed him there and broke down the door. Johnston jumped out of the back window to escape. Marie called a policeman in uniform who had been drawn to the house by the noise of the fight and she begged him to prevent a murder. That cop refused to help. The story told by Mr. and Mrs. Johnston was corroborated by several witnesses. Policeman Keon (the refuser) was called as a witness. He said that he saw no fighting and that when he asked Walsh what the trouble was Walsh replied, "I'm here on police business and can attend to this matter myself." Walsh faced a maximum sentence of one year in prison and/or a fine of $500.[144]

On March 6, Thomas Walsh was sentenced to serve 30 days in the Tombs prison. When the officer was arraigned for sentencing, Assistant District Attorney Pinchot asked the court to impose a severe sentence. He said the case was not deserving of leniency. Pinchot characterized the assault as "unwarranted, brutal and wholly unprovoked" and aggravated by the fact that it was the special duty of the man who committed it to protect citizens. The prisoner, a police officer, had entered the house of a respectable citizen and attacked him with his club and revolver, forcing him to jump from a window to escape. Pinchot added that "scores of policemen had committed perjury in their testimony for Walsh." Presiding Judge Mayo declared Walsh's offense was without extenuating circumstances and "the court found that it must punish him severely."[145]

1907 February 5 *[135] Jackson, Michigan, death.*

Jackson, Michigan, policeman Isaac Lewis walked into the office of police captain Holzapfel in the station on February 5, 1907, and without a warning or any cause, so far as could be ascertained, killed his superior officer by shooting him through the heart. Lewis then fired a shot at Police Chief Boyle but missed him. Lewis, it was said, had been drinking of late and it was thought, said a reporter, "he must have been insane." After the shooting Lewis became violent and "fought like a mad man" against being locked up in a cell. In an incoherent statement later Lewis said he shot Holzapfel because he got tired of seeing him "strutting around." The shooter had been on the force for 11 years and it was said he had a "good record."[146]

Judge Parkinson, in Jackson, Michigan, sentenced the by then former cop Lewis, on December 10, to life imprisonment after the ex-cop was convicted of murder. Parkinson commented that the murder never would have happened (meaning the bad feeling and envy) had it not been for drink. Concluded the judge: "Policemen are entrusted with the enforcement of the laws, and that is the reason they should never accept favors from saloon keepers. The mayor, the council, and the police commission, who did not interpose to put an end to wrong tendencies, must shoulder their share of the blame."[147]

1907 March 26 [136] *Philadelphia, death.*

William McElroy was reportedly shot and killed by a policeman in Philadelphia on March 26, 1907, while resisting arrest for stealing bread. The officer detected McElroy robbing a grocer's bread box and placed him under arrest. He attacked the officer and the latter drew his pistol. In the scuffle the pistol was discharged, with the bullet entering McElroy's brain. He was 18 years old.[148]

1907 April [137] *New York City, assault.*

New York City patrolman Stephen S. Walsh told a police trial board on May 2, 1907, he was beaten by three cops who set upon him without the slightest provocation. He detailed how he had been assaulted in the section room of the police station and later dragged out of bed in the dormitory area and beaten again, yet the three accused officers, a lieutenant, and 15 patrolmen all declared under oath that they saw no assault. All of them were called to the stand to testify, yet each one said he had heard nothing and saw nothing. Deputy Police Commissioner Hansen declared, "Nearly every man that has testified has lied and deliberately perjured himself. They are the worst set of liars I ever saw in my life." The condition of the face and body of Walsh showed the result of the assault. Hansen added, "This is not a new practice in the Police Department—hazing good men off the force and then lying by platoons to save the guilty ones."[149]

A few days later, on May 7, Hansen found three officers attached to the Oak Street station guilty of hazing and assaulting a brother officer in the station house and recommended that they be dismissed from the department. He also said that he would recommend that all the men in reserve at the time of the assault be transferred to outlying precincts. Officers convicted were Eugene Z. Clinton, Frederick Unger, and Christopher T. Fitzgerald. Walsh had said that after the beating he went to complain to Captain Walling, the man in command of the precinct, but the captain had done nothing except to tear up his complaint. It was reported that the accused cops declared that Walsh had been acting "in a peculiar manner and had dreamed he was assaulted."[150]

New York City police commissioner Bingham dismissed the above named three officers from the force on June 8, 1907. It was said herein that Walsh was unpopular with all the men and one night after picking a quarrel with Walsh the three beat him until he was nearly unconscious. Bingham also had the remaining entire platoon transferred to the Park Street police station.[151]

Stephen Walsh was dismissed himself from the police force on July 31, 1907, for cowardice in permitting Frank Warner the murderer to escape from the building in which he had been hiding. Independent witnesses corroborated the story and Walsh did indeed seem to have been guilty of cowardice, at least by police definitions. That development inspired the three dismissed cops who had beaten him to take legal steps for the recovery of their old jobs as cops. At the police trial board hearing for Walsh it was established that the seeming cowardice might have been caused by mental weakness, and thus the legal action. After his previous success at the trial board and winning his assault case Walsh was moved to various stations, but, said an account "the record he had made of a 'squealer' stuck by him."[152]

Initially that legal action involved just the one officer, Eugene Clinton. Police Commissioner Bert Hansen received a scolding at the hands of Justice Frank C. Laughlin of the Appellate Division on January 11, 1908, who delivered the unanimous opinion of the court sustaining Clinton in his appeal from Hansen's action in dismissing him from the police force back in May 1907. Laughlin declared that review of the proceeding conducted by Hansen showed him that it "bristles with improper conduct on the part of the Deputy Commissioner." He noted that the record was barren of any evidence to sustain the finding that Clinton was guilty of the charge of assault. Laughlin ruled that Clinton should be reinstated to the police department with back pay from the date of his dismissal. Clinton's case went alone as a test case with the other two expected to follow with suits of their own, in light of Clinton's victory. But those other trials proved to be unnecessary. On April 6, 1908, Police Commissioner Bingham returned all three of the men, Eugene Clinton, Frederick Unger, and Christopher Fitzgerald, to the police force and to active duty.[153]

1907 May 11 *[138] Butte, Montana, death.*

Patrol wagon driver Charles Jackson of the Butte, Montana, police force shot and killed Harry Cole on May 11, 1907, while Cole was attempting to escape from custody. As a result of the public indignation that arose from that killing a mob of some 2,000 people led by brothers of Cole made an attempt to lynch Detective Charles McGarvey under the impression it was McGarvey who did the shooting. Cole was said to have been suspected of being one of two bandits who several days earlier robbed a train. After he was taken into custody on suspicion of that crime and while he was being "sweated" about his knowledge of that robbery it was reported that Cole said he knew all about the holdup and then made a dash from the interrogation room. Jackson then shot and killed him.[154]

Cole had been arrested by McGarvey not only on suspicion of the robbery but also for an alleged forgery charge. His brother George Cole was then serving a term in the penitentiary for robbing a train two years earlier. When Harry made his dash for freedom from the station he reached the door and then ran off down an alley leading away from the police station. An unnamed cop supposedly started after Cole but tripped over the door threshold and fell down. McGarvey was also in on the chase, and as he was following the first officer who fell McGarvey fell over the prostrate form of that first policeman. Jackson heard the commotion and shot the fleeing man in the back, killing him instantly. An immense and angry mob formed up also immediately after the killing, estimated in this account at 5,000, under the impression it was McGarvey who did the shooting. That mob that was intent on lynching McGarvey was held back but rioted in the streets until 11:00 p.m. or so, when it finally dispersed. During the rioting the crowd, among other things, raided a gun store. In this account Harry Cole was described as a "bad one" who "figured in police circles for some time and has been suspected of complicity in several cases." On about May 18 a coroner's jury exonerated Jackson of all blame in the killing of Cole.[155]

1907 May 23 [139] *Sterling, Illinois, death.*

In Sterling, Illinois, on the afternoon of May 23, 1907, policeman James Sheehan shot and killed Michael Grady, who had been placed under arrest and was being taken to the police station. Reportedly, Grady pulled away from the officer and started running toward the railroad tracks. When he refused to halt he was shot dead. Sheehan was ordered held by the coroner on May 24 for action by the grand jury. He was locked up and denied bail. On October 9, 1907, Sheehan was indicted by the grand jury for manslaughter.[156]

Later in 1907 Sheehan stood trial for manslaughter, with the result apparently being a hung jury. The report on the outcome stated: "The first trial resulted in a disagreement and it is deemed quite likely the second will bring an acquittal." That second trial for manslaughter took place in January 1908 and it did indeed result in a verdict of not guilty.[157]

1907 August 13 *[140] Oakland, California, death.*

California state policeman J. B. Burke shot and instantly killed F. A. Duman, a switchman at the West Oakland railway yards. The shooting took place on the morning of August 13, 1907, with the policeman claiming the switchman was stealing a bottle of whisky from one of the Southern Pacific freight cars. A chase resulted in which Duman was killed. Reportedly, Burke called out to the switchman, but the latter started to run and refused to halt at the command of the officer, who said he was at last forced to fire his weapon.[158]

1907 October 1 *[141] St. Landry, Louisiana, death.*

On October 1, 1907, in St. Landry, Louisiana, Gerizim Levergne went to town and drank too much. While intoxicated he became boisterous and went into the store operated by Marius Smith, where Levergne continued to cause a disturbance. The town marshal, Carlisle Jordan, heard the noise of the drunken man and went to arrest him. In effecting that arrest Jordan struck him on the head with his club. Levergne was jailed and that evening he was released. He went home, but soon it became necessary to call in a doctor and his condition kept getting worse until he died a day or so later. The sheriff was notified of the death and in the meantime Jordan surrendered. The coroner's jury came to a verdict that Levergne came to his death as the result of a blow struck by Jordan, a blow that produced a concussion. Jordan was released on $500 bail the following morning. Levergne left a wife and several children.[159]

1907 October 7 *[142] New York City, death.*

Isaac Jaffe, junior member of the firm of Jaffe and Company, cigar manufacturers of Brooklyn, was shot and killed instantly by Patrolman Alfred Shuttleworth in Saratoga Park, Brooklyn. The officer was locked up and charged with homicide. Shuttleworth declared the shooting was accidental. He said about 12 young men were annoying people in the park, among them Jaffe. He placed Jaffe under arrest and started off to the station with him when several of the friends of the prisoner came to his rescue. They kicked the officer and beat him with his own club, said the officer. During that melee Jaffe broke away and ran across the grass, at which point Shuttleworth drew his revolver and fired, he said, into the air. However, Jaffe dropped down dead with a bullet to the brain.[160]

Shuttleworth shot Jaffe in the presence of hundreds of people. The youths had been skylarking when the officer told them to "move on." Jaffe protested that order and was arrested. John O'Malley, a companion of the deceased, said the cop started to beat Jaffe with his club, but Jaffe managed to get clear. Then

Shuttleworth drew his revolver and fired one shot, hitting Jaffe at the base of the brain with the bullet coming out of his right eye. Shuttleworth declared Jaffe had tried to get his club away from him and that the prisoner's friends also attacked him. Shuttleworth was doing special duty in the park because the police had received many complaints of rowdy behavior in that park. According to the officer, when he arrived in the area he had found Jaffe shouting and insulting men and women. Shuttleworth ordered Jaffe and his friends to desist, but they just laughed at him. Then he arrested Jaffe. On October 7 Shuttleworth was arraigned before Magistrate Furlong and held for examination on a charge of homicide in the death of the 23-year-old Jaffe. The policeman was released on $2,000 bail.[161]

Shuttleworth was also suspended from the New York City police force in October 1907 and, according to a journalist, "the policeman grieved more over the death of his victim than over his own unfortunate position. It seemed to cheer him up only a little when the indictment against him was quashed, and he was ordered back to the Ralph Avenue Station for duty on May 26." Almost daily he told his wife, said the reporter, how he regretted the shooting, meaning only to frighten Jaffe. Shuttleworth's health failed and after doing duty for only 13 days he collapsed at the dinner table at his home on June 8. He was confined to bed with a "stroke of paralysis" and on the afternoon of July 21, 1908, Alfred Shuttleworth died. He had been a member of NYPD since October 22, 1896.[162]

1907 November 23 [143] *Portland, Oregon, death.*

Albert Engvall was shot and killed on November 23, 1907, in Ashland, Oregon, by Police Chief C. A. Simmons of Ashland. Engvall was one of a number of unemployed men who had been going southward since the cessation of work in the Northwest. On the evening of November 23 Simons ordered some of those men to stop. No attention was paid, reportedly, to that command and

FATAL BATTLE WITH

GANG OF TRAMPS.

Policeman Kills Innocent Man

How to spin a story. The top headline is from the *Capital Journal* (Salem, Oregon), while the bottom one is from the *Los Angeles Herald*. Each was published on November 25, 1907, and each described the same incident. The bottom headline was closer to the truth, while the top was an example of demonizing the victim, even in the headline.

the peace officer fired, not intending to hit anyone, he declared. A different account described the men heading south to try to find work as "tramps" and said that Engvall was in a group of 40 or so men. According to this account, Simmons fired several times into the air to frighten the "gang" and then "accidentally lowered his gun and shot again," with the bullet striking Engvall. That group of men was near the city's railroad depot and was said to have been "terrorizing the railroad men."[163]

1907 December 25 *[144] Newport, Tennessee, death.*

At Newport, Tennessee, on December 25, 1907, Robert Knowles, a special policeman, tried to arrest William Allen for drunkenness. A scuffle ensued during which Allen fell on top of Knowles and the officer pulled out his pistol and shot Allen, who survived for about two hours.[164]

1908 February 12 *[145] Portland, Oregon, death.*

F. D. Hepner was a new policeman in Portland, Oregon, who had been on the force for only one week when he shot and killed his best friend and neighbor, John G. Wettle, on the evening of February 12, 1908. For a joke Wettle jumped out at the new officer from a clump of bushes in a Portland suburb and held his pipe pointed at Hepner's head while at the same time ordering the officer to throw up his hands. Hepner pulled out his revolver and fired, with the result that Wettle fell dead, shot through the heart. Hepner immediately surrendered himself but was not arrested. A reporter exclaimed that public sentiment was that the officer was justified in his actions, as the city for several weeks had been overrun with holdup men and "bad characters." Portland police chief Gritzmacher, Coroner Finley, and seven of Wettle's own relatives held the policeman Hepner blameless.[165]

1908 February *[146] Muskogee, Oklahoma, assault.*

After a trial lasting two days I. S. Butler, a Muskogee, Oklahoma, policeman, was found guilty in February 1908 of assault upon Nora Graves, his 14-year-old sister-in-law. The maximum penalty for that offense was 20 years in state prison. Nora had testified that Butler had threatened her life and his wife's life if Nora told on him. Mrs. Butler accidentally discovered her husband's actions and caused his arrest. She was then suing for divorce. According to a reporter, "He is considered one of the best officers on the force."[166]

Nothing more about Butler surfaced until November 2, 1908, when it was reported that W. S. Graves shot and killed the policeman on that date. At that time Butler was described as a "former" policeman. It was also reported that Butler had been tried twice for rape and had been convicted of the charge each time, but in both instances Butler was granted a new trial. At the time he was murdered he was out on bail awaiting a third trial. On the day of the shooting Graves saw Butler at the train station and without a word walked up to the officer and started shooting. Graves fired four bullets into his target. Graves, the brother of Nora, gave himself up at once and was placed under arrest. The killing took place before some 200 people at the Missouri-Kansas-Texas Railroad depot. Said W. S. Graves, "He ruined my sister and I tried to take his life." According to this second account the second trial ended in a hung jury and not a conviction. Butler's third trial had been scheduled for February 1909.[167]

1908 March 1 *[147] Portland, Oregon, death.*

Portland, Oregon, patrolman N. H. Suitter shot and killed Henry Shaffer, a 35-year-old longshoreman, in the latter's home in Portland on the night of March 1, 1908. That night a party in honor of Mrs. Shaffer's birthday was in progress and Suitter was called on by the neighbors to stop the noise. Reportedly, Shaffer assaulted the cop, who responded by drawing his gun and firing, inflicting a mortal wound. That incident took place on the second visit by the officer to the Shaffer household that night. After the cop had warned the revelers once he went to a phone to summon help. Suitter and his fellow officer returned to the house, whereupon Suitter confronted six male guests in the kitchen and placed them under arrest. He sent his companion officer to call for the patrol wagon. According to Suitter's story, Shaffer started to throw him out of the house. According to the policeman, Shaffer struck him on the chest and then he was compelled to shoot in self-defense. Shaffer was struck by two bullets, one of which pierced his heart. One day later the coroner's jury held an inquest into the death and declared that Shaffer came to his death at the hands of Suitter and that the shooting was not justified. Immediately after that verdict District Attorney John Manning ordered Suitter arrested and said he would seek to indict him at the grand jury.[168]

1908 May 12 *[148] New York City, death.*

On May 23, 1908, New York City patrolman George Maher was arrested and sent to the Tombs prison without bail on a charge of having killed Gaetano Trotti. The latter was shot on May 12 and died on May 14. At the time of the death police captain Corcoran sent out two detectives to hunt down the killer, but they reported back to the station that they had been unable to learn anything about the crime. That caused relatives of the dead man to go to the District Attorney's office and accuse policeman Maher of the shooting. Coroner Acritelli, after hearing the evidence, ordered the cop's arrest and sent him to jail. Maher explained, in his own defense, that he had been chasing a number of boys on the day Trotti was shot and that he intended to frighten them by firing his gun into the air. He drew his pistol, he said, but it got caught in the lining of his coat and accidentally discharged, killing Trotti.[169]

Bail for Maher was soon set at $5,000. Trotti was hit by a bullet while he was sitting on the steps of his home. When detectives Flynn and Higgins conducted their investigation they reported that Trotti had been shot by some "unknown" person. Their report made no mention of Maher. Relatives of the deceased, however, conducted their own independent investigation. Maher admitted his revolver dropped from his pocket while he was chasing some boys and "exploded." He did not know, he claimed, that the bullet hit anybody. In explaining the report he received from his detectives, police captain Corcoran said an "honest investigation" had been made but that no one connected the "exploding" of Maher's gun with the death of Trotti, especially since Trotti's home was some distance removed from where the cop was chasing the boys. Those relatives of the deceased managed to find half a dozen witnesses who said they had seen Maher pursue a crowd of boys and shoot after them.[170]

1908 June 29 *[149] Chicago, death.*

Because he objected to the arrest of a man by a black policeman and led a number of men in an attack upon that officer, Edward Smith, a teamster, was shot and killed by Officer Mirtell Parker on the night of June 29, 1908. A week and a half later an inquest was held into the death of Smith wherein Parker was exonerated by the coroner's jury. The killing followed a quarrel over the arrest of a man named Thomas Quigley. Parker testified that Smith knocked him down twice. He added that he fired his weapon into the air and did not intend to shoot Smith.[171]

1908 July 22 *[150] New York City, death.*

Some of the mystery regarding the death of a young woman found with a bullet hole was cleared up on July 23, 1908, in New York City. The victim was a 30-year-old woman named Barbara Reig. City policeman David Shellard was part of the investigating team looking into the woman's death, but he was forced to admit on the afternoon of July 23 that he had a six-month friendship with her, that he was with her when the bullet ended her life, and that it was his pistol that killed her. But, Shellard insisted, she killed herself. Reig died at one o'clock on the morning of July 22. Shellard, who was married, was arrested on a charge of homicide. A reporter stated: "The police, particularly those connected with Shellard's station, have seemed bent from the beginning on proving the case an ordinary one of suicide." Newspaper reporters and two or three detectives from distant police stations were said to have uncovered what little was known about the case at that point. Reig had been employed in a lithograph factory and was paid $8 a week, said her mother, Mrs. Eva Reig. Also, she said her daughter had become engaged some months ago to Adolph Hack, a trucker. She admitted her daughter had become a mother about eight years earlier, but the father of the child failed to marry her. On the evening of July 22, continued her mother, Barbara left home saying she was going to see a girlfriend who also worked in the factory. On the morning of July 23 Barbara did not show up at the breakfast table at home. Her family were not especially worried, though; they thought she had stayed overnight at her friend's place and that the two had gone on to work that morning. A married sister named Mary Thompson remembered she had heard Barbara speak of a policeman acquaintance named Dave. The family then remembered an Easter card Barbara received on April 17 that was signed "Dave." A friend of the dead woman, Sadie Lee, said she knew about the affair Barbara was having with the cop, that it had been going on for six months, and that the cop in question was David Shellard. When his name surfaced reporters working on the case recalled Shellard as the cop "who was most abusive in telling them to mind their own business" when they sought information from the police investigation team.[172]

Shellard had one child and joined the NYPD on January 7, 1907. He told his story of the incident to police inspector Hussey. He claimed he was on duty at about one o'clock on the morning of July 22 and was approached by Reig, who said she wanted to talk to him. They went into a shelter house in a nearby park and talked for a bit. Then they went into a small toolroom in the shelter— the cop had gotten a key made for it specially some four months earlier. He took off his pistol and club and laid them down. Barbara suggested that he leave his wife and marry her, according to the cop. He replied that was a foolish idea, as he was a married man. Finally, just before 2:00 a.m. he suggested he had to go to get back to work. While he had his back turned to her to put on his shirt and hat he heard a shot. Shellard picked up his stuff and left the shelter. Then he met Patrolman Rudolph Kohler running through the park. That cop asked Shellard if he had heard a shot and he said he had heard one. They went into the toolroom together and found the girl, still alive. Kohler ran for an ambulance and Shellard went to call the station house. On his way as he looked for a phone he stopped and went into a saloon and into a rear room there, where he stopped to clean his pistol. He had already thrown the empty shell away in the park. After reporting the crime to the station house he was assigned to the case. He didn't tell the truth at that time about his relationship with Reig because, he said, he knew he would be implicated and feared his family would be disgraced: "It was she who sought me. She pestered me about marrying her." Said a journalist: "Many of the detectives, despite all this, were still loud in their arguments that it had been a suicide. They said they believed every word Shellard had said."[173]

Another reporter wrote an article that implied cops from Shellard's station (Hamburg Avenue Station) were devoting their time to proving his innocence while it was the investigators from the distant stations who were the ones who seemed to be really trying to find out whether or not Shellard killed the woman. When the funeral was held for Reig a few days after her death those in attendance delivered jeers for the platoon of officers detailed to keep order at the funeral. Women predominated in that large crowd and it was all said to be a manifestation of public sentiment.[174]

Coroner Brewer held his inquest into the woman's death on July 29. The verdict delivered by that jury was that Reig died from a self-inflicted wound. Shellard was present but was not "allowed" to testify. The family and friends of the deceased who were in attendance at the inquest created such a scene after the verdict was announced that the police were obliged to clear the courtroom. Among the conflicts introduced in the evidence was the fact that Barbara Reig had a crippled right hand that was partially useless and it was unclear if she would have been able to even hold a gun in that hand. She died from a bullet wound to her right temple. One of her friends, Mary Krug, swore that just a couple of days before Reig's death she told Krug that she was in fear of a cop called Dave who had threatened her life. Dr. Samuel Hubbard testified that he had examined Reig two years earlier and that she had lost the power to bend her second, third and fourth fingers on the right hand but retained complete command of her index finger and thumb. Acting District Attorney Eller declared on July 30 that the result of the inquest would have no effect on future action in the case. Shellard remained in jail. As a result of the poor efforts put forward by the investigation team in the immediate aftermath of the woman's death six patrolmen and all the lieutenants, sergeants and Captain Wormell, all of whom were attached to the same station as Shellard, were transferred to other precincts. Internally, charges of neglect of duty and of being off post without permission or notification were preferred against Shellard. On the afternoon of August 13 Shellard was released from jail on $10,000 bail.[175]

On August 21, 1908, David Shellard was dismissed from the NYPD by

Deputy Commissioner Baker, who conducted the police trial board of the accused man. He was judged guilty of violations of the police manual including being off his post, not notifying his superior that he would be off post, and having no entry in his notebook that he had been off post.[176]

The Kings County Grand Jury handed down an indictment on September 10, 1908, for murder in the first degree against David Shellard, a now "former" cop. While he had been out on bail, that was canceled in the wake of the indictment and he was committed back to jail without bail on the afternoon of September 10. A journalist observed that "the trial of the case promises to develop a big police scandal. Detectives have been at work ever since Shellard confessed he was in the shelter house with the girl. A police conspiracy to hide the identity of the girl and protect Shellard has been established and will be exposed by testimony in court." Reig had suffered her hand injury some years earlier in a streetcar accident. She met Shellard through a girlfriend, and although Reig was engaged to a man at the time she spent much time in Shellard's company. She frequently told her mother and sister that a policeman named "Dave," who was married and had a child, was annoying her with his attentions. When Reig left home late in the evening of July 21 she told her mother she was going to a party in the neighborhood. The night was stormy with heavy showers off and on. At about one o'clock early the next morning a policeman was standing on a street corner one mile from Reig's home when he heard a pistol shot. It came from a shelter house in a park and the officer ran to it. As he reached the door, according to his statement, Shellard ran out from a clump of shrubbery nearby and joined him. The two cops found the body of Reig inside with a bullet wound in the head. Among the cops detailed to work on the case was Shellard and it was not until the next day that the girl was identified. Her mother saw a photograph in the paper of the belongings found with the body and

Mother of Girl ex-Policeman Shellard Is Accused of Killing

Sketch of the mother of Barbara Reig, the girl involved with policeman David Shellard. This case also involved wholesale lying and obstruction on the part of the police.

recognized them. A reporter soon learned, after her identity was established, that Barbara had been on friendly terms with a cop named "Dave" who was attached to the same station house as Shellard and that the girl had been killed by a bullet from a policeman's revolver. That reporter quickly came to uncover Shellard. Those facts were laid before Inspector Hussey, who summoned Shellard to his office. At that meeting, reportedly, the cop broke down and made a confession but claimed Reig committed suicide.[177]

As of January 18, 1909, the trial of Shellard was under way. Three policemen who were with Shellard on the night that Reig died were on the stand that day and, with respect to their testimony, a journalist observed; "Their failure to remember what Shellard said that night astonished Justice Crane. Several times he stopped the trial to rebuke the officers when their memories failed on important matters." One cop named Hahneman said he talked to the accused shortly after the body of Reig had been discovered and had asked Shellard if he knew the girl. But Hahneman said he did not remember what his brother officer replied. When Justice Crane asked him that question again and got the same "don't remember" reply Crane stated, "How do you men get on the force anyway. You look in the faces of those jurymen, all taxpayers, and tell them you can remember the questions that were asked Shellard that night and not the answers."[178]

On the one hand, Dr. Charles Wuest, a coroner's physician, gave testimony that it would have been possible for the girl to have shot herself, while on the other hand Dr. Hubbard said the condition of her hand would have made it extremely difficult for her to have fired the shot that killed her. When Shellard took the stand he told the same story as on previous occasions. Commented a reporter: "Several more policemen with bad memories were examined yesterday."[179]

Shellard's trial came to an end on the evening of January 21, 1909, when the jury entered the courtroom and announced that it was impossible for them to agree. The case before the jury gave them two options, besides acquittal, murder in the second degree and manslaughter; the judge had ruled out murder in the first degree. It was believed that the jury had taken two ballots and that each one ended at six votes to six. Shellard was then taken back to jail to await a second trial. In his summation Assistant District Attorney Roy bitterly scored the police connected with the case, saying, "It is not the usual one of the People on one side and the defendant on the other, but of the People on one side and an organization on another." He added, "It is not a question of this defendant being convicted of killing Barbara Reig, but of the community being exposed to a reign of terror from the uniformed men charged with the duty of preventing such crimes as these." Roy continued by stating, "Men have gone on the stand

and been sworn, and as soon as their testimony approached the point where it was to throw light and truth on the case their memories have been crippled by some insidious influence. Men were at the shelter house that morning who knew the dead girl and said they did not, and lied in saying so. Isn't it remarkable that such a condition of affairs should exist?" Friends of Shellard succeeded on March 19, 1909, in raising $15,000 for his bail and he was released from jail, where he had been since the jury had disagreed.[180]

1908 August 25 *[151] Denver, assault.*

John Bradley (alias John Bremen), a cowboy who was arrested in Denver on August 26, 1908, on suspicion of having murdered policeman William P. Stephens one day earlier, was set upon by a number of peace officers at police headquarters and narrowly escaped being beaten to death at their hands. Detectives who had charge of the prisoner were said to have fought off their furious brother officers and dragged their prisoner to a place of safety.[181]

1908 August 30 *[152] Parsons, Kansas, death.*

A race war was reported to have been narrowly averted at Parsons, Kansas, on August 30, 1908, when city policeman John Williams shot and killed Matt Matthews, a black man. After the killing, black people began to gather in the neighborhood and plan vengeance against the cop and city officials. According to a report, "The better class of the negroes at once took the affair in charge and persuaded the leaders from any rash action and the mob was dismissed without trouble." Matthews was a train porter on the Missouri-Kansas-Texas Railroad and worked the run between Parsons and Kansas City. The trouble was said to have begun when the porter resisted the officer and a scuffle broke out that culminated in Matthews' death. Wrote a journalist: "Matthews was considered a bad man. He killed a Negro in this city four years ago and was known as a prize fighter and a bully."[182]

1909 March 5 *[153] Washington, D.C., death.*

Capt. William H. Mathews of the Fifth Police Precinct in Washington, D.C., was shot and killed while sitting at his desk in the station house on the night of March 5, 1909, by policeman John W. Collier. It was alleged that Collier had been reprimanded for a breach of the police rules. The tragedy took place behind the closed doors of the captain's private office in the station house at about 7:45 p.m. The two men were alone at the time. Collier fired a total of five shots, two into the forehead and three into the right temple. Several cops from the reserve room ran into the office at the sound of the shots and found Collier bending over the captain. Those arriving officers overpowered Collier, disarmed him and locked him up. That there was some kind of feud between the two was the opinion of the Fifth Precinct men. Collier remained silent after the shooting. In the opinion of some of the policemen the feud had its origins on the night of March 3. Collier had evaded reserve duty on the night before Inauguration Day and had been expecting a reprimand ever since that time. But for those few days following Matthews had not had a chance to speak to Collier about his dereliction of duty. Collier had been on the Washington police force for about four years and according to members of the police trial board he had appeared before that body for internal discipline on several occasions on minor charges. Nonetheless, he was said to be "known as an efficient policeman." The 32-year-old Collier was single, while Mathews was a married 52-year-old with grown children and had been on the force since 1886. One theory was that since he faced a potential dismissal from the force for the aforementioned infraction that may have prompted his action. On the day of the shooting Collier was due to report for duty at midnight. However, at around 4:00 p.m. he sent in a telephone message that he was ill. Mathews was apparently irritated at that request for leave and ordered Collier to come to the station house and prove that he was ill. And Collier did appear there, at 7:45 p.m. The coroner's jury ordered him held on a charge of murder.[183]

The district commissioners for the District of Columbia approved on April 1, 1909, the sentence of the police trial board in ordering the removal from the police force of Collier. That was so ordered because he was absent without leave on March 3, 1909, between 10:00 p.m. and 6:00 a.m. and "did absent himself from reserve duty without permission." He was also deemed convicted of a number of other violations pertaining to the police manual, including that on March 5 at about 7:45 p.m. he "did show disrespect

Capt. William H. Mathews was slain in his office by one of his own patrolmen. Bizarrely, in this case, the killer attempted to demonize his own superior. Demonizing often worked when it was an ordinary citizen being demonized, but it did not work in this case.

for and to his superior officer, namely, the late Capt. W. H. Mathews." By this time Collier had been indicted for murder in the first degree.[184] At the coroner's inquest, according to police lieutenant J. L. Sprinkles, Collier, within a minute after he had entered the private office of Mathews, had fired the five shots at him. When asked by fellow officers about the shooting, all Collier said was: "It is done and that's all there is to it." Reportedly, Collier seemed to be normal and in good spirits that day, with nothing wrong. No alcohol was involved. By this account he had been a member of the force for four years and prior to October 1908 he had been up before the police board on minor charges eight to ten times. He had made no appearances before that board since the previous October. Friends of Mathews admitted he was a strict disciplinarian and was not popular with his men. Mathews was born in 1856 and Collier herein was said to be 26. Around this time, early March, with Collier charged with murder in the first degree one report that circulated was to the effect that when Collier entered the office of Mathews the captain made an attempt to assault him and that Collier drew his revolver and fired in self-defense.[185]

Several months later, in August 1909 Collier broke the silence he had maintained since the shooting. In a petition to secure his release from jail pending his trial he argued his release was necessary to prepare a proper defense. Collier declared in that petition that he shot Mathews after the latter had threatened him and had assumed a "menacing position," saying, "I will fix you for that, damn you." After declaring that Mathews once drew his pistol on policeman J. F. Cotton and threatened to shoot him and that the captain had on several occasions kicked or otherwise abused one or more of the officers under his command, Collier detailed his actions on the day of the shooting. He said he was uncertain as to his reserve duty and called Mathews on the phone to find out what to do. Mathews swore at him, he declared, complaining he had not seen Collier for three days. Nevertheless, Collier went to his captain's office at 7:45 p.m., whereupon Mathews chewed him out and Collier, thinking Mathews was reaching to draw a pistol, drew his own weapon and fired. No bail was allowed for the accused.[186]

On the stand at his trial in December 1909 Collier claimed self-defense. He exclaimed, "It was his life or mine." He took the stand after ten fellow officers had testified one after the other as to how peaceful Collier was, a quiet man of good character who was not given to quarreling. Collier insisted Mathews was a quarrelsome man: "He was known as a man who would not hesitate to kill when the occasion arose." On December 5 the jury convicted Collier on a charge of manslaughter. Jury deliberations lasted three hours and 45 minutes. Bail was fixed at $10,000 pending an appeal. John W. Collier was released on bail on December 10.[187]

Justice Gould on January 7, 1910, sentenced Collier to 15 years in the penitentiary. That was the maximum sentence for manslaughter under the law. In the middle of March it was reported that Collier had abandoned his appeal of the conviction and would thus head off to prison at Leavenworth with the next batch of prisoners detailed to go. He had been in jail ever since the sentence was imposed, having been unable to renew his bail bond on which he had been at liberty for a few weeks between the verdict of the jury and the imposition of the sentence. Late Tuesday afternoon on March 29, 1910, Collier was transported to the federal prison at Leavenworth, Kansas, to begin his 15-year term.[188]

John W. Collier, who shot and killed his superior officer, was sentenced to 15 years in the penitentiary.

1909 March 8 [154] *Boston, death.*

Daniel G. Spillman had been a cop in Boston for 21 years when, on the morning of March 8, 1909, he shot and killed his wife and then wounded himself. He was found at his home, reportedly dying from a self-inflicted gunshot wound, while the body of his wife lay on the floor beside him. He died later at the hospital. It was said he had been deranged for the past two years from brooding over the death of a 19-year-old daughter. Apparently the shootings took place while breakfast was being prepared. Other families in the apartment house heard two quick revolver shots. Those neighbors forced open the door and found the dead Mrs. Spillman and the dying Daniel. He had his pistol in his hand.[189]

1909 March 20 [155] *Chicago, death.*

Joseph Finn, 26, was shot and killed in Chicago by a city policeman, Alexander Scott, who said he mistook Finn for "Pickles" Gilroy, a suspected robber, and shot him. Immediately after the shooting Scott realized his mistake, notified his station and surrendered himself. He was held in custody pending the coroner's investigation. Finn left a wife and an eight-month-old child. Scott claimed he fired his gun only after Finn refused to stop upon being ordered to surrender and that he had made a motion as if to draw a weapon. Gilroy was said to have been much older than the man who was shot.[190]

Chicago police chief Shippy, in a notice issued on April 1, asked the members of his police force (about 4,700) to contribute 50 cents each toward a fund for the widow of Joseph Finn. If the chief hoped to deflect criticism by that action he found that it did not work. Sentiment against the police department aroused by the killing of Finn "by mistake" fueled violent demonstrations in the city in two separate instances on the night of April 4 when policemen in the performance of their duty in widely separated parts of the city were attacked by bystanders. Some of the exclamations uttered by the crowd included, "Lookout that he don't give you what Finn got" and "He may be a hair trigger cop." Riot calls were issued when both encounters were in progress.[191]

In Chicago on March 25, 1909, the coroner's jury held Scott to the grand jury on a charge of manslaughter. It declared the shooting to have been "unwarranted and unjustifiable."[192]

1909 April 27 [156] Pocatello, Idaho, death.

Gus Travis, a black Pullman railroad porter, was shot and killed at about 5:30 p.m. on April 27 in Pocatello, Idaho, by city policeman Tom Dickins while, supposedly, resisting arrest. It was reported that Dickins found Travis and another black man engaged in a fight near a saloon. Dickins ordered them to stop, but instead of quitting Travis began an attack on the officer, who warned him that he would shoot if he advanced upon him. Travis paid no attention to the warning and he was shot as he came on for the fight, dying in a few moments. Dickins was placed under arrest while the case was investigated. Travis was a dining car waiter on the Oregon Short Line Railroad. The train had stopped in Pocatello for a few hours and four of the crew wandered over to different saloons in the city. While they were drinking, an altercation arose between members of the crew and the officer arrested two of the dining car men and started for the jail. Travis was alleged to have interfered with the officer in the discharge of his duties and a "rough and tumble fight is said to have occurred in which Travis was shot by the policeman," noted a reporter.[193]

At the coroner's inquest on the following day evidence brought out the fact that several employees of the dining car were engaged in a brawl when the cop attempted to quell the row and arrest the participants. In the struggle the officer pulled out his gun to knock one of the fighters down (not Travis), when Travis interfered to prevent that man's arrest. Dickins attempted to strike Travis and in the scuffle the gun was "accidentally discharged" and Travis lay dead. That coroner's jury ruled the death to be an accident and policeman Tom Dickins was discharged. The whole affair was laid down to black dining car crew members drinking too freely cheap whisky.[194]

1909 April? [157] Spokane, Washington, assault.

A jury in Judge Webster's court in Spokane, Washington, on the night of May 3, 1909, found peace officer Norris Wallace guilty of assault and battery on the person of Ernest Eklund, whom he struck three times with his club while attempting to arrest the man. Wallace had recently been given a ten-day suspension by the police trial board because of his brutality toward Eklund. On July 20 of that year Wallace turned in his resignation and the Police Commission accepted it. At his sentencing in criminal court Wallace was fined $100 and costs for his treatment of Eklund. The grand jury had also recommended his dismissal to the Police Commissioner, something that was said to be in process when Wallace decided to quit.[195]

1909 May 2 [158] New York City, death.

New York City policeman James F. Dillon shot and killed 19-year-old Louis Probber on Sunday May 2, 1909, while attempting, he said, to arrest the boy's father, Isaac Probber, for violating the Sunday law by keeping his grocery store open that day. According to the story, as told by Dillon to his superiors, he had warned Probber to close his store, as he was violating the Sunday law. When he returned to the store an hour later the grocery was still open and doing business. He waited until two customers had made their purchases and left and then arrested Isaac. Dillon said Probber asked him, after the arrest, to be allowed to go back for his coat. In the store at that time were Mrs. Probber, Louis, and another son Max, age 12. While Isaac was going for his coat, said Dillon, the youngest son locked the store door. Dillon told Max to open it and was about to lead Isaac away when Mrs. Probber and Louis tried to intervene. Dillon then drew his revolver and Louis made a grab for his arm. Dillon said Mrs. Probber had a cheese knife in her hand and the whole family joined in the scuffle, which ended with Louis being shot in the abdomen. The officer explained to police captain Fennelly that he had no intention of shooting the boy and that his revolver went off in the struggle with the family. All three family members were locked up in the Adams Street police station and later in the day released on bail. Louis was still alive at that point, lying in a hospital bed. The coat the policeman had been wearing at the time of the attack was cut in several places, which Dillon stated had been done by the knife that Mrs. Probber had in her hand and tried to use on him.[196]

However, from what he learned from the family Inspector Holohan found the cop to be at fault. Probber and his wife said Dillon entered the store and ordered Isaac to remove the vegetable baskets from the doorway and then arrested Isaac. Louis, who was in the back, came to the front of the store to see what the trouble was. At that point Louis turned to go to the telephone, whereupon the cop drew his revolver. While the boy had the receiver in his hand and was calling up police headquarters, said Isaac and his wife, Dillon shot Louis. Two customers were in the store at the time. When Mrs. Probber was asked if she had attacked Dillon with a knife she denied it. She said she was standing behind the counter with a butter knife in her hand when her son was shot. The couple said none of them interfered with the cop at all. They said the coat was torn deliberately in the patrol wagon as the family was being taken to the police station. And that he did so to add evidence to the idea that Mrs. Probber had attacked him with a knife. The family was in the back of the wagon but could see Dillon in the front compartment as he slashed his own coat with his own knife. Thirty-year-old Dillon was married with a family and had been on the force for about two and a half years. Later that day in the hospital Coroner Brewer took an ante-mortem statement from the dying Louis. The young man said the only cause of the quarrel between him and the cop was that he had not given the cop duck eggs of late. Louis had been accustomed to giving him eggs (for free) every Saturday, he explained. When the officer came by and ordered the vegetables taken inside he then told Isaac to close up, as he was under arrest. Then Dillon struck both Louis' parents. Louis thought at first Dillon was just joking, but then he saw it was serious and telephoned police headquarters for help and they promised to send it. "After I telephoned the policeman took out his revolver and shot me," said Louis. Also, he said his father asked the policeman why he did not close up the other stores in the neighborhood that were also open, but that only made the cop angry.[197]

At 5:00 a.m. on May 3 Louis Probber died. Dillon was to be charged with homicide. Assistant District Attorney Francis L. Carrao said the police at the Adams Street station "were apparently conspiring to make the killing of the young man appear to have been an accident." And, he added, "we have been told that Dillon's coat was slashed after he left the Probber store, to deceive the investigators." Dillon denied that Louis, at the time of the alleged assault upon him, was at the rear of the store making a phone call to police headquarters. However, police records indicated that such a call had been made and received at headquarters. As well, several independent witnesses confirmed the family's story, more or less. Although Dillon's fellow cops in his precinct asserted he was always "a good officer," stories floated around about misbehavior. It was said that he had been reckless in the use of his pistol and that, for example, he had fired two ineffective shots at a small boy whom he was chasing two weeks earlier. On another occasion, it was asserted, Dillon beat three small boys who were playing ball in a park. Also, there were stories to the effect that Dillon had been indulging in petty grafting by taking shoes, turkeys, and other tribute from the stores of the small shopkeepers on his beat. Brother officers of the accused man denied those stories.[198]

When Dillon stood trial in June 1909 it was alleged by the prosecution that Dillon shot Louis Probber because he was in a rage over the refusal to give him more free duck eggs. New York policeman Sergeant Kuhlman was one of those who testified. When a neighbor heard shots coming from the Probber store he rushed out and summoned Kuhlman, who was walking an adjacent beat. He got to the store after the alleged assault and shooting were all over. He testified that there were no cuts, or other damage, on Dillon's coat when he reached the store.[199]

James Dillon was convicted of manslaughter on June 25 after the jury deliberated for about 45 minutes. According to the testimony, Dillon was in the habit of levying tribute on the grocery store. A day before the shooting the deceased boy had refused to give the officer the duck eggs he demanded. Dillon returned the next morning and apparently extracted his revenge. In his summation District Attorney Clarke declared that "the policemen who had appeared on the stand in Dillon's behalf, with a couple of exceptions, had perjured themselves." On June 29 Justice Maddox sentenced him to a term of not more than 14 years and not less than seven years in Sing Sing prison; the maximum term was 20 years. On July 7, 1909, orders were issued from police headquarters dismissing Dillon from the NYPD.[200]

1909 May 8 *[159] Glade Springs, Virginia, death.*

At Glade Springs, Virginia, on the night of May 8, 1909, policeman Humphreys went into a black restaurant to arrest Jake Fullen, black, for raising a disturbance. The latter reportedly resisted the cop and Humphreys in self-defense struck the man in the head with his revolver. The weapon accidentally discharged and the ball passed through Fullen's brain, killing him instantly.[201]

1909 June *[160] Claremore, Oklahoma, death*

In a very brief report it was related that at Claremore, Oklahoma, a policeman by the name of M. E. Moseley killed his wife in the presence of their three children and was then not long after killed by the sheriff while he was resisting arrest. Nothing more was reported except that Moseley had had a quarrel with his wife.[202]

1909 June 17 *[161] Macon, Georgia, death.*

At around 1:00 a.m. on June 17, 1909, Officer Oscar Abel of the Macon, Georgia, police force shot and killed Emma Raymond in the red-light district of Macon. At the time of the shooting Abel was in uniform and no motive was known. Raymond was shot three times in the chest. The policeman, after killing Raymond, shot himself in the head and lived only a short time.[203]

1909 June 22 [162] San Francisco, death.

At an early hour on the morning of June 11 in San Francisco Bernard Lagan, described as a "prominent" young man of the city, was shot and probably fatally wounded by police captain Michael Joseph Conboy of the San Francisco Police Department. According to the ante-mortem statement made by Lagan, the attack made upon him by the cop was entirely unprovoked. According to the story, Lagan was on his way home when he saw a drunken man fall and he stooped down to pick him up and help him. Conboy, allegedly highly intoxicated, saw Lagan and started for him, thinking he was intent on robbing him. Lagan resented the charge that he was a robber and started to take his coat off to fight the cop, whereupon Conboy threatened to shoot and when Lagan approached nearer he fired, piercing Lagan's legs. When Conboy was arrested he was still under the influence of alcohol. He had been on the police force for 31 years. Edward McKenna and George Greenwood, who witnessed the shooting, said Lagan was helping Conboy to stay on his feet when the officer shot him. The policeman had been out celebrating the birth of his granddaughter.[204]

Police captain Michael Conboy was born on June 14, 1854, in Ireland and joined the San Francisco police on April 24, 1909. On October 11, 1880, he was ordered to appear before the Police Commission trial board on a charge of "unofficerlike conduct" but was exonerated. On September 21, 1886, he was ordered before the Police Commission on a charge of intoxication but was exonerated. On July 30, 1880, he was ordered before the trial board on a charge of intoxication but was exonerated. On March 25, 1889, he was ordered before the board on a charge of "unofficerlike conduct" and reprimanded. On April 28, 1890, he was ordered before the board on a charge of being under the influence of liquor but was exonerated. On February 1, 1895, he was made a sergeant. On March 4, 1902, he was ordered before the Police Commission on a charge of unofficerlike conduct and exonerated. On August 1, 1902, he was made a lieutenant. On October 11, 1906, he was made a captain. In the wake of his shooting of Lagan he was suspended from the force for drunkenness by Police Chief Cook and held at the city prison pending the outcome of Lagan's injuries. Conboy was a widower with five children and all agreed that on the day of the shooting he was very drunk.[205]

Conboy continued to maintain that he believed Lagan stooped down not to help him but to rob him as he lay on the sidewalk and it was with that thought in mind that he drew the revolver and sent a bullet into the young man's chest. It was reported, though, that Lagan's reputation was clear of any suspicion that he would do such a thing. Conboy had spent nearly the entire evening in a café not a block from the scene of the shooting drinking with friends as they came and went. At around 1:00 a.m. the officer left the café and wandered to the corner of Ellis and Fillmore. Neither Lagan nor his friend Charles Greenwood, with whom he was walking when he stopped to assist Conboy, was under the influence of liquor. Lagan was the eldest of three brothers running the family coal business they had carried on since the death of their father several years earlier. Those three brothers (Daniel and John were the other two) supported their widowed mother, Mrs. Annie Lagan, and their sister Annie (a child). An older sister, Margaret, was a trained nurse who lived on her own. Witness Edward McKenna was less than 40 feet away when the shooting happened. He saw a man he later learned to be Conboy leaning on a lamppost. He was swaying back and forth and finally did fall to the sidewalk, on his back. Then Lagan came along and seized Conboy under the shoulders, evidently to lift him up. Greenwood stood back watching. Conboy and Lagan had some sharp words, but witness McKenna would not hear them and then, as Lagan walked away, Conboy called after him, saying he was a thief and swearing at the young man. At that point Lagan started back and Conboy said, "Keep away from me or I'll shoot you," and as he said those words he drew his revolver and fired. Lagan stopped at the first shot and fell to the sidewalk at the second.[206]

On June 24 Conboy was charged with assault to commit murder. He was released that same evening on $1,250 bail. He had been in custody for about three hours before his release. All the friends of the accused streamed in and out of the lockup area to see him and, said a reporter, "the jail corridor was blocked all day by the friends of the imprisoned man." Those visitors "came from all walks of life, lawyers and bankers." His daughters stayed with him all day to "keep him from brooding over his predicament." On the afternoon of June 26 charges of intoxication and unofficerlike conduct were filed against him with the Police Commission.[207]

Bernard Lagan died at 4:30 a.m. on October 6, 1909, and his slayer was locked up at the city prison in San Francisco on a charge of murder within two hours of the young man's death. Conboy had been brought before the Police Commission on July 23, convicted of being intoxicated on the night of the shooting and dismissed from the force. All of Lagan's friends had testified that he never drank, that he was a total abstainer. Conboy himself, those friends of the deceased declared, had called on Mrs. Ralston, at whose house Lagan along with 15 others were gathered just before the shooting, and been told there were only three bottles of beer in the house when Lagan was there and that the young man touched none of it. Lagan was 28 years old at the time of his death.[208]

Margaret Lagan, the sister of the slain man, protested to Coroner T. Leland on October 12 that the inquest into her brother's death was conducted in a manner unfair to her brother's memory. No one from the District Attorney's office was present to represent the people in the action, while Conboy had two lawyers present "to handle the witnesses in such a way that young Lagan's memory would seem to bear much of the odium of the tragedy," observed a journalist. Conboy's lawyers tried to show Lagan was responding aggressively to Conboy's charges that he was a pickpocket. One material witness was Miss M. L. Payne of the Hotel Congress, "who had not before appeared in the case yet suddenly turned up and

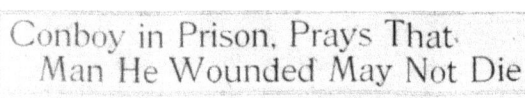

Left: Conboy and his victim, Lagan, along with a sketch of the shooting. This was at a time when Lagan was still alive after the shooting. *Right:* Lagan's sister, shown here, complained bitterly that the prosecution had not bothered to show up for the first day of the coroner's inquest, a highly unusual response. That was one of many examples in this book of a negligent prosecution. Prosecutorial neglect and/or substandard performance was one of many methods used by the state to increase the likelihood of a policeman being exonerated for a crime when he should not have been freed.

"testified that Lagan had almost taken his coat entirely off and was threatening" the officer when the cop fired the shots. Another of the more curious witnesses was Louis Kropp, a waiter, who claimed to have witnessed part of the trouble between the two men. "Kropp's recollection seemed generously bestirred by the grateful memories of gratuities received form his former patron," wrote the reporter. Kropp was a waiter at the establishment where Conboy had been drinking for much of that day. Despite that, Kopp testified that when the policeman left the establishment (30 minutes before the shooting) Conboy was "sober, but jolly." Said Kropp, "I thought the young man was going to hit him in the eye; I would have done the same thing as Conboy did." The reporter commented: "The Coroner rebuked Kropp for his obvious bias." That coroner's inquest was very unusual in that no assistant district attorney was present when it was held on October 11, as was usual in cases where a murder charge was one of the potential outcomes.[209]

Despite the lack of enthusiasm on the part of the state to properly prosecute at the coroner's inquest, that jury came to a verdict that Conboy caused Lagan's death by gunshot and that the officer should be charged with the crime of murder. An assistant District Attorney was present on the second day of that inquest. The only split in the jury room was over whether the charge against Conboy should be murder or manslaughter. It took four ballots, 7–4, 6–5, 8–3, and 11–0, with the majority favoring murder each time. Conboy had argued justifiable homicide on the ground that Lagan had threatened him.[210]

On November 16, 1909, Conboy came to trial for murder. It was the start of a legal nightmare and 30 months would pass before Conboy was taken away to prison to begin his sentence, which happened on May 12, 1912. Over that time a total of five trials were held; that is, the same man was tried on the same charge on five separate occasions. On February 17, 1910, the first trial ended in a hung jury. The second trial culminated on April 2, 1910, with a conviction for manslaughter and a sentence of seven years imposed on Conboy (reduced from 10 years when the judge took into consideration the jury's recommendation for mercy). Conboy appealed and got a new trial, with trial number three ending on August 4, 1911, with a hung jury. The fourth trial ended on September 1, 1911, also with a hung jury. The vote stood at six in favor of conviction and six for acquittal in both trials three and four. The fifth trial ended on April 18, 1912, with Conboy being convicted of manslaughter. That jury deliberated for about five hours. With its verdict the jury also issued a "recommendation for the mercy of the court; if possible, probation." With respect to that fifth trial a journalist observed: "During the trial which closed yesterday Conboy frequently tripped over the testimony he had given before, while the prosecution presented an array of evidence that was overwhelming."[211]

Over the course of those trials the prosecution threatened to charge some of the witnesses for Conboy with perjury and, reportedly, some charges were filed, although nothing seemed to have happened with respect to those charges. At one point during his many trips to the stand Conboy suddenly claimed to back his argument of self-defense that Lagan "had a shiny object in his hand." Conboy had never made such a claim before that time. One of the assistants to Conboy's lawyers was Judge Robert Farrell, who spoke for four hours in a summation. During that oration he remarked several times that Conboy had never discharged his revolver while a member of the force. Farrell failed to mention the Sunday morning Conboy shot the top off a Kearney Street transit vehicle and scattered the passengers in all directions and his subsequent appearance before the Police Commission for drunkenness at the time of that shooting.[212]

After the conviction was registered at his fifth trial Conboy launched another appeal. He was sentenced to three years and was taken into custody immediately after that conviction. For unexplained reasons Conboy dropped any and all appeals and declared he was ready to "take his medicine." He was taken to San Quentin on May 11 to begin his term of incarceration. By early in 1913 his application for parole had been filed and was in the works. On August 24, 1913, at its monthly meeting, the Prison Board denied Conboy's application for parole. He was on the wrong end of a 3–1 vote by that board. At the hearing Conboy made an appeal on his own behalf, noting that he had spent one year and 11 months in custody in the county jail before going to San Quentin.[213]

Another headline in the Conboy case, this one just after Lagan had died.

1909 June 29 *[163]* Cincinnati, death.

Cincinnati policeman Monty Lowenstein found himself in a cell at that city's central police station on June 29, 1909, with a charge of murder registered against him. Nellie Marts, 19, was dead as a result of a bullet allegedly fired by the cop. The shooting took place in a house and Lowenstein admitted to having met the girl frequently in the past few years, but the policeman claimed the shooting was an accident. Lowenstein had a wife and several children.[214]

1909 September 10 *[164]* Ridgeway, South Carolina, death.

Joe Murphy, black, was shot and killed on the night of September 10, 1909, by policeman J. C. Crumpton. The shooting occurred in the black section of town, just outside of the house occupied by Lilla Coleman, black. That house had been reported as a nuisance, and when Crumpton attempted to make an arrest Murphy, reportedly, resisted, cursing the cop and throwing rocks, whereupon Crumpton fired twice, with one shot "entering the back" and causing the death of Murphy. A coroner's jury considered the case on September 11 and rendered a verdict that the deceased came to his death from a pistol shot fired by Crumpton, "an officer of the law, in discharge of his duty and in defence of his life." Magistrate Heims let Crumpton out on $1,500 bond to appear at court at Winnsboro, South Carolina, soon thereafter. When J. C. Crumpton appeared in court he was found not guilty.[215]

1909 November 13 *[165]* Monroe, Louisiana, death.

S. D. Newman a member of the Monroe, Louisiana, police force, was arrested and placed in jail on the night of November 13, 1909, charged with the killing of Kitty A. Watson, black. According to the police, Newman, who was off duty that night, went to the woman's house and, finding a man there, who made his escape, fired four shots into the woman's body, each shot taking effect. Noted a journalist: "This makes the fourth negro who has died as a result of pistol wounds inflicted by Newman since he has been a police officer." Kitty Ann Watson was killed between 9:00 p.m. and 10:00 p.m. while lying on her bed in her cabin in the backyard of the J. S. Handy residence, where she was employed as a cook. She died instantly from the, in this account, five shots that struck her. Besides herself there were present in her room at the time of the shooting her two sons, 12 and 14 years of age.[216]

A different account described Kitty (perhaps Katie), with respect to her relationship with the cop, as "his concubine for several years" and said that his murderous deed was prompted by jealousy. This account stated that Watson was the sixth "human being" Newman had killed in recent years. He had a wife and several children. The editor of this newspaper said; "The murder of this woman, if a negress, demands that the law shall be applied fairly and fearlessly and that Newman shall be prosecuted and convicted regardless of the fact that he is a white man." He then added a comment that had appeared in another newspaper: "Any white man who lowers the standard of decency and becomes the associate of negro women, forfeits all claim to the sympathy and respect of honest people." When he appeared in court S. D. Newman pled guilty to manslaughter and was sentenced in May 1910 by Judge Madison at Monroe to ten years' imprisonment.[217]

1909 December 20 *[166] Seattle, death.*

Seattle police shot Antonio Portipillo on the evening of Monday, December 20, 1909, while he was fleeing from Patrolmen Thomas Walsh and McGaw. The victim was still alive at that time but in the process of dying. The Italian consul took Portipillo's ante-mortem statement and it was reported that all Italian residents of Seattle were incensed. Those two officers professed to be at a loss as to how the man was shot. They claimed they did not shoot him. Walsh stated he fired into the air and could not possibly have hit Portipillo. In his dying statement he said one of the cops shot him but that he did not know which one.[218]

Portipillo was just 17 years old. A newspaper account published a few days after the shooting exclaimed: "As this poor lad lies gasping out his life, the police are scurrying about in their efforts to defame his reputation. They are trying to justify this cold blooded crime, the shooting of a harmless boy who had done no wrong." He was described as poor, friendless, unarmed and a person who barely spoke English. He was shot in the back and reportedly ran in terror from cops whose intentions he did not understand. Two shots struck him. According to the police, Portipillo attempted to draw a revolver. Both officers said they saw him drawing it; no one else did. Original source of the trouble was said to be a woman named Miss Florence Davis. She had gone to the theater with him and had accepted presents of candy. In a confused account Davis complained to the police that the young man was annoying her and threatening her, and that was what brought the police into the affair.[219]

On the complaint of the Italian consul the prosecuting attorney's office issued on January 18, 1910, a warrant for the arrest of Thomas Walsh. While Walsh continued to deny the allegations that he fired two shots into the boy, two eyewitnesses swore they saw the cop shoot Portipillo. Within a day or two

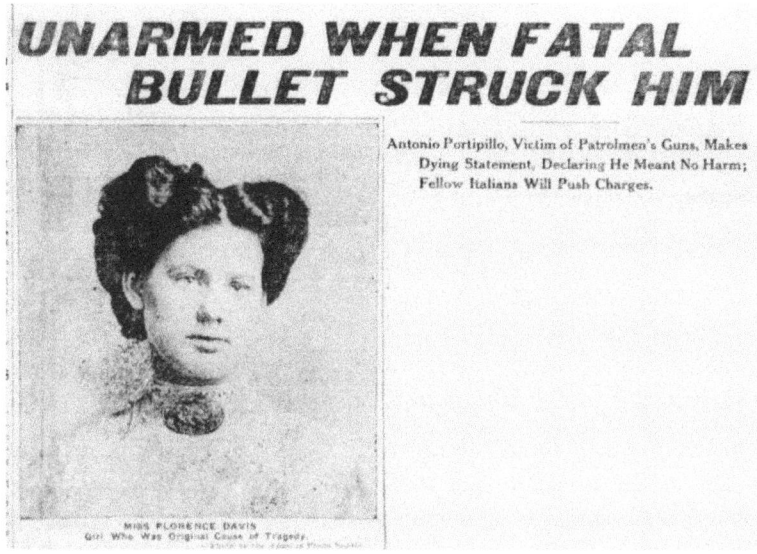

Florence Davis was the young woman who was an indirect catalyst for yet another shooting to death of an unarmed citizen by the police.

it was announced that fellow officers had established a fund to raise money to help Walsh pay for his defense. Each of Seattle's 282 officers were asked to subscribe $1 to start the fund and to contribute more if needed in the future. The trial of Walsh for murder in the second degree began on June 21, 1910. Walsh had been trying to arrest the boy just before the shooting. After 16 hours of deliberations the jury returned to the courtroom on June 25 to report that it could not reach a verdict. That verdict should have led to a second trial but probably did not. The only mention of Thomas Walsh over the next two years came in a July 1, 1910, in a brief item about an accident that happened to James Walsh. He was reported to be "the brother of Patrolman Thomas Walsh—which made him sound like a serving and active officer.[220]

FIVE

1910–1920

1910 January 8 *[167] Albuquerque, death.*

On January 8, 1910, in Albuquerque, New Mexico, policeman Antonio Guavara became involved in a quarrel with Francisco Vargas over the possession of a horse that an animal control officer was trying to take away. Vargas reportedly resisted arrest and Guavara shot him. The wound was not thought to be, noted a reporter, "particularly dangerous but Vargas failed to take care of it, with the result that he died early in February [it was actually April]." Immediately after the shooting Guavara was held on a charge of assault with intent to kill, but he was allowed to continue in active duty as a peace officer and to carry arms. That incensed one journalist who fumed about "both the police chief and the city administration being apparently entirely indifferent to the fact that Guavara is under a charge of assault with intent to kill." He continued by noting that if the allegations of Vargas were true the cop used his gun without provocation and at a time when his life was in no danger "and upon no more excuse than that he thought a motion of Vargas meant an effort to draw a revolver." That the policeman was continued on duty and in possession of a revolver "aroused sharp criticism and indignation against the administration which allowed it." Guavara was then out on a $1,000 bond and it was said of the wounded man's condition: "His wound is not serious and he will recover."[1]

Early in February it was reported that Vargas was still in the hospital and "is in a dangerous condition and may die." A reporter added there had been no investigation of the case "by the council or any of the city officers or, in fact, by any other competent authority." On the night of February 7 the city council of Albuquerque adopted a report from the police committee to the effect that it could not find any ground for suspending Guavara, although the report stated frankly that the only testimony the committee had heard in connection with the case was the policeman's unsupported statement given at the committee's hearing some days earlier. The committee stated further that the reason it had not made a more thorough investigation was because the witnesses it had notified of the hearing had not attended. Police Chief McMillin had the task of notifying those witnesses, but rumors circulated that he had told them not to attend.[2]

Vargas died at his home at around 7:45 p.m. on April 1, 1910. Soon thereafter Guavara was charged with murder. On April 30 the jury hearing the case deliberated for a little more than one hour before delivering a verdict of guilty of assault with a deadly weapon, an offense that carried a maximum of not more than three years in jail. He was sentenced to serve an indeterminate amount of time of from one to three years in the penitentiary. An appeal was immediately in the works, but a pardon issued by the governor of New Mexico closed the incident. On July 21, 1910, Antonio Guavara was pardoned by Governor Mills as the result, said an account, "of numerous requests made to him by prominent citizens of Albuquerque and other parts of the territory."[3]

1910 February 26 [168] New York City, assault.

A newspaper story reported that at a police trial board in New York City that took place around February 18, 1910, three of five NYPD policemen charged variously with assaulting a woman whom they had plied with liquor in the rear of a barbershop and with suppressing a report of the incident had been found guilty by that police commission board and were recommended for dismissal from the force. It was reported that the case attracted attention by the energy with which New York City mayor William Gaynor took it in hand and because of the exposure it afforded of the methods of "the system"; that is, police department corruption. Wrote a journalist: "One of the convicted policemen had an ample supply of witnesses to swear an alibi." By that it was meant fellow officers who would and did lie for a brother cop.[4]

1910 February 26 [169] Clinton, North Carolina, death.

On February 26, 1910, a number of farmers had gathered in Clinton, North Carolina. What was described by a reporter as a "trivial disagreement" broke out between two of the farmers and soon involved a number of other farmers in the melee. The mayor of the town and a number of policemen tried to quell the dispute and in the course of that attempt Officer John K. Tew shot and instantly killed George Jones after the policeman, it was said, had three times been knocked down and "roughly handled" by the crowd.[5]

1910 March *[170] Mayfield, Kentucky, death.*

On the morning of March 23, 1910, in Mayfield, Kentucky, it was reported that the jury in the murder trial of John Lewis, a then former Mayfield policeman, returned a verdict of guilty. Lewis was sentenced to ten years in the penitentiary. Back sometime in the summer of 1908 Lewis arrested James Puckett. The prisoner escaped from Officer Lewis and, he claimed, he fired a shot in the air to stop the fleeing Puckett. However, a bullet struck the man in the head and he died in a short time. Reportedly, Lewis was defended by 11 attorneys. Two years later, in March 1912, it was reported that John Lewis was issued a pardon by Kentucky governor McCreary.[6]

1910 March 29 *[171] Philadelphia, death.*

William McGuire was a young auto tire salesman who died from injuries received in Philadelphia when, according to witnesses, Frank Connelly, a recently appointed policeman, attacked him without provocation and fractured his skull with his club. Connelly was then under arrest, held without bail while they awaited the results of McGuire's injuries.[7]

1910 June *[172] Nelsonville, Ohio, death.*

Thomas Cline was a member of the Nelsonville, Ohio, police force who shot and killed John Lanning in June 1910. He was soon thereafter charged with murder and was hurried from Nelsonville to Athens, where he was lodged in a cell and protected against the actions of a threatening mob. Cline had shot and killed Lanning, the father of four, whom he had been called upon to arrest on a charge of drunkenness. In attempting to capture the man Cline fatally wounded him as he tried to evade the officer's grasp. Neighbors had been annoyed by the boisterous and drunken Lanning and had summoned the police to arrest him. When Lanning saw Cline approach he attempted to escape. Cline fired two shots with the second shot striking the man in the back and killing him instantly. At first the cop was arraigned on a charge of manslaughter, but then the charge was changed to murder in the second degree, in the wake of public feelings running high against the officer. At Athens, Ohio, Thomas Cline was found guilty of manslaughter on February 27, 1911, after the jury deliberated for 12 hours. On March 6 the 55-year-old Cline was sentenced to two years in the penitentiary.[8]

1910 September 2 *[173] New York City, assault.*

New York City mayor William Gaynor and his crusade against assault by the policemen of his city made the papers again in September 1910 when it was reported that in order to put an end to brutality, corruption and negligence in the NYPD Mayor Gaynor had taken the affairs of the police department into his own hands. All complaints were to come to his desk. Within a few weeks, it was said, he dismissed about 25 members from the uniformed force for assaulting citizens or "shirking" duty. He made it known he would break every one of the 10,000 New York cops if that should be necessary "to put an end to the clubbing and assaulting of citizens." As well, it was reported: "The mayor announced that he would not only dismiss the policemen guilty of unjustifiable clubbing, but would have them prosecuted in the courts like other criminals."[9]

1910 September 17 *[174] Kansas City, Missouri, death.*

While he was chasing two black "chicken thieves" through the streets of Kansas City, Missouri, on September 17, 1910, Patrolman Charles Cook, black, fired a total of eight shots at the fleeing men. It was believed that one of those bullets killed Mrs. Karl B. Schaefer in the washroom of her home. Cook fired into the air and it was thought that it was one of those errant shots that struck and killed the woman. Her dead body was discovered by her husband when he returned home from work some three hours after the shooting. Cook was arrested but then ordered released by the prosecuting attorney.[10]

1910 October 1, 1910 *[175] Washington, D.C., death.*

After shooting his wife to death on the sidewalk near his home at 8:45 p.m. on October 1, 1910, and then ineffectually firing the last bullet in his weapon at himself, Washington, D.C., policeman Charles G. Baston sat down and waited for his arrest by fellow officers. He had fired four bullets into his wife's head. The brim of his police helmet, half an inch from his forehead, was shot partly off. At the time of his arrest Baston refused to talk except to say, "I've done it now; I've fixed it all right. I'm only sorry that I didn't have another bullet to fix myself." Baston was 38 years old.[11]

Catherine Baston and her husband had been married nine years earlier. On the night in question the couple quarreled on the street over money. Charles would not give her his recently received pay that he had hidden in one of his shoes. His wife feared he would spend the money on alcohol. During their quarrel on the street he turned on her and fired those four shots into her. That quarrel had started while the couple were still at home and when Charles got tired of it he left the house. Mrs. Baston followed and caught up with him in the street and turned him back toward the house. They had walked a few steps only when Catherine dealt him a blow and she struck him several times, reportedly.

Throughout all this they continued their argument and when the couple were not far from their house he pulled out his gun and fired. The first two bullets dropped her to the ground and then he fired the other two shots into her as she lay on the ground. Baston was appointed to the force on July 1, 1901. Just a few weeks before the shooting Charles had appeared before the police trial board on a charge of intoxication and was fined $50. The couple had fought over money many times in the past. Before becoming a policeman Charles Baston had spent 11 years in the U.S. Navy.[12]

On October 3 Baston was formally dismissed from the Washington police force. It was done using the technical charge that he had violated a section of the police manual that forbade officers to use their clubs or revolvers except in the most urgent cases of self-defense and "when the circumstances justify such action." Witnesses testified to the cop's illegal use of his revolver. The coroner's jury held Baston for action by the grand jury. Several witnesses at the coroner's inquest told of the couple's marital troubles. The couple had a two-year-old child.[13]

Baston was convicted of murder in the second degree on February 7, 1911. He had been indicted on murder in the first degree. His defense was that Mrs. Baston came to her death in a scuffle with her husband while she was trying to gain possession of his revolver; that is, it was a case of self-defense. He went so far, at the trial, as to claim his wife took the pistol from his pocket and in the ensuing struggle she was shot. A few days later at his sentencing hearing Baston made a plea for mercy. However, Justice Wright declared he thought the jury had already shown leniency with the murder in the second degree conviction and he sentenced Baston to life in the penitentiary, the maximum allowable term. He was thus due to spend the rest of his life at Leavenworth Penitentiary in Kansas.[14]

As was to be expected, the attorneys working for Baston had filed an appeal as soon as the conviction was registered. But in the middle of June 1911 it was reported that Baston had abandoned his appeal and would be transported to Leavenworth on June 26. From the penitentiary he intended to appeal to U.S. president

Charles G. Baston was a police officer who shot his wife to death. This photograph was taken much earlier when he was in the U.S. Navy, where he spent 11 years. In defending himself he went so far as even to try to demonize his own wife.

William Taft for commutation of his sentence. One plea made to Taft was to be on the ground of Baston's ill health, said to have been contracted during his confinement in the District of Columbia jail. He planned to also point out his nine years of service as a policeman and his 11 years in the U.S. Navy, including service under Admiral Dewey at the battle of Manila. On January 5, 1917, U.S. president Woodrow Wilson commuted Baston's sentence to eight years. With time off for good behavior he would be eligible to leave the penitentiary in May 1917. At the time of the announcement of the commutation Charles Baston was reported to be dying of tuberculosis.[15]

1910 October 28 [176] New York City, death.

New York City mayor William Gaynor's crusade against corruption in the NYPD, which included the clubbing of citizens by policemen, made it into the newspapers again in October 1910. Early in the morning of October 28 NYPD officer Thomas Kelly committed suicide by shooting himself in the head with his service revolver. He was to have gone on trial that day, before the police trial board, for being absent from his precinct without permission. Another cop who did make it to that trial board session was William F. Waddell. He was sent to the workhouse by Magistrate House for 60 days for shooting up a barbershop a few days earlier. Kelly was the patrolman mixed up in a saloon brawl in the Bronx back on June 28, 1909, when Sebato Basso was beaten to death. Kelly and two other men were afterward arrested and charged with murder. However, at the coroner's inquest all three were discharged. Early in 1910, though, indictments were made against all three of them with respect to Basso's death and each of them was held on $20,000 bail. After two juries had failed to agree in their trials all were discharged. Since the indictments had been dismissed Kelly had, reportedly, "been acting strangely and many charges were preferred against him" before the police board. Kelly was appointed to the force on March 27, 1907. When Waddell appeared in criminal court evidence showed that the cop entered the barbershop on a Monday morning and asked for a drink of whisky. When he didn't get it he was alleged to have drawn his revolver and fired "right and left." Magistrate House in sentencing the officer said he did not believe the story offered by the defense "and was sure the witnesses had been tampered with." While Waddell was in the barbershop a total of five shots were fired by the policeman. As the barber explained to a passerby, "There's a policeman out there and he says if I don't give him a drink he will kill me. I told him we did not serve drinks, and he drew a pistol on me."[16]

That fact that Thomas Kelly came to trial at all for the Basso killing had to do with Mayor Gaynor's crusade. For a time he had all the complaints that citizens tried to register with the police routed to his office first. In March 1910 one of those letters that came to him contained charges with respect to the death of Basso and policeman Kelly. The mayor referred that letter directly to the District Attorney and as a result Kelly stood trial on May 12, 1910, on a charge of manslaughter, along with the other two men. Basso was a porter in a saloon and on June 28, 1908, he got into a row with John De Wald, the bartender, over the allowance of eight glasses of beer a day, which constituted part of the man's wages. He returned to his home that night badly battered and died there from a fracture of the skull. Rocco Savino, a musician, testified he saw Basso being dragged into the saloon by Kelly. There with the aid of the bartender the man was carried upstairs, where it was understood Mrs. De Wald (who had been involved in the fight) refused to make a complaint against Basso. A few minutes later Basso landed in a heap on the front landing of the building. At that point Kelly and De Wald were joined by the third man, John Hayne. Savino said the three men propped Basso against the wall. He said that Kelly hit Basso across the head with his club and held him while one of the others punched him several times in the face. But, as noted earlier, no one was convicted.[17]

1910 November 6 [177] *San Francisco, death.*

Raymond Cullom, a bartender in San Francisco, was shot and killed early in the day on November 6, 1910, by city policeman Justus while the latter was attempting to arrest him. Cullom was at a masked ball at a city auditorium and when he was accused there of taking a woman's purse he started to run. Justus pursued him for several blocks and after firing a shot into the air, which failed to stop the fleeing man, Justus fired at Cullom with fatal effect. The investigation into the death of Raymond Cullom reportedly brought out the fact that he had been arrested for petty theft several times before and that "reports by several policemen were received to the effect that Cullom was a bad character and had frequently had trouble with the police department." As he ran off, it was said, he dropped an overcoat and satchel belonging to others.[18]

1910 November 21 [178] *New York City, assault.*

James T. Welsh, a New York City policeman, was arrested on November 25, 1910, and charged with homicide. According to information, Welsh was the man who shot Lucie Chabenat as she was going up the steps to a house on the evening of November 21. It was believed that he did not intend to shoot the woman and probably did not even see her when he fired what turned out to be the fatal shot. Lucie had reached the top step at about 10:30 p.m. when a shot was fired and she dropped down dead. Another policeman by the name of Devlin told acting police captain Clark that although he had reported the shooting as having been done by an "unknown man," he believed he knew the man and he was an officer. Devlin found that man at a saloon and questioned him. Devlin said that Welsh told him that while he was off duty and walking with a woman he went into a store for a moment and when he came out the woman told him an Italian had insulted her. She pointed him out and Welsh confronted him. The Italian picked up a club and made for the cop. Welsh, thinking to scare him, fired his revolver into the air. Someone shouted that a woman had been hit and then ran away. Devlin went to check on the condition of the woman and found her dead. He went back to the saloon, but Welsh was gone. Since that night Welsh had continued to work his regularly scheduled shifts but made no report of the shooting. Detectives finally went to Welsh's home on November 25 to arrest him. He was then suspended without pay but, on the advice of his lawyers, refused to make a statement. Welsh, 32, had been on the force for seven years and, noted a reporter, "His record is said to be good." Chabenat was 31 years old. On November 28 Welsh was released from custody upon posting $10,000 bail. By then seven witnesses told of Welsh firing at an escaping man.[19]

At the coroner's inquest that was held in January 1911, Coroner Feinberg held Welsh until the District Attorney could review all the evidence. Five of the inquest jurors were in favor of freeing Welsh on the ground there was no criminal intent. Welsh testified that his pistol accidentally discharged. According to his story, he had been dining at a restaurant with a woman. As they walked along a street he knocked down a man who had insulted his companion. A little farther along the street, said Welsh, he was struck on the head from behind. Half-dazed, he drew his pistol as he turned and found the same man raising a three-foot-long club for another blow. The club struck Welsh's arm and the pistol went off. Mrs. Cora D. Myler was his companion that night and she verified that story. Welsh added that he did not know the bullet had killed anyone until four days later. On February 28, 1911, James T. Welsh was dismissed from the NYPD for having shot and killed Chabenat.[20]

1910 November 26 *[179] Washington, D.C., assault.*

Washington, D.C., peace officer George H. Armstrong was arraigned in police court on December 13, 1910, on two charges, one of assaulting William Weaver and another, separate, charge of assaulting Mrs. Elsie Armstrong, his wife. Weaver was assaulted on the morning of November 26, when the officer went to the man's house to arrest someone else for a minor offense. Armstrong was convicted in court on December 22 of having assaulted Weaver and superintendent of Washington police Richard Sylvester declared, in the wake of the conviction, that steps would be taken to remove Armstrong from the force. Armstrong was then under suspension from duty without pay. The jury took just 20 minutes of deliberations before returning the guilty verdict. Meanwhile, Mrs. Armstrong had dropped her charge of assault against her husband. On January 10, 1911, George Armstrong was sentenced to pay a fine of $75 or serve three months in jail for assaulting Weaver. Armstrong paid his fine. At the same time his motion for a new trial was denied. A day or two after that he was dismissed from the Washington police force. On March 28, 1911, Armstrong was arrested during a fire. He was one of several people arrested for looting during the excitement caused by the fire. The charge was petty larceny, as he had stolen eight neckties with a value of $8 from a store.[21]

1910 November 28 [180] San Francisco, assault.

Policeman George H. Ryan, accused by Edward Cheri of assault with intent to commit murder, appeared before police judge Weller in San Francisco on December 1, 1910. Ryan was charged by Cheri with trying to shoot him during a drunken spree at the Casino Café on the afternoon of November 28. As well, charges were filed against Ryan by Capt. John Mooney, his superior officer. Nothing more was heard about the officer except for a brief one-sentence report that was published on August 9, 1911. That item noted that George H. Ryan had been moved from one San Francisco police station to another.[22]

1910 December 25 [181] Salisbury, Maryland, death.

Many riots and affrays that reportedly had occurred over the previous few months in the eastern section of Salisbury, Maryland, culminated on the night of December 25, 1911, when city cop John C. Brittingham shot and instantly killed Herman Parker, age 25. The incident took place in a restaurant. Parker, his brother Carl and three other men went to a restaurant at 6:30 p.m. for a meal. Shortly after that time Brittingham entered the place; soon thereafter Carl Parker struck him in the face. The officer hit back and then Herman joined in the scuffle. During that ensuing tussle the officer drew his pistol and fired, hitting Herman in the heart. After the shooting there was said to have been a "general riot" that was caused by the friends of the dead man. Many threats were issued against the peace officer, who by then was lodged in jail. For his safety extra armed guards were placed at the county jail to protect him. Brittingham made the usual plea of self-defense and said that Parker reached into his pocket, causing the officer to fear he was going for a gun.[23]

1911 January 19 [182] El Paso, Texas, death.

Frank Richard, an infantry bandsman, was shot and killed on the night of January 19, 1911, in a restaurant in El Paso, Texas, by Henry C. Bernauer, a member of that city's police department. It was said that Mrs. Bernauer was dining with Richard at the time. Richard, with two bullets in his head, died in a booth at the Eastern Grill restaurant on El Paso Street shortly after 1:00 a.m. on January 19. He had arrived at the grill a few minutes earlier with Mrs. Lola Bernauer. Henry was immediately arrested and taken to the police station where he was locked up. A warrant charging him with murder was issued and he was bound over to the grand jury with his bond placed at $1,000. The killing took place after the couple had attended a dance. Richard called for Lola at the apartment of the couple; Bernauer was present at the time. He told the pair to be home before midnight and they would all have some beer together. The couple returned to the apartment shortly before midnight, but the officer wasn't there. Richard looked around outside but did not see him. He finally returned and the three people had some beer. Bernauer then said he would go out for sandwiches and left, saying he would be back in an hour. After waiting for a while, with Bernauer not returning, the other two left and went to the Eastern Grill. They were sitting there when Bernauer entered and started shooting. Richard was 26. Immediately after the shooting Bernauer called the police and asked that a cop be sent to arrest him. Bernauer was appointed to the El Paso police on September 20, 1910, and in his time on the force had not missed a shift. Lola was 25 and the couple had a three-year-old son. Bernauer had posted bond and was released shortly after twelve noon on January 19.[24]

When he came to trial in March 1911, Bernauer, who had been suspended from the force since the shooting, took the stand to explain his action. He said he found evidence of "improper relations" between Richard and his wife when he returned to the couple's apartment. He also said he had found his wife in the booth at the Eastern Grill with Richard and she had her left arm around his right shoulder when Bernauer shot the man. On March 21 the jury returned a verdict of not guilty. Three ballots had been taken, with the first one standing at 9–3 in favor of acquittal. A reporter observed: "Although the defence was what is commonly known as the unwritten law, yet it is a written statute of the state of Texas which makes homicide justifiable when a man finds another violating the sanctity of his home, or in a fit of passion, believing that another has violated his home, kills him. All of this was contained in the judge's charges and in that regard only did it differ from the stereotyped charge."[25]

1911 May 27 [183] *Englewood, New Jersey, death.*

An 18-year-old student by the name of Roland Ruddock was mistaken for a burglar, reportedly, by policeman Michael O'Neill on the night of May 27, 1911, in Englewood, New Jersey, and shot in the back while running away. O'Neill was in plainclothes. The shooting took place at about 9:00 p.m., with the boy dying a few hours later in the hospital. The policeman had been sent to guard the residence of a man named Cameron Blakie because two attempts had been made to break into his home in the recent past. O'Neill was hiding in the bushes when he saw two figures crossing the Blakie lawn and heading toward the house. It was, in fact, two schoolboys taking a shortcut across the lawn. Stepping out into the open, O'Neill called on the two to halt. It was dark and the boys, fearing O'Neill was a highwayman, started to run off. That caused the cop to think they were suspicious characters, at the least. He drew his revolver and gave chase. The boys were outrunning the policeman, so he fired a shot into the air, but that only made the boys run faster. Then came two more shots aimed at the runners. Ruddock continued to run for a couple of hundred more yards before he fell to the ground.[26]

At Coroner Tracey's investigation into the death of Ruddock, held two days later, the jury rendered a verdict that Ruddock came to his death from a bullet wound and, while there was no evidence to show that O'Neill fired the fatal bullet, the officer had not denied the fact. O'Neill remained under arrest on a murder charge as of May 29.[27]

1911 September 17 [184] *Coatesville, Pennsylvania, death.*

On Sunday night, September 17, 1911, in Coatesville, Pennsylvania, a black man named Zachariah Walker was dragged out of his hospital bed by a mob and lynched—he was burned to death by that mob. It was alleged that Walker had shot and killed a special policeman named Edgar Rice as part of a larger race riot. When cornered by his pursuers Walker tried to commit suicide by shooting himself, but the bullet did not kill him and, hence, he was in the hospital. On September 20 warrants charging two members of the mob with murder and two policemen with involuntary manslaughter were issued by Judge Butler upon the recommendation of the special grand jury. That grand jury had been in session for three weeks and it was said they were reluctant to take action. Policeman Stanley S. Howe was on guard at the hospital that night and it was claimed that he did not exert himself to prevent the mob from seizing the man he had under his care and did not prevent that mob from lynching Walker. The other officer under indictment was Police Chief Charles E. Umstead, who, it was claimed, failed to perform his duty properly. The grand jury report censured the entire police force of Coatesville for failing to further the ends of justice. Nothing more was reported on those two cops until two months later when a brief item published on November 21, 1911, noted that a posse in Coatesville was after a rapist and that posse was led by Chief of Police Umstead.[28]

1911 September 20 *[185] Vancouver, Washington, death.*

Shot through the back while attempting to escape arrest for what was termed "a minor offense" in Vancouver, Washington, on September 20, 1911, Pvt. Harvey Llewellyn of the Vancouver barracks died later that same day. Reportedly, the troopers at the barracks were aroused and there was much talk of prosecuting policeman Roy Burchardt, who did the shooting.[29]

1911 October 12 *[186] New York City, death.*

Michael J. Aspell of New York City was shot and killed on the morning of October 12, 1911, by NYPD cop Jon Clifford. Aspell had been arraigned before Magistrate Cornell in Manhattan a few days earlier and ordered to pay his wife $5 a week in support payments. On October 11 he went out drinking and at a bar he had stopped at he stole a statue from the place when the barkeeper was in the back and left the saloon with it. When Aspell failed to return with the merchandise the barkeeper called the police and Clifford was sent to his house. When he got there Clifford waited outside until Aspell came out carrying a bundle. Aspell started to run when the officer tried to arrest him. Clifford gave chase and fired two shots into the air, at which point Aspell stopped and surrendered. As the officer escorted his prisoner to the station Aspell made another dash for freedom after the pair had walked a block or two. Again the officer gave chase. This time he was being outrun and so Clifford fired two shots at the fleeing man. One of them hit the man in the back and penetrated his lung.[30]

1911 November 13 *[187] New York City, assault.*

Fourteenth Street and Sixth Avenue in New York City was crowded with shoppers, mostly women, around 2:00 p.m. on November 13, 1911, when suddenly there was a commotion near the entrance to the elevated train station. A cop stood over a woman whom he had just struck twice in the face, once with his fist and the second time with his club. Angry men sprang toward the cop, who held his ground, waving his club threateningly. The woman got up and ran screaming to policeman Wohle, who was out in the street directing traffic. Wohle started to tell the woman to go to police headquarters with her complaint when he noticed another commotion near the train entrance. It appeared the attacking policeman was still brandishing his club and now also had his pistol drawn and was pointing it toward the crowd. Wohle went to his rescue and disarmed him. He then escorted him part of the way toward the police station with the crowd still in pursuit. Wohle came to an office building and pushed his fellow officer into its lobby, from where he called for reinforcements, who eventually came. The prisoner was NYPD policeman Joseph D. Borgman, 35, a cop since October 21, 1905. Borgman refused to say anything and police doctor Jennings was summoned to examine the man. Jennings pronounced his patient to be intoxicated. He was then locked up and when news of his arrest reached headquarters Police Commissioner Waldo immediately suspended Borgman from duty. In court, where he was held over on $1,000 bail, Magistrate House chastised Wohle for not getting the name of the female victim, who had since disappeared. House was skeptical and wondered if that action by Wohle was a deliberate act of a cop protecting another cop and asked Wohle, "Is the system at work here?"[31]

That missing woman surfaced on the next day. Mrs. Mary McCullough had seen in the newspapers that she was wanted and thus had made herself known to the police. She said she had been shopping and was walking toward the train station when she saw Borgman waving his club in the air. He appeared intoxicated, she said, and she stopped to watch him. She saw him knock the crutches from beneath a crippled beggar and beat the man with a club. Suddenly, she explained, Borgman saw her watching and, leaving the cripple, strode toward her swearing and exclaiming, "Are you looking for some of the same then! Get up those steps now," indicating the stairs to the elevated. She started to do that but apparently not fast enough, for he struck her with his club and blood began to flow from her ear. A woman friend helped her out into the street and over to traffic cop Wohle. One of the reasons she fled, Mary explained to Magistrate House, was that "he had his revolver in his hand and I was afraid he would shoot me." She agreed it was not the fault of Wohle he didn't get her name; she did not give him the chance. House increased the bail amount to $2,000.[32]

Joseph Borgman was indicted for assaulting McCullough and came to trial in February 1912, at which time he was referred to as an "ex-cop." On February 16 he was convicted of assault in the third degree and remanded one week for sentencing. Several independent witness verified McCullough's story.

Five • 1910–1920   169

This graphic displays the police "system." That was the name given to the fact that policemen usually united together to bail one another out of trouble and protect one another, with the men going so far as to engage in egregious lying whenever and wherever necessary.

He was dismissed from the NYPD after a police trial board had him appear before it on the same charge. In court Borgman testified that he had been under the influence of opium, which had been given to him as a medicine.[33]

1911 December 24 *[188] Abingdon, Virginia, death.*

Brad Henry, a liveryman in Abingdon, Virginia, was shot and instantly killed in that city on December 24, 1911, by city policeman Jack Clark. Henry's two sons, Joseph and Milton, were both seriously wounded in the same incident.

The trouble reportedly started when Clark undertook to make an arrest. In doing so the officer slapped a little girl, whereupon Henry interceded, pushing Clark backwards off a house porch. In response the officer fired five shots, killing Henry instantly and wounding the two sons.[34]

1912 April 29 *[189] Florence, South Carolina, death.*

A black man named Doc Lerk was shot and instantly killed in Florence, South Carolina, on the afternoon of April 29, 1912, by policeman J. L. Haselden. According to the story, Lerk had come to Florence from his work camp to "liquor up" and "he is said to be very ugly when drinking. He is a big negro over six feet in height and over 200 pounds in weight." The story "as accepted by the coroner's jury" was that he was with disorderly black women, got into a quarrel with them, and knocked one of them down. As the cop placed him under arrest and led him off Lerk suddenly turned on the cop, choked him, wrestled with him, and finally drew a knife, at which point Haselden shot and killed him. Conveniently, the knife was found beside the dead man. The coroner's jury declared the homicide was justified.[35]

1912 May 18 *[190] Pomaria, South Carolina, death.*

Will Eichelberger, black, was shot and killed in Pomaria, South Carolina, by peace officer Henry B. Richardson late on Saturday afternoon, May 18, 1912. It appeared from the testimony taken at the coroner's inquest that the shooting took place while Richardson was having trouble with Will in arresting him for disorderly conduct. Wasting no time at all, the inquest into Eichelberger's death was held that Saturday evening, May 18. The verdict was that the black man came to his death from pistol wounds at the hands of Richardson. According to witnesses, the pair were walking along the street and Richardson told Will to get out of town and the man replied that he would. Richardson continued to follow Will as he moved along, but then Will stopped to light his pipe and was cursing. Richardson told him not to curse. They exchanged some words and then Richardson took Eichelberger by the arm and said he was going to take him to the lockup. Will told the officer to leave him alone and to go away. They scuffled and Will grabbed for the cop's gun. At that point Richardson fired and Eichelberger fell dead. Another witness told a similar story.[36]

1912 June 16 *[191] Rock Hill, South Carolina, death.*

Henry H. Putnam, about 20 years old, an employee of the Victoria Cotton Mill in Rock Hill, South Carolina, was shot and killed by policeman Eubanks on the railroad tracks near the mill at about 5:00 a.m. on June 16, 1912. Coroner Louthian held an inquest four days later wherein, it was said, evidence showed that Putnam and three other young men were in front of the mill and that Putnam hopped a passing freight and rode it for a bit and that Eubanks came out from the other side of the train and arrested Putnam when the train passed. After the pair got out of sight as they marched toward the city lockup a shot was heard and Putnam's companions ran up to find their friend had been shot. He died in a few minutes. There were no witnesses to the shooting. Eubanks admitted to the shooting, but the officer claimed it was self-defense. The coroner's jury declared that Putnam came to his death by pistol shots at the hands of Gus Eubanks while the latter was in the discharge of his duty as a peace officer of the city of Rock Hill. Eubanks surrendered immediately after the killing and was held in custody until the bail amount was set.[37]

A few days later employees of the mill had reportedly started a subscription for a fund to help in the prosecution of policeman Eubanks. They felt the killing was unjustified and they wanted to see the cop punished.[38]

Eubanks was tried for the murder of Putnam on November 30, 1912. The story to that time was that there was no other reason for the shooting of Putnam than that the deceased had squatted down in the road while he was being escorted to the lockup by the officer and refused to go on. In habeas corpus proceedings later, the claim of the defense was that the defendant had reason to believe the deceased was trying to draw a weapon, and fired in self-defense. At the trial the defense was somewhat different. Eubanks claimed that Putnam broke away from him and started to run. He pursued his prisoner and because Putnam had his hand in his pocket in a threatening attitude, said an account, "the cop's pistol was discharged. The defendant claimed that he had no intention of shooting the deceased and could not explain just how it was done. He gave the impression of inadvertence and disclaimed all thought of intent or malice." At the end of the one-day trial the jury returned a verdict of not guilty.[39]

1912 July 16 *[192] New York City, death.*

The story of NYPD lieutenant Charles A. Becker began with a small article that appeared in the newspaper In New York City on July 15, 1912. The item related that New York City police commissioner Rhinelander Waldo was demanding, on that day, that an immediate investigation be launched by the District Attorney into the stories that corruption in the form of shakedowns and grafting was widespread in the Tenderloin area of the city and that uniformed police officials had been taking protection money from Herman Rosenthal and other gamblers.[40]

One day later the aforementioned Rosenthal was murdered in a sensational, gangland-style killing. This article referred to him as a "cheap gambler. He was the representative of a politician of nationwide prominence." Recently, it was reported, Rosenthal had violated the ethics of the gambler's code because "he squealed to District Attorney Charles Whitman, saying that Police Lieut. Becker was holding him up for a percentage of the profits to his gambling house." From that time onward the gambler was in fear for his life. At close to midnight on July 15 Rosenthal made a tip to see Whitman. A meeting was arranged for 8:30 a.m. two days later. For safety's sake the meeting was scheduled for Whitman's home. However, Rosenthal never made it. At about 2:00 a.m. he was called outside from a hotel where he was relaxing in one of the public rooms. A car drew up as Rosenthal emerged from the hotel and several men armed with automatic weapons jumped out of the vehicle and began shooting at the gambler. He died in that proverbial hail of bullets.[41]

New York City mayor William Gaynor had before him, at a meeting, on July 18, Becker along with NYPD patrolmen Charles Foy and Charles Steinhardt. They were there in response to a letter written by the mayor to Police Commissioner Waldo requesting them to come and explain themselves to the mayor with respect to their friendship with Rosenthal. In part Gaynor's letter said: "I cannot understand why Lieutenant Becker should sit down at dinner with such a scoundrel. That he did so seems to be admitted." The letter continued: "I

Above: Charles A. Becker pictured at the time he was first arrested. *Right:* A sketch of Becker at the time of his first conviction and sentencing to death.

found that Rosenthal and his associates who called on me were the worst gang of men that I had ever seen. That is why I am so surprised that Lieutenant Becker should sit down to dinner with any of them or associate with them in any way." No reports about that meeting were published. Those three policeman summoned to see the mayor had all been near the Hotel Metropole on the night the gambler was shot. Rosenthal was in the Metropole when he received the call that lured him out into the street. It was a sensational case that occupied New York City newspapers with headlines off and on for several years. In due course the four gunmen who were in that car were identified, tried and convicted and all four were executed in 1914. District Attorney Whitman made no secret of the fact that he thought Becker was the man who had orchestrated and paid for the murder. Becker was arrested on July 29, 1912, and convicted and sentenced to death along with the gunmen in 1914. However, he was awarded a new trial but was again convicted and sentenced to death. By then it was revealed that Becker had used his position to extort substantial sums of money from gamblers that totaled more than $100,000. At the age of 45 Charles Becker was put to death in the electric chair on July 30, 1915, in Sing Sing prison. Newspapers were unanimous in considering Becker to have been guilty.[42]

Becker (inset) and a crowd of witnesses lining up for admittance to the death house to observe the execution in the electric chair of Charles Becker.

1912 October 29 *[193] Seattle, assault.*

A farmhand by the name of Leslie Pepper was shot and seriously wounded in a lodging house in Seattle, Washington, on October 29, 1912, by a Seattle city detective, M. J. McNamee. About one month later the officer was charged with assault. Then, on December 10, 1912, the Seattle City Council by a vote of seven to one passed, over Seattle mayor George F. Cotterill's veto, the bill curtailing the power of the police to make arrests without warrant. The bill was introduced following the shooting of Pepper, a Missouri youth who refused to open his door when the police demanded admittance at night. That bill restricted the power of the police to enter private apartments or make arrests without a warrant in felony cases unless an offense was committed in the presence of an officer. That law was to go before the voters in a March referendum.[43]

At the trial in January 1913 it was revealed that McNamee mistook the room in which Pepper and his brother were sleeping for one in which he expected to find a burglar for whom he was looking. He broke into the room and shot Pepper when the youth protested and would not admit the cop. The jury, on January 22, found the officer guilty of assault in the third degree after deliberating for two hours and 15 minutes. The maximum penalty for that felony was not more than one year in jail and/or not more than a fine of $1,000. In another news account it was stated that McNamee was found guilty "despite the efforts of the whole Seattle police force to clear him." On February 2, 1913, McNamee appeared before Judge Ronald, who sentenced him to a fine of $200. Ronald held that the officer, having received an anonymous letter stating that holdup men occupied certain rooms in a lodging house, had the right to make an arrest without a warrant and that he also had a right to break open the door. The court also held that the officer was guilty of a mistake in judgment and nothing else and that he shot in the fear that the two men he beheld in the room were desperate strangers. Up to the time of the shooting, Judge Ronald declared, McNamee was a "brave, fearless officer" and if he had not broken down the door he would have been derelict in his duties. The court also lauded the officer for his courage in view of the fact, said the judge, "that a certain Seattle newspaper had been advising people to shoot through their doors at policemen who were trying to force entrance."[44]

1912 December 15 *[194] Riverside, California, death.*

Riverside, California, policeman Bert Barrett shot and killed his superior, Acting Chief of Police John R. Baird, on December 15, 1912. After shooting Baird the officer was taken to the county jail and there he unsuccessfully tried to commit suicide. Reportedly, the two men had been vying for the office of chief of police, a post that had recently been left vacant by the death of Chief Coburn, and the shooting was the outcome of the rivalry. The two men were alone at the time of the shooting. Officer Lucas, in another room at the station, heard three shots and rushed into Baird's office to find the acting chief dead on the floor and Barrett standing over him with a revolver in his hand. While he was in the lockup he tried to cut his throat with a fragment from a drinking glass. Baird was slated to be named the permanent police chief on the day after the shooting.[45]

Barrett broke his silence about the shooting for the first time on December 16 to declare that the killing was not a result of any rivalry between the two men for the office of chief but was the result of Baird's alleged persecution of Barrett's two nephews. Those two boys, said Barrett, were constantly being arrested and he believed Baird was pursuing them to harass himself.[46]

1912 December 17 [195] Central City, Kentucky, death.

At about ten o'clock Tuesday morning, December 17, 1912, Robert Glenn, a policeman on the force at Central City, Kentucky, shot and instantly killed Frank Smith, a black man It was reported that Glenn went out in response to a call that Smith had beaten up a black woman. Finding Smith, Glenn put him under arrest and started walking back to the lockup with his prisoner. Smith tried to make an escape, and as he ran Glenn began firing at him, with one shot striking him in the back of the neck and killing him. A news account declared: "It is the opinion that Glenn is in serious trouble over the killing, as he had no warrant, was making an arrest outside the city limits where he had no authority, and in no event was justified in shooting at a prisoner who was making an attempt to gain his freedom by running away. Glenn surrendered himself and was released on a $1,000 bond.[47]

1913 January 4 [196] Marion, Iowa, death.

At the beginning of January 1913 in Marion, Iowa, a prisoner in the jail by the name of Harvey Lee was attempting a jailbreak. In the scuffle that followed, Charles P. Gillin of the Cedar Rapids Police Department was shot and killed by a bullet through the chest and Detective John Cook was shot through the hand. Lee denied having any weapons and the officers who searched him did not find any weapon. That death of Gillin remained a mystery until nearly the end of January, when it was reported that the cop was accidentally killed by one of his brother officers. One of the officers at the scene struck Lee on the head during the scuffle surrounding the attempted escape and that blow caused the weapon to explode and it was then believed that the bullet passed entirely through Gillin's body and wounded Cook in the hand. Lee was an alleged bank robber.[48]

1913 March 17 [197] Philadelphia, death.

Philadelphia policeman Frederick Kilmer was found guilty of involuntary manslaughter on October 27, 1914, in a courtroom in that city for shooting to death 17-year-old William Murphy on March 17, 1913. After the jury returned its verdict Judge Martin "severely criticised" Kilmer for using his revolver when there were no more serious charges against Murphy than "skylarking." Murphy and a number of his friends had been playing about the street corners in their neighborhood when Kilmer and a sergeant appeared and tried to apprehend them. Murphy fled and the cop chased him and when he saw the lad was gaining ground on him Kilmer fired his weapon. The bullet entered the back of the boy's head, killing him almost instantly. Said Judge Martin to Kilmer, "A man of your sort is not a safe man to have a revolver. It made no difference if this crowd of boys were singing and making a racket, you had no right to resort to the use of your revolver under any circumstances, even if they were trying to escape." Martin continued, "Men are chosen for the police force because they are supposed to be cool-headed and do not get excited under conditions that would affect some other persons. It is plain, however, that you, instead of keeping your head, get excited or angry. You evidently fired in the air in this case, but when this boy did not stop you got angry and then tried to wing him. When policemen get the impression that they can draw their revolvers on any occasion it becomes a great danger to the community." Kilmer was then under suspension by the police board. Martin postponed sentencing pending an investigation of the officer's police record. On October 30 Kilmer was sentenced to one year in prison.[49]

Frederick Kilmer was present to hear his own application for a pardon on November 18, 1914. While he had been sentenced to jail he was still free on the outside, as he "was released on parole." Accompanying him to the hearing were several police officers from his station and a number of friends. He wanted a pardon so he could be restored to the police force. His case was presented by John H. Fow, who contended Kilmer had shot into the air to stop Murphy but that he stumbled and the revolver, while it had been held in a perpendicular position, was thrown to a horizontal position and the bullet hit the boy. Fow also presented letters, said a reporter; "from every banker in Germantown and from the Revs. C. Wesley Burns, Wayne Channel and Martin Hastings Dodd together with other prominent men of that section asking for a pardon." At its executive session on November 18, the Pennsylvania Board of Pardons recommended Frederick Kilmer for a pardon.[50]

1913 March 18 [198] Chicago, death.

Dressed in his uniform Joseph Smith, a member of the Chicago Police Department for over 20 years, walked into a police station on March 18, 1913, and announced, "I've killed my sister-in-law Mrs. Smith, over in her home. You had better send someone over there." When officers arrived at the house they found the woman shot to death with three bullet wounds in her head. "She ruined my home, disgraced my name and brought shame upon my sons," explained Smith. He was reportedly drunk when he killed Mrs. Rosie Smith and explained further that she caused the arrest of his son for theft. When he came to trial on a murder charge in December 1913 Joseph Smith was found guilty and sentenced to 14 years in the penitentiary.[51]

1913 June 16 [199] Chicago, death.

Patrolman Fred E. Wooster of the Chicago Police Department shot and fatally wounded Chester Robinson, a 40-year-old black man, on June 16, 1913, when the latter reportedly attacked him in an alley. The shooting took place shortly after 9:00 a.m., with Robinson being pronounced dead in a hospital 30 minutes later. It was said that Wooster's nose was broken and that he was cut about the head. The incident started when neighbors complained that a crowd of black men had congregated in the alley and were drinking beer. Wooster was sent to disperse them. When he arrived at the spot he found Robinson and four other men and told them to disperse. All went peaceably except Robinson. Wooster said he took hold of Robinson's coat and threatened to arrest him if he did not leave. Then, said the cop, Robinson grabbed his club off him and beat him about the head with it, knocking him down. Robinson continued to strike Wooster and the cop drew his revolver. While lying on the ground Wooster fired four shots, with two of them striking Robinson.[52]

1913 August 7 [200] Denver, death.

An application for a pardon filed by Frank Campbell, a Denver policeman who had been convicted in the court on a charge of murder for having struck a prisoner a death blow with his club, was not taken up by the Colorado Board of Pardons at its August 1913 meeting and was postponed until the next meeting of that board.[53]

1913 September 25 *[201] Chicago, death.*

A bullet fired by Chicago policeman William Allen at three highwaymen early on the morning of September 25, 1913, struck an iron trolley pole, deflected and killed William Lorimer, a tobacco agent. Three friends who were talking with Lorimer when he was shot seized the cop and took him to the station where he was placed under arrest. Another cop nearby heard the shots and arrested one of the three highwaymen.[54]

1913 November 3 *[202] New York City, death.*

In a fusillade of shots fired by New York City police officers early in the day on November 3, 1912, to try to check the mad rush of 16 steers that had escaped from a railroad stock pen on the west side of the city those officers managed to kill one man and wounded another with errant shots; both were innocent bystanders. George Beattie toppled from the seat of an express wagon when a stray bullet pierced his brain. Another bullet went through the foot of Walter Wagenheim, a waiter. A different news story stated that the number of steers that had escaped was eight. It all started around 4:00 a.m. Reportedly, some of the cops commandeered two taxis and as they rode down the street opened the windows and started shooting.[55]

1914 February 4 *[203] New York City, death.*

An unidentified thief was shot and instantly killed by NYPD officer George Wangerman on the afternoon of February 4, 1914. He had chased the thief for two blocks and caught up to him while he was scaling a fence in a backyard. The cop yelled, "Stop," but it had no effect and then he fired a warning shot into the ground. He yelled again at his suspect, but by then he was almost over the fence. So Wangerman fired again, hitting the man in the back. Wangerman said he did not mean to hit the man but had aimed at the fence near him. The officer had been on his beat with another cop when cries of "Police!" drew them to a store where a robbery had taken place. They reached the scene in time to see two men fleeing the area. Without stopping to make inquiries Wangerman started after one man while his partner chased after the other one. Reportedly, the two robbers had entered a junk store and struck the proprietor on the head, but the junk dealer had fought back and yelled for help. Wangerman had been on the force for six years and, it was said, "had a good record." The deceased was later identified as Robert Downie, age 21. Junk dealer James Rooney had pointed out Downie to Wangerman. After the incident was reported, Police Commissioner McKay conducted his own investigation and concluded that Wangerman would not be suspended but would stay on duty and that he had been justified in using his revolver when he did.[56]

1914 March 10 *[204] Tucson, assault.*

The trial of Tucson, Arizona, policemen Smith and Devant who were charged with malicious assault on the person of Leon Sera took place on March 10, 1914, before Justice of the Peace Comstock. Both officers were convicted. Smith was sentenced to a fine of $50 or 50 days in the county jail while Devant was sentenced to a fine of $150. A jail sentence of six months had been asked for each of them.[57]

1914 June 12 *[205] New York City, death.*

Aaron Hirsch was killed on June 12, 1914, by New York City patrolman Joseph R. Wallace when he resisted arrest and, reportedly, put a hand to his hip pocket as if to draw a pistol. As Hirsch ran away, the cop fired once into the air. A second bullet struck the sidewalk behind the fugitive and bounced up and into him. Hirsch dropped to the ground but got back up and continued running away. Wallace fired again and the bullet ricocheted off the sidewalk once again and hit a 19-year-old bystander named Frank Gottwald, injuring him slightly. Meanwhile Hirsch had again dropped to the ground and was dead when the officer reached him. The shooting took place on the street where Wallace had arranged to meet Bertha Zora in response to a letter saying that he wished to make amends for "a petty theft" committed by him a few days earlier. Zora complained to the police and Wallace went with her when she went to meet with Hirsch. However, when Hirsch saw the policeman he started to run. Hirsch was 40 years old and it was said he had been in and out of jail since he was 18 and described as a "notorious criminal." After details of the case were investigated by his superiors, Aaron Hirsch was allowed to go back on duty.[58]

1914 July 18 *[206] Fulton, Kentucky, death.*

Hal Ferguson, acting city marshal in Fulton, Kentucky, shot and killed Jack Johnson (alias James K. Polk), a black man, in that city on July 18, 1914. Johnson had been separated from his wife and had reportedly had some trouble with her. On Saturday night, July 18, he passed her on the street and it was said he struck at her or assaulted her in some way. A few minutes later Ferguson met Johnson on Church Street, whereupon Johnson started cursing him and made, reportedly, a threatening motion as if he would draw a pistol. The cop did not wait any longer but drew his gun and began shooting. He shot twice, with Johnson dead in a few minutes.[59]

1914 July 25 [207] *Charleston, South Carolina, death.*

Joseph Roper, a black man, was shot and killed on July 25, 1914, in Charleston, South Carolina, by policeman George McNaughton, who fired his weapon while lying on the ground at the victim, who, said an account, "was large and powerful and attacked him and was beating him over the head." The trouble arose when McNaughton ordered Roper and three other black men to move on. To this order, it was testified to at the coroner's inquest, Roper became offensive and refused to move on. Upon being placed under arrest Roper offered resistance and a fight ensued. At that inquest, the coroner's jury returned a verdict of justifiable homicide. Samuel Sanford (one of the other three men) testified at the inquest that Roper was intoxicated and acted "distastefully" upon the officer's command. Two shots were fired at Roper. A reporter observed: "Policeman McNaughton also testified and his story, in substance, was identical with Sanford's."[60]

1914 August 1 [208] *Harrisburg, Pennsylvania, death.*

Trouble started in Harrisburg, Pennsylvania, at about ten o'clock on Saturday night, August 1, 1914, on the street near the home of Nathan Banks, a black man. A fight reportedly took place that involved Banks and a few other men. City peace officer Robert F. Scott (also black) ordered Banks to move on, but Banks refused to go. A scuffle followed and Banks, it was said, grabbed the officer's club and started to run away. Then Scott drew his revolver and fired at the fleeing man, killing him. Scott was immediately placed under arrest at the order of the coroner.[61]

Scott came to trial in January 1915 facing a charge of murder in the first degree. The prosecutor declared he would show the shooting of Banks occurred after the victim had threatened to expose the cop and not because the deceased had tried to evade arrest. Scott now claimed the shooting was accidental. When court adjourned for the morning a dozen or more city patrolmen, friends of the accused, filed up the aisle, shook his hand and wished him good luck. It was also reported that Scott's wife "occupied a chair at the side of her husband during the morning session." Herein it was reported that the cop chased Banks about one block and Banks was standing in the doorway of his house when the officer fired the fatal shot and that remarks made by Banks led to the chase.[62]

At the trial a dozen or more character witnesses, mostly cops and other people connected with the city of Harrisburg's police department, testified as to Scott's good reputation as both a cop and a civilian. Two dozen others, mostly businessmen of the city, were slated to testify to the same thing later in the day. Scott still claimed the death was an accident and as to his excuse for drawing his weapon the officer said he did it "in the excitement of the moment and also in view of the fact that he knew Banks to be a bad character—a lawless citizen of the Tenderloin." Several officers, including Police Chief Joseph B. Hutchinson, testified that the killing took place in a section of town "where the percentage of lawless characters exceeds that of law abiding citizens" and that Banks had a police record and was reputed to be a "bad character." Speculation had it that Banks had threatened to tell Scott's wife that the cop had been "down in the park with that woman." Half a dozen black witnesses all testified that the policeman fired the fatal shot after he had dared Banks to repeat the assertion connecting his own name with that of a woman not his wife.[63] On January 18 the jury convicted Robert Scott of murder in the second degree after four hours of deliberations. The jury recommended the man to the mercy of the court. On February 18, 1915, Judge McCarroll sentenced Scott to a term of not less than 12 years nor more than 20 years in the penitentiary. The clemency recommendation of the jury, said the judge, resulted in Scott not receiving the full maximum term of 20 years. McCarroll, who saw the shooting as a personal matter, declared the killing was "inexcusable" and "You had a personal quarrel with Banks and for that you had no right to use any weapon. Police officers are permitted to carry a gun and mace so that they may perform their official duty and secure the arrest of persons for whom they have warrants and prevent the escape of those who have been arrested and are trying to get away." He added, "When police officers use weapons they must be cautious about the way in which they use them." Scott had been appointed a police officer in March 1914 and had a wife and two sons, aged six and eight.[64]

1914 August 7 [209] Raven, Virginia, death.

In August 1914 in Raven, Virginia, a man named Ira Harless was causing a disturbance at a show. The police were called and city officer Clapp Osbourne responded. He approached the man and told him to quiet down, but that only led to a row between the two men. Reportedly, Harless drew a gun, but then Osbourne drew his revolver and fired two shots into Harless, killing the man. A day or two later Squires (Justices of the Peace) G. R. Thomas and Thomas Harrison sat on the Clapp Osbourne case at Raven, Virginia. Osbourne was acquitted. Given the number of witnesses likely present, the deceased may well have been armed and thus should not be included in this book. However, a reporter remarked, with respect to Osbourne on the job as a cop; "This was his third man."[65]

1914 October 18 [210] Greenville, South Carolina, death.

Judson Brooks, 19, was shot and fatally wounded early on the morning of October 18, 1914, near Greenville, South Carolina, by the chief of the rural police, Reuben Gosnell. According to the officer, the shooting was accidental. Brooks, he said, was resisting arrest and so the cop struck him over the head with his .38-caliber automatic revolver. The first blow did not quiet Brooks, so the cop hit him again. When he did so the pistol discharged and the bullet entered the young man's brain. Gosnell informed other officials and he was lodged in jail. It all started when Brooks and policeman Macaulay were scuffling and Gosnell came to the officer's aid. It was also reported that Brooks slashed Gosnell several times with a knife and then Gosnell struck him on the head. After being taken into custody Gosnell was released upon posting $3,500 bail. When Gosnell appeared in the Court of General Sessions for Greenville in January 1915 he was acquitted in the killing of Brooks.[66]

1914 October 24 [211] Union, South Carolina, death.

Another very brief item reported that policeman J. W. Sanders of Union, South Carolina, shot and killed a black man named Cornelius Shell, who resisted arrest on the night of October 24, 1914.[67]

1915 January 28 [212] Portland, Oregon, death.

On January 28, 1915, in Portland, Oregon, much of the city's police force was searching for a stolen automobile. After police sergeant R. H. Stahl recovered the vehicle he drove it slowly past Patrolman C. E. Klingensmith. Apparently Stahl was conducting some kind of a test to see if the officer would recognize the car. The sergeant did not stop the vehicle promptly when Klingensmith recognized the auto and ordered it to stop and so Klingensmith shot Stahl through the head, killing him instantly.[68]

1915 February 25 [213] Jersey City, New Jersey, death.

Jersey City, New Jersey, policeman Charles Hill was shot and killed on February 25, 1915, by brother cop Vincent D. Cash following an altercation. Five shots were fired at the victim, with one bullet penetrating the heart. Cash was arrested and admitted to killing Hill. For some time, claimed Cash, there had been bad blood between them. Hall had tormented Cash because he had been on the force only 19 months. The shooting took place at around 2:00 a.m. He then began to claim that he had killed Hill in self-defense, as Hill had beaten Cash over the head with his club. For some time the two men had walked adjacent beats in the city. On the evening of February 24 Cash had been out and happened to meet Hill on Hill's beat, whereupon Hill demanded to know what Cash was doing on Hill's beat and said that his proper place was on the other side of the street (the site of Cash's beat). Then Hill struck Cash on the head with his club, whereupon Cash pulled out his gun and fired several shots into Hill. That night Cash had worked an extra shift and was later relieved but wandered around the area still in his uniform. Cash had been on the force for three years. On May 13, 1915, Judge Mark A. Sullivan sentenced Vincent Cash, after he had been convicted of murder in the second degree, to serve not less than 30 years in the penitentiary.[69]

1915 April 6 [214] *New York City, death.*

NYPD officer Andrew Zalena, 31, told his wife on Monday, April 5, 1915, that he was going to kill her and himself. He carried out that threat on April 6. The shooting took place at around 10:00 a.m. A neighbor found their bodies lying across the bed in their apartment in New York City. They were not found until 5:00 p.m. and when they were found the revolver was still in Zalena's hand. The neighbor who found them recalled that Mrs. Zalena had spoken to her on Monday and told her of the husband's threat. Apparently he said he was going to kill them both if the pains that he complained of did not go away. Mrs. Zalena was frightened and told her neighbor she had taken her husband's gun. There was no reported trouble between the couple. Zalena had been off duty since April 4 owing to ill health. He had become a policeman in November 1909 and he had been taken ill from an attack of malaria in December 1914 and was off on sick leave all during January and February in 1915. Since then he had only worked intermittently. He was 33 years old and his wife was 40; they had no children. Toward the end Zalena kept telling his wife, "I can't stand the pain."[70]

1915 June 12 [215] *Philadelphia, death.*

In Philadelphia on June 12, 1915, John Murtaugh, 22, was slain by city Patrolman John Archibald as he was running from a pawnshop. He was described as a former Marine who was shot while fleeing from a pawnshop where he sought to pawn a ladies' gold watch. It was stolen the day before from a house in South Philadelphia. The shooting happened after he had been chased by two policemen who had several times yelled at him to stop running before Archibald finally drew his revolver and fired at the fleeing man, killing him instantly. Murtaugh had entered the pawnshop, presented the watch, and asked for $5. However, earlier that day the pawnshop had received a message from the police department to watch out for a watch of that description. The clerk was immediately suspicious and went into the back room where he called the police. Archibald and Louis Booker were dispatched to the scene and when they arrived and entered the store Murtaugh dashed out. Archibald had been on the force for just three months. After the shooting he was placed under arrest pending an investigation. Two days later the police produced "evidence" showing Murtaugh had a long criminal record and sometimes used the alias of John Murphy or Dugan Murphy. According to the police, he had been sent to the Catholic Protectory in 1908 for robbery and was arrested later in that same year for robbing gas meters. He was released on probation on that occasion but was sent back to the Catholic Protectory in 1909 for robbery and to a prison in Glen Mills, Pennsylvania, in 1910.[71]

John Murtaugh, later shot to death in Philadelphia by police. A former member of the U.S. Marines, the 22-year-old is shown here in that uniform.

1915 August 24 *[216] Winchester, Kentucky, death.*

Winchester, Kentucky, police received a telegram on August 23, 1915, telling them to keep a lookout for two black men who had robbed a man and thrown him from a train near Corbin. Policemen John Ballard and W. R. Strode stationed themselves near the depot and early on the morning of August 24 saw two black men leave a freight train and when the officers called for them to surrender both of them started to run away. At that point both cops opened fire on them, killing one instantly and wounding the other man. At the coroner's inquest later in the morning of August 24 (the shooting had happened at 5:00 a.m.) the bullet from the dead man was matched to Ballard's gun. However, noted a journalist, "the jury immediately exonerated Ballard."[72]

1915 October 14 *[217] Greenville, South Carolina, death.*

An editorial that appeared in a South Carolina newspaper in October 14, 1915, declared: "It has been several months since a Greenville policeman killed anybody. Since the above was written we notice that an old negro woman, who was shot some time ago by a Greenville deputy sheriff, died Monday from the wound."[73]

1915 October 22 [218] Los Angeles, death.

Chester Nolen, 17, was killed and Frank Ward, 19, probably fatally wounded by a single bullet fired by one of two Los Angeles policemen who began shooting at the boys as they sped away on a motorcycle, either ignoring or failing to hear a command to halt. The incident took place on October 22, 1915, in Los Angeles. The fatal bullet first struck Nolen in the back, killing him almost instantly, passing through his body, and then it pierced Ward in the back. The cops involved were Sgt. William Cahill and policeman Samuel Shammo. They declared the boys had stolen the motorcycle and that they had chased them some two miles. Ward, in what was thought to be an ante-mortem statement, said he bought the bike from a man named George Singleton in San Francisco a month earlier. He admitted to hearing the command to halt but decided to "beat it," thinking he was wanted for speeding. Both boys had been wards of the juvenile court for five years.[74]

When the coroner's jury investigated the shooting it reached a verdict that the shooting was unjustified and that Nolen was killed by one of the two cops. On October 30 both policemen were charged with manslaughter and released the same day on bail of $5,000 each. The charge of murder had been reduced at the preliminary hearing held earlier in the day. On February 2, 1916, the jury acquitted Samuel Shammo of all charges. He had been tried alone and following the verdict the District Attorney for Los Angeles County offered a motion (accepted) dismissing the same charges pending against William Cahill.[75]

1916 January 15 [219] Chicago, death.

Chicago Police Department officer Harry Baird shot and killed his two children and then killed himself in that city on January 15, 1916. Mrs. Baird told the coroner that her husband had been brooding for several days. The family had just eaten dinner and Mrs. Baird had left the room when the shooting of Charles, ten, and Bodine, six, took place. She heard the shots and hurrying back into the room found the three bodies on the floor. Both boys had been shot in the head, while her husband had shot himself in the heart. Mrs. Baird explained that her husband had been acting in a strange manner for several days and seemed to be brooding. None of his fellow officers knew the nature of his apparent mental distress, but all had noticed a change in him.[76]

1916 October 26 *[220] New York City, assault.*

NYPD detective Alexander McConeghy was convicted on December 14, 1916, by a jury in New York City of assault in the third degree and remanded one week for sentencing. On October 26 the officer arrested John Manning, charging him with disorderly conduct on the subway platform. The platform was jammed with a theater crowd at the time and McConeghy created a panic when he suddenly drew his revolver and knocked down and beat Manning. A traffic cop arrived at the scene and took McConeghy's weapon away from him and Manning was locked up. Passengers followed McConeghy and his prisoner to the station house and demanded that the cop himself be arrested. McConeghy was later indicted for the assault.[77]

1916 November 24 *[221] Kansas City, Kansas, death.*

A black man by the name of Harrison Thomas was shot and killed on the afternoon of November 24, 1916, in front of a police station on Jane Street, on the Kansas side, when he tried to escape from police sergeant James Dooley. Thomas had been arrested for, allegedly, cutting a black woman about one month earlier. In front of the police station Thomas broke free and when four blows from Dooley's club failed to stop him the officer then pulled out his gun and fired. A shot hit Thomas in the wrist, but he kept running, so Dooley fired again. That shot hit him in the thigh, but it still did not stop the fleeing man. Then Dooley aimed at the head of Thomas and fired a third shot, which killed him.[78]

1916 November *[222] Philadelphia, assault.*

Four Philadelphia policemen, Edward Keegan, Sherman H. Clark, Edward Bellerby, and John H. Weaver, were convicted in court in that city before Judge Carr on June 26, 1917, of conspiracy and aggravated assault in connection with the beating inflicted upon two sailors in the cell room of the station house in November 1916. The policemen were to be sentenced after a motion for a new trial was dealt with.[79]

1917 February 9 *[223] Aurora, Minnesota, death.*

B. C. Belcher and Julius Gullickson were both members of the Aurora, Minnesota, night police force. At the village hall in the town the two got into an argument on February 9, 1917. In the course of that argument Belcher shot and killed Gullickson. Belcher surrendered himself immediately after the shooting.[80]

1917 February 27 *[224] New York City, death.*

Percy Harris, a 24-year-old black man, died early on the morning of February 28, 1917, in New York City from a bullet wound inflicted on February 27 by policeman Charles Secord, who had arrested Harris on a charge of assault made by Frederick Treadwell, who said he had been slashed in a fight. Secord apparently left Harris' cell unlocked in his hurry to arrest another person and that allowed Harris to walk out of the police station. Later he was recaptured on the street by Secord. Harris, it was said, broke away and ran a mile before Secord brought him down with a shot from his revolver. The cop was paroled by Coroner Livingston. After Harris walked out of his cell he went directly home. Secord was sent out to recapture him. When he did that only to have Harris break away and run off Secord fired eight shots into the air and then two more at the running man. Harris ran two more blocks before he finally collapsed.[81]

1917 July 12 *[225] Greenville, Mississippi, death.*

Police Chief William A. Chipman of Greenville, Mississippi, was shot and killed on July 12, 1917, by Wallace Mullens, a patrolman on that force. It was reported that Chipman was sitting at his desk when Mullens fired three loads of buckshot into him. Mullens said that Chipman had attempted to assault his 13-year-old daughter Mullens surrendered himself and was placed in jail.[82]

1917 August 14 *[226] Bristol, Rhode Island, death.*

Nicholas J. Golden was a real estate dealer in Bristol, Rhode Island, who was shot and killed in front of his home on the evening of August 14, 1917, by his son James Golden, a city policeman. He surrendered himself after fellow officers convinced him to give up his gun. The father was taken to the hospital, where he died later. James told the authorities that his father had upbraided him about some work and had struck him over the head with a hammer. In the district court of Bristol on August 16, 1917, James Golden pled guilty to the murder of his father.[83]

1917 October 12 *[227] Chicago, death.*

Lee Legg, a 25-year-old black man, was shot and killed in Chicago on October 12, 1917, by city policeman George Teeling when Legg reportedly fled after his attempt to holdup a black man by the name of James Hill.[84]

1917 October 13 *[228] Columbia, South Carolina, death.*

Coroner Jack A. Scott was shot and killed on the night of October 13, 1917, by Jesse W. Helms, a rural cop in Richland County. The shooting took place near midnight about four miles from Columbia, South Carolina. The two men were described as friends and had gone out for the day. As they returned to the city they, said an account, "became involved in a difficulty" that resulted in the death of Scott. The deceased man left a wife and six children.[85]

1917 November 13 *[229] Clifton, New Jersey, death.*

Two-year-old toddler Dorothy Ackerman was shot dead on the morning of November 13, 1917, in Clifton, New Jersey, as she stood beside her mother, Mrs. George Ackerman, in front of a school in Clifton where they were waiting for Dorothy's sister to emerge, and then the family of three would walk home. The bullet came from the revolver of city cop Henry Prall, who was pursuing a thief who had escaped. Not until Prall reached his police station after giving up the chase did he learn what harm his bullet had done. Mrs. Ackerman did not hear the shot and was bewildered when her child fell dead at her feet. Prall and another officer had gone to a grocery store when the owner reported three suspicious characters in the area. The police arrested two of the three men they found hiding behind a tree and Prall fired five shots at the third, who escaped. Nothing more was heard about Prall except for a brief item that appeared in print in August 1925. It told briefly of an arrest made by Sgt. Henry Prall at Clifton, New Jersey. Not only had nothing happened to him by way of punishment, since he was still on the force, but apparently he had been promoted.[86]

1917 November 19 *[230] Kansas City, Missouri, death.*

Joe Muco and "Cap" Gargetto were found carting a quantity of cigars and other tobacco products away from a building in the early-morning hours of November 19, 1917, and were shot and killed by policemen. Both victims were shot through the head. Another member of the gang was captured, while a fourth man escaped. The two deceased were killed in the chase that followed their discovery.[87]

1918 January 10 *[231] Chicago, death.*

As of January 11, 1918, no charges had been made against the policemen who fired upon and killed 15-year-old Herbert Walker when he was trapped on January 10 while he was, reportedly, trying to rob a fruit store. Another boy who was with him escaped after being wounded by gunfire. Those two boys were trapped by the police and were fired upon as they fled the store.[88]

1918 March 9 [232] *Detroit, death.*

A very brief report declared that Harry Deering, a 13-year-old "bandit," was shot and killed in Detroit by a city patrolman on March 9 when he was caught rifling a cash register in a saloon located on Russell Street.[89]

1918 April 4 [233] *Minneapolis, death.*

Martin T. Walsh was said to have been the fourth member of a holdup gang that had operated in Minneapolis. He was shot and instantly killed by Patrolman Adolph Hanson in that city on April 4, 1918, when he attempted to escape from the officer after being arrested.[90]

1918 June 6 [234] *Philadelphia, assault.*

Philadelphia cop Emanuel Auerbach was charged in June 1918 with having assaulted Benjamin Yonowitz, who was a witness for the Commonwealth in the trial of two men in a Fifth Ward election case. The grand jury indicted the officer on three counts of aggravated assault and battery, with the other two victims being Mrs. Yonowitz and a waitress named Dora Landy. According to Benjamin Yonowitz, the cop told him he had "better get out of this trial" and when he refused Auerbach returned and beat him and the two other people with his club. Later in June Judge Bonniwell sentenced Emanuel Auerbach (no longer a cop) to a term of two years in jail.[91]

1918 July 14 [235] *New York City, death.*

After a running chase over the rooftops of several buildings in New York City two NYPD plainclothes officers who had raided a crap game on one of those roofs shot and killed 16-year-old James Cushing on July 14, 1918. Reportedly, several young men were shooting dice on the roof when Officers Cornelius J. Flood and Robert O'Brien emerged on the roof. Immediately the boys all took off jumping over roofs and, according to the police, "several of the fugitives stayed their flight long enough to fire shots at their pursuers. For this reason, Flood and O'Brien returned fire." Apparently neither cop saw the boy drop down after being shot, for they continued on with their chase, eventually arresting two of the boys.[92]

That case lay dormant until February 10, 1921, when the grand jury in New York City returned an indictment for murder in the first degree against Flood and O'Brien. The story then presented was somewhat different. It was reported the two cops had their attention drawn for some reason on that July day to a number of girls and boys playing on the roof of a building. Those young people were watching a boy fly his pigeons—he kept them in a coop on the roof. Suddenly two men both flashing revolvers appeared on the roof. Some of those youngsters recalled a number of incoherent remarks from the gunmen and then a number of shots. Everyone fled except Cushing, who dropped to the rooftop from a gunshot wound. A witness (not one of the group of young people) saw the kids playing and testified they were doing nothing when one yelled, "Cop!" and they jumped to other buildings, except for the boy who was shot. The police let him lie there while they beat two of the other boys "unmercifully." Then the police took those two boys away but still paid no attention to the injured boy.

That witness was Mrs. Alice Smith Kenny. Another witness came to the aid of Cushing as he lay dying. She had to go down to the street to find another cop and that policeman called for an ambulance. Only later when the District Attorney's office launched an inquiry to find out who killed Cushing did the two cops admit the shooting. Cushing's companions—the two boys taken to jail—were fined $15 each, in lieu of which they went to jail for three days. The case had been submitted to the grand jury back in 1918, but the two cops were exonerated. Reportedly, Cushing's body lay on the roof for three hours before receiving any attention.[93]

Flood was placed on trial for murder, but as the trail neared completion in March 1921 the court ordered that a charge of manslaughter be substituted. Flood testified he tripped and fell and his revolver discharged accidentally. He said he reported the incident to his superiors as an accident, swearing he did not know he had shot the boy. Flood was convicted on the manslaughter charge and on March 24, 1921, Judge Charles Nott sentenced Flood to serve from three to 10 years in the state prison. O'Brien awaited trial on the same charge. Both were released from custody that night on a certificate of reasonable doubt, with appeals pending. Bail was set at $10,000 each. During the trial of Flood it was shown that the statements of the witnesses to the 1918 grand jury did not tally with what they told Judge Nott in 1921. In many cases the witnesses denied that they had made the statements read back to them from the 1918 record. During that trial Flood admitted firing one shot and O'Brien admitted to firing two shots. On December 9, 1925, New York State governor Al Smith pardoned Flood, then serving time. Herein Cushing was listed as 18 years old.[94]

1918 September 13 *[236] Philadelphia, death.*

James Gray was a Philadelphia peace officer who shot and killed a man who, he said, attacked him when he discovered him and a companion trying to scale a fence on the morning of September 13, 1918. The dead man was David Cassidy and his companion was Charles Kelly, who was put under arrest and charged with assault and battery. Gray was held without bail by Magistrate Pennock. Police said Gray came upon the two men shortly after 6:00 a.m. He ran up to them and they turned on him. The cop was being beaten when he managed to draw his revolver. Cassidy dropped down dead with a bullet to the chest.[95]

1918 October *[237] Honolulu, assault.*

Honolulu policeman Henry Eli shot and wounded William Thomas following a quarrel in October 1918 over 20 cents in a Honolulu crap game. It was reported that the cop had been drinking. He was arrested, held for the grand jury, and dismissed from the police force. On December 1, Judge Heen sentenced the former cop to a term of not less than two years at hard labor. Attorney Rawlins said the only defense was that the officer was drunk. Heen replied that intoxication was no excuse.[96]

1918 November 22 *[238] Washington, D.C., assault.*

On March 4, 1919, Washington, D.C., policeman Fitzhugh F. Woodward was indicted by the grand jury for assault with a dangerous weapon. It was alleged that while he was in a physician's house on November 22, 1918, he shot Leo Nachman. One year later Woodward, then called a former cop, pled guilty to the shooting and Justice Stafford sentenced him to serve three years in the penitentiary.[97]

1918 December *[239] Pittsfield, Massachusetts, assault.*

On December 16, 1918, policeman Michael F. Callahan of Pittsfield, Massachusetts, was sentenced to three months in the house of correction on charges of assault and battery, and drunkenness. He was arrested earlier that month on a complaint by Ernest Wheeler. Callahan appealed his sentence and furnished $500 bail. Pittsfield police chief John L. Sullivan had already suspended the officer and upon his conviction Sullivan recommended that the city council discharge Callahan from the police department.[98]

1919 April 24 *[240] Tucson, Arizona, death.*

Early in the morning of April 24, 1919, in a neighborhood in Tucson, Arizona, residents believed that someone was in the process of attempting to rob homes in the area and called the police. Fecundo Martinez, a suspect in the murder of a Chinese merchant several months earlier and later convicted of bootlegging, was found in the area and shot and killed by Tucson patrolman Shumarer, who arrived in response to the calls for help from the residents in the area.[99]

1919 April *[241] Butte, Montana, assault.*

The trial of Butte, Montana, motorcycle cop Philip Prlja was slated to begin on April 30, 1919. The officer was charged with assault in the first degree upon Mike Burzan. That charge grew out of the shooting of Burzan by Prlja following an attempt by the former to escape from the latter. Prlja had placed Burzan under arrest on a charge of carrying concealed weapons. While waiting at the patrol box for the police wagon to arrive Burzan scuffled with Prlja in an attempt to escape. During the scuffle a revolver was discharged and Burzan fell to the ground wounded. At the trial two physicians testified as to two bad wounds on Burzan's head where he had evidently been struck by blows from the officer's gun. Prlja argued his actions were self-defense.

On May 3 the jury deliberated for less than one hour before it returned a verdict of guilty of assault in the second degree. Prlja was then in custody and would remain there until sentence was passed several days later. Penalty on that charge was a term of not less than one year nor more than five years in prison, or a fine not to exceed $500, or both. Evidence indicated that during the row Burzan was struck twice over the head and shot once in each leg.

On May 8 the officer was sentenced to a term of not less than 18 months nor more than three years in the state penitentiary at hard labor. In passing sentence Judge Lynch pointed out the serious injury done to society by the unlawful brutality often inflicted upon prisoners by officers who got the notion that the badge of authority gave them the right to abuse and manhandle other citizens at their pleasure. It was conduct such as that, said the judge, that was largely responsible for the prevailing and growing dislike for law and order. Lynch thought that the unlawful and outrageous acts by constituted officials were making Bolshevists.[100]

With a view to further the defense of Philip Prlja, brother officers started a subscription fund early in May and before a single night had passed they announced they had collected "a handsome sum." Individual policemen had reportedly contributed from $5 to $25. District Judge Lynch had permitted

Prlja to be released from the county jail under a $5,000 bond pending an appeal. When Prlja gave notice of appeal the lower court refused him bail until it was ordered to do so by the higher court. Prlja was then at liberty in the spring of 1919.[101]

Prlja wasted no time in getting a new job and was soon the duly accredited security guard for Con F. Kelley of the Anaconda Copper Mining Company; specifically, he was the guard at Kelley's summer home. It was understood that after his release from the county jail Prlja learned that Butte mayor Stodden refused to reinstate him as a member of the police force. As was noted by a newspaper headline that told of his new job, "Kelley Takes Care of Faithful." Early in August Prlja's motion for a new trial was denied, but he remained released on bail pending his appeal to the Montana Supreme Court. Judge Lamb of the district court issued an order requiring Mayor Tom Stodden to reinstate Prlja as a member of the city police force or to show cause why the order was not obeyed. Earlier, the City of Butte had given Prlja $300 to help him pay to take his case to the state supreme court. On March 29, 1920, at Helena, Montana, that state supreme court ruled against the cop and confirmed his sentence. The case showed, they held, that Prlja had placed Burzan under arrest for no apparent reason and, although Burzan submitted peacefully, Prlja scuffled with the man and shot him. It was also said, at this time, that Prlja had made open boasts that nothing would come of the charges filed against him. In this account it was reported that the amount the city gave to Prlja for his legal expenses in taking his fight to the Supreme Court was $800.[102]

On April 7, 1920, Montana governor Stewart recommended a pardon for Prlja, declaring, "Influential citizens of Butte signed petitions for the pardon and it is said later evidence shows extenuating circumstances." Following that recommendation from Stewart the Montana Board of Pardons, on April 30, issued an unconditional pardon to Prlja. That petition for a pardon was said to contain the names of more than 100 "of the most prominent men and women of Butte." Prlja had served no jail time apart from a couple of short periods while awaiting bail being posted or renewed.[103]

Montana District Court judge Edwin Lamb, on September 11, 1920, ordered that Prlja be reinstated on the Butte police force. He was to be reinstated as a traffic sergeant, the position he held until May 2, 1919. At that time Prlja was dropped from the police rolls when he was convicted. Lamb held that the City of Butte erred by not giving Prlja a trial before the police commission, as was required under the metropolitan system under which Butte operated, before they dismissed him. Prlja stated that once he was reinstated he would begin legal action for back pay for all the time he was off the force. The City of Butte declared it would appeal.[104]

Before those legal battle played out something else happened. On the afternoon of March 21, 1921, Prlja was shot six times by Mike Burzan and later died. The shooting occurred in the center of town and was witnessed by a score of people. Burzan gave himself up to the police immediately. Since the legal actions had not played out, Prlja had not been reinstated to the force at the time of the shooting. On November 10, 1921, Mike Burzan was acquitted in the killing of Prlja. The jury deliberated for 41 minutes. Attorneys for Burzan introduced evidence that the former cop had persecuted Burzan for some time and had made threats to kill him. Both men were armed at the time of the killing, although neither man was legally allowed to carry a weapon. Prlja did not draw or show his gun when Burzan shot him. And finally, in March 1922, the City of Butte's appeal against reinstatement was dismissed, but an attempt to substitute the administrator of Prlja's estate in place of the deceased was also denied, as no money was involved.[105]

1919 May 10 *[242] Kansas City, Missouri, death.*

A man whose papers identified him as Homer Horn was shot and killed on the night of May 10, 1919, in Kansas City, Missouri, by a patrolman as he was being taken to the police station. The officer said Horn tried to pull a knife while riding in the patrol wagon and in the scuffle for the weapon he was shot and he died on the way to the hospital. Horn was arrested on the complaint of a garage owner, according to the police. He was to have been held for investigation and no formal charge had been made against Horn.[106]

1919 May 28 *[243] Columbia, South Carolina, death.*

Columbia, South Carolina, motorcycle cop Eugene M. Lancaster emptied two revolvers on the afternoon of May 28, 1919, shortly after 4:00 p.m. As a result Newton S. Lorick, a Lexington County farmer, and Mrs. E. M. Lancaster (the cop's wife) died in an automobile from their wounds. Lancaster fired 11 shots in all, seven into Lorick and five into his wife. According to witnesses, Lancaster was in a moving police car when he recognized his wife in a car with Lorick. Lancaster left his car and got on the running board of Lorick's car and began to fire his gun repeatedly. It was alleged that Mrs. Lancaster was receiving attentions from the unmarried Lorick. It was also reported that the couple did not get along. The couple had four children ranging in age from seven to 15.[107]

Lancaster came to trial for the double murder in September 1919. He testified that his mind was a perfect blank after he fired the first shot at the couple when they approached in an automobile. He said when the couple saw him

Lorick threw his hand from the steering wheel to his hip pocket and when he did that the officer fired "and from that my mind is a blank" until he came to himself several days later at the police station. He detailed several instances in the six weeks or so prior to the shooting that made him doubt his wife's fidelity, with Lorick then posing as one of Lancaster's best friends. Just before he fired a shot he said he saw her put her arm around Lorick in the car and kiss him. At the time of the incident Lancaster was recovering from a broken leg sustained while on duty some seven weeks earlier and, as a result, he had a driver, James Harmon. When he testified Harmon stated that after the first shot he helped Lancaster into the car and drove him up to the Lorick auto, then stopped, and Lancaster fired the remaining shots in that first revolver and those of another revolver into the bodies of the pair. The couple's eldest son (age 16 herein) testified by affidavit, as he was too sick to attend in person. He told of several compromising situations he had found his mother and Lorick in. The son added that on two occasions his mother gave him firearms and urged him to kill his father, but the son said he could not do it. At that time Lancaster was confined to bed with his broken leg. On September 10 the jury returned a verdict that Lancaster was not guilty in the murder of his wife. He had been on trial only for the murder of his wife and, in theory, he was still to be tried for the murder of Lorick.[108]

1919 July 9 *[244] Washington, D.C., death.*

In Washington, D.C., in the early-morning hours of July 9, 1919, 17-year-old Leo A. McLeod and three of his friends were riding around in a car. Henry A. Starr, a city policeman, was on duty and he heard a racket coming from inside the car made by one of the boys who was intoxicated. Starr heard shots such as "Help!" and "Police!" from the car and ordered the vehicle to stop, but it did not do so and he fired at the auto, at a rear tire, he said. Only one shot was fired, but it struck and killed McLeod. Starr was new to the force and had been appointed only on June 25, 1919, a little more than two weeks before the shooting. Washington police major Pullman stated, "The shooting of the boy was not justifiable, for police have been instructed that never should a revolver be drawn unless their lives depended on it, and to go slow then." The shooting took place at around 3:40 a.m.[109]

Following the shooting Starr, 27, was suspended from the force. He obtained employment at the Liggett drugstore chain and on September 18 he was sent to a bank with a deposit and when he failed to return several hours later the police were called in to find him and the $532 he had disappeared with. He had been employed by the drugstore for some two months. Starr was arrested in Cincinnati on September 19. At this stage he was described as "formerly" a cop.[110]

On October 1 the grand jury returned an indictment for manslaughter against Starr. On October 19, 1920, at his trial ex-cop Starr was found not guilty of manslaughter. Earlier he had pled guilty to embezzlement and received a two-year sentence that he was then serving. After he was found not guilty Judge Gould remanded Starr back to jail to continue to serve the embezzlement term.[111]

1919 July 23 [245] New York City, assault.

New York City traffic policeman John J. Higginson was drawn from his post on July 23, 1919, by cries of "Mad dog!" In an alley he found a dog making vicious rushes at one group of children, then at another. Higginson fired one shot that struck and killed the animal, but it went through the dog's body and struck and wounded 13-year-old Thomas Burke. The cop rushed the injured boy to the hospital.[112]

1919 August 6 [246] Des Moines, Iowa, death.

Joseph A. Reich, a recently discharged soldier, was fatally shot on the night of August 6, 1919, in Des Moines, Iowa, by peace officer George Walsh when, police officials said, he attempted to prevent Reich and a companion from entering a dance hall. Reich died an hour after being shot. Blanche Pike, cashier of the dance hall, said she refused two men admittance because she thought they were intoxicated. Reich, the police said, was accidentally shot in the struggle when Walsh tried to use his gun as a club to make Reich stop biting the cop's thumb.[113]

1919 August 31 [247] Cedar Falls, Iowa, assault.

In Cedar Falls, Iowa, on September 16, 1919, a jury of six men found Peter J. Rock, a Waterloo, Iowa, policeman, guilty of assault and battery upon Henry W. Terrel, state agent. Rock was fined $25 and costs or 15 days in jail. The case started with an encounter between the two men on the night of August 31. On September 2, Rock caused a warrant to be issued for the arrest of Terrel charging the latter with assault and battery. He was arrested and later tried and found guilty in municipal court. A few days later Judge Willis Birdsall imposed a fine of $100 and costs on Terrel. In the meantime Terrel had filed a charge of assault against Rock.[114]

1919 September 18 *[248] New York City, death.*

Mistaken for a man who had fired five pistol shots, Peter Jeribola, 15, was shot and killed inside his family's apartment in Brooklyn, New York, on September 18, 1919, by NYPD policeman Frank G. Lisa. Lisa claimed that Jeribola made a motion as though he were going to draw a weapon from his hip pocket. The boy was not armed. He was shot over the left eye and died almost instantly. It all started when an unidentified person came into the garage where the boy worked and said he wanted to take out a touring car. However, Peter refused to let it go. That man got into a car anyway and started it up. Peter closed the garage door and stood outside. The enraged man then ran into the office and fired five shots at the boy through the window. Jeribola was not hit but ran away and headed for home. Meanwhile a man named William Daly told Lisa that he had seen someone run into the apartment building where the boy lived. Lisa entered and found Jeribola on his balcony and ordered him to throw up his hands. Instead of obeying, he made a motion to draw a gun, insisted Lisa, and then the cop fired. According to a different account, Jeribola (perhaps Jerabek) ran home after the shots were fired at him, to escape the shooter. Jeribola lived nearby the garage where he worked. Lisa followed him, thinking the boy was the gunman who had shot up the garage. The cop entered the apartment the boy had just entered. Peter's mother said the policeman came into the apartment and shot her son without a word of warning—she was in another room. Jeribola had one arm in a sling due to an earlier fall.[115]

On September 24, 1919, following the testimony of two witnesses and upon the recommendation of Assistant District Attorney John P. Hurley, Patrolman Lisa, 28, was discharged from custody by Magistrate Steers and the charge of homicide against him was dismissed. On October 8 the application made by Lisa for full pay while he was under suspension was approved by the police department. It covered the full period that he was suspended, from 1:45 a.m. September 18 to 12:47 p.m. September 24.[116]

1919 November 2 *[249] Seattle, death.*

In Seattle city police sergeant Guy Carleton was shot and killed by motorcycle policeman Charles A. Roselius at 8:15 p.m. on November 2, 1919. Roselius admitted to killing the man after an automobile chase. Carleton was out driving with Mrs. Jennie Roselius, 29, when Roselius overtook the car and shot the sergeant through the heart. Other officers said Roselius had warned Carleton not to continue paying attentions to his wife. Mrs. Roselius and Mrs. Carleton were both said to have threatened to take divorce proceedings. On the evening of November 2 Roselius overheard his wife make a date with Carleton over the phone and when she left the house he followed. A car chase ensued, with Roselius firing three shots at the car, and when it came to a stop he fired two more shots into Carleton in the vehicle. Another cop arrived on the scene thinking to arrest both vehicle occupants for speeding. It was believed he may have stopped Roselius from killing his wife. Carleton was 41 years old and had been on the force for 15 years.[117]

One day later the prosecutor stated that Roselius told him, "I tapped the telephone wire and heard my wife make the date with Carleton Sunday night." Roselius told the prosecutor that he followed them but did not intend to kill Carleton. The two men got out of their cars in front of a gas station and the gun went off accidentally, explained the cop, who did not say anything to the prosecutor about shooting at Carleton's car and causing it to stop. Carleton was warned three times to stay away from Mrs. Roselius—once by Police Chief Warren, once by his wife, Mrs. Carleton, and the last time by Roselius himself. Each time Carleton gave his word to quit seeing the woman; each time he went back on his word. On January 7, 1920, a jury of five women and seven men deliberated for just 20 minutes before they returned a verdict that declared Charles Roselius to be not guilty in the death of Carleton. A reporter thought it might have been because the jury was in sympathy with the slayer of an alleged home wrecker.[118]

1919 November 14 *[250] New York City, assault.*

Thomas Rowan was a detective with the NYPD and on February 9, 1920, he was convicted in court of assault in the third degree, with the victim being truck driver Solomon Blumberg. Photos were introduced as evidence to show the effects of a beating allegedly administered by Rowan to Blumberg on November 14, 1919. His flesh had been severely lashed by a whip of some kind. Blumberg told his employer that he had lost a large case of tobacco from his truck and Rowan and another detective accused him of stealing it. In order to get a confession, Rowan cut a piece of rope from the case, took Blumberg into the detective's room at the station and proceeded to beat him by turns and to demand that he admit his guilt. A charge of larceny was dismissed a few days later and it was then that Blumberg caused the arrest of Rowan. From the photos it could be seen that 47 distinct lash stripes could be counted on Blumberg's flesh, a week after the whipping. One month later a citizens' group wondered why it took so long to try Rowan and why, one month after Rowan's conviction, he was still on the police force. A little over a year later, in April 1921, a brief report noted that several NYPD detectives were investigating a crime—one of them was Thomas Rowan.[119]

1920 March 31 *[251] New York City, death.*

A bullet fired in the early-morning hours of March 31, 1920, in New York City by city cop Abraham Martling in the direction of a stolen taxi in which two store thieves were escaping with two bags of bread and a can of milk struck and killed one of the occupants of the vehicle, Dan Houlihan. According to the cop, he saw the two men steal the bread and milk from in front of a store. There had been several complaints of similar thefts in the neighborhood and when they drove off in the stolen car, ignoring the officer's command to halt, Martling fired four shots, but the cab disappeared. An hour later another cop found the abandoned cab containing the body of Houlihan, who had been struck by one of the bullets. An account in a different newspaper called the deceased a "west side gangster" known as "Red Dan" Houlihan, a member of the "notorious" Gopher gang on the Lower West Side. That notorious and dangerous gangster had stolen a bit of bread and a bit of milk and was 20 years old. An August 1929 report noted that Patrolman Abraham Martling was involved in the investigation of a certain crime.[120]

1920 May 28 *[252] Madison, Wisconsin, death.*

Sophomore student at the University of Wisconsin in Madison Carl Jandorf was shot and killed on May 28, 1920, by a policeman. The shooting reportedly resulted from an argument with students whom the cop attempted to stop from taking a barber pole, intended to be burned during an undergraduate frolic later that night. According to witnesses, the cop saw students steal the pole and then chased them into an alley where he arrested one of the students. At that point Jandorf came up and started to argue. Those witnesses said the cop tried to kick Jandorf in the shins before he raised his pistol and shot the student, killing him instantly. Abandoning their party preparations, a mob of some 500 students demanded that something be done about the cop, Matthew Lynaugh. The officer said he warned the boy twice before he fired his gun.[121]

Following a coroner's inquest into the death of the 22-year-old Jandorf, on June 1, 1920, District Attorney Roman Heilman declared that Lynaugh had to stand trial for murder. At the preliminary hearing on June 17 the charge was set at murder in the first degree. Bail of $10,000 was set at that time and furnished by the accused. On January 14, 1921, the jury found Matthew Lynaugh not guilty in the murder of Jandorf.[122]

1920 May 22 *[253] New York City, assault.*

On September 1, 1920, a grand jury in New York City returned two indictments against Patrolman Henry J. Coleman, each alleging assault in the second degree. He was accused of beating and gouging out the right eye of Michael H. Taylor, 25, and of assaulting and gouging out the right eye of Harry Jaffe, 23. Coleman was notified that $1,000 in bail would be required. Those alleged assaults took place on May 22, 1920, and June 6, 1920. In court Jaffe and Taylor each showed Magistrate Sweetser the empty sockets of their right eyes. Jaffe said his trouble dated back to an attack Coleman made 18 months earlier upon Charles Dunton. The suit brought by Dunton was dismissed in court. Jaffe had witnessed that assault and had been threatened by the police if he testified as to what he saw. Cops told him they would plant a gun on him and frame him. Jaffe went ahead and testified in court against Coleman. Taylor also witnessed the assault on Dunton.[123]

After 10 months the trial of Coleman had still not taken place. It was reported that he had succeeded in obtaining seven postponements of his trial on assault charges. Until his indictment a year earlier he had been a detective first grade in the NYPD. He was then under suspension by the NYPD pending the outcome of the case. He was said to then be employed as a detective for the New York Central Railroad Company. After an eighth postponement the trial was finally held. On June 28, 1921, the jury in Coleman's assault trial was dismissed when it reported itself to be hopelessly deadlocked. Coleman was continued in bail for a supposed upcoming second trial.[124]

1920 September 14 [254] *Mt. Sterling, Kentucky, death.*

Mt. Sterling, Kentucky, policeman Rufus Stockdale shot and killed John Fay, who, it was said, had been "terrifying" a neighborhood and who had then attacked the officer and attempted to draw a revolver. It was said that Fay had been in much trouble, having killed one man and injuring another. As well, Fay was reportedly intoxicated. Stockdale surrendered after the incident. The examining trial of Stockdale was held on September 17. Evidence produced showed that the office acted in defense of his own life. Stockdale was exonerated and he at once resumed his duties as a police officer.[125]

1920 September 15 [255] *Chicago, death.*

A state primary election in Chicago produced bloodshed on September 15, 1920, when Michael Fennessey, a worker for a Democratic candidate for state senator, was shot and killed by city policeman Thomas Powers. The shooting followed an argument over a voting booth. Powers was arrested.[126]

1920 November 25 [256] *St. Louis, death.*

Morris Edwards, black, was shot and killed in the Webster Groves police station on the second floor of the City Hall building in St. Louis on November

25, 1920, by peace officer Burns Harris when Edwards resisted an attempt to put him in a cell. He had been arrested by two other cops when they saw him on the street carrying off a load of boards that they thought he had stolen. They took him to the station, where they said he struck Fire Chief Lanz and was making a rush at policeman Bush when policeman Harris entered the room and drew his revolver. Edwards grabbed that revolver from the cop, who then secured another from a desk drawer and fired twice at Edwards. The first shot hit him in the chest and spun him around, with the second bullet hitting him in the back. A coroner's jury returned a verdict of justifiable homicide.[127]

Chapter Notes

Chapter One

1. "Murdered by a policeman." *Nashville Union and American*, August 26, 1869.
2. No title. *Indianapolis Journal*, December 30, 1869.
3. "Police murders." *New Albany Daily Ledger* (IN), August 30, 1869.
4. "Facts and figures." *Plymouth Democrat* (IN), April 7, 1870.
5. "Police court." *Star* (Cincinnati), January 5, 1875; "Law report." *Star* (Cincinnati), January 25, 1875; "Latest local." *Star* (Cincinnati), February 15, 1875; "Police court." *Star* (Cincinnati), October 9, 1876.
6. "Police murders." *New Albany Daily Ledger* (IN), August 30, 1869.
7. Ibid.
8. "A Philadelphia policeman kills two men." *Evening Star* (Washington), April 27, 1870; "Latest telegraphic brevities." *National Republican* (Washington), April 29, 1870.
9. "Sparks from the wire." *Charleston News* (SC), May 23, 1871.
10. "Killed." *Knoxville Chronicle* (TN), July 25, 1871; "Chattanooga road." *Knoxville Chronicle* (TN), July 27, 1871.
11. "The Chattanooga police." *Knoxville Chronicle* (TN), July 27, 1871.
12. "Assault and battery." *Charleston News* (SC), March 28, 1872.
13. "Sad tragedy in Georgetown." *Evening Star* (Washington), July 16, 1872.
14. Ibid.
15. "The Georgetown tragedy." *Evening Star* (Washington), July 17, 1872.
16. "Condensed locals." *Evening Star* (Washington), July 25, 1872.
17. "The three men convicted of murder." *Evening Star* (Washington), November 16, 1872; "Renewed efforts to save O'Brien from the gallows." *Evening Star* (Washington), February 12, 1873; "O'Brien's commutation." *Evening Star* (Washington), March 26, 1873; "A pardoned convict's child." *Evening Star* (Washington), January 16, 1879.
18. "Conviction of a policeman." *Evening Star* (Washington), February 6, 1874.
19. "Local items." *State Journal* (Jefferson City, MO), January 5, 1877.
20. No title. *Highland Weekly News* (Hillsborough, Ohio), February 14, 1878; "State items." *Athens Messenger* (Ohio), February 14, 1878.
21. "Not even suspended." *Stark County Democrat* (Canton, Ohio), February 21, 1878.
22. "Policemen arrested for murder." *New York Times*, November 18, 1878; "Murderers bailed." *Evening Star* (Washington), November 20, 1878.
23. "A police kills a planter." *Evening Star* (Washington), June 24, 1879.
24. "The tragedy in Columbia." *Anderson Intelligencer* (SC), July 3, 1879; "Murder in Columbia." *Anderson Intelligencer* (SC), June 26, 1879.
25. "Found guilty of manslaughter." *New Orleans Democrat*, November 8, 1879; No title. *Weekly Union Times* (Union, SC), November 21, 1879; "South Carolina news." *Yorkville Enquirer* (SC), November 20, 1879.

26. "A policeman kills a man, and shoots himself." *Stark County Democrat* (Canton, Ohio), August 28, 1879.
27. "Local items." *Charlotte Democrat* (NC), October 18, 1875.
28. No title. *Sun* (NY), January 27, 1878.
29. "What policeman cannot do." *Evening Star* (Washington), September 17, 1879.

Chapter Two

1. "Blood again." *New Orleans Democrat*, March 9, 1880; "It was manslaughter." *New Orleans Democrat*, March 10, 1880.
2. "Crime." *Weekly Chillicothe Crisis* (MO), May 13, 1880.
3. "Brooklyn." *New York Tribune*, August 17, 1880; "No jurisdiction." *Brooklyn Eagle*, August 21, 1880.
4. "The morning's news." *Sacramento Record-Union*, January 2, 1882.
5. "Killed by a policeman." *St. Paul Globe*, March 12, 1883.
6. "Bloody deeds." *Omaha Daily Bee*, March 12, 1883.
7. "Murdered by a policeman." *New York Times*, March 12, 1883.
8. "The Comisky inquest." *New York Times*, March 16, 1883; "The Casey jury disagree." *New York Times*, April 26, 1883; "Murder in the first degree." *New York Times*, May 24, 1883; "Sentenced to be hanged." *New York Times*, May 25, 1883.
9. "Casey to have new trial." *New York Times*, May 10, 1884; "City and suburban news." *New York Times*, June 24, 1884.
10. "A murderous policeman arrested." *Bismarck Tribune* (ND), August 31, 1883.
11. "Policeman McNamara held." *Sun* (NY), September 4, 1883; "McNamara admitted to bail." *Sun* (NY), September 11, 1883.
12. "A murdering policeman dismissed." *New York Tribune*, September 13, 1883; "Officer McNamara dismissed." *New York Times*, September 13, 1883.
13. "Murdered by a policeman." *Boston Post*, August 31, 1883.
14. "A brute gets off with a ridiculous sentence." *New Albany Ledger* (IN), October 18, 1883.
15. "A brute with a billy." *Omaha Daily Bee*, November 5, 1883.
16. "Ending with a murder." *Sun* (NY), November 5, 1883.
17. Ibid.
18. "Killed by a policeman." *New York Tribune*, November 5, 1883.
19. "The verdict in the Keenan inquest." *New York Tribune*, November 9, 1883.
20. "Our letter from Broadbrim." *Donaldson Chief* (LA), November 17, 1883.
21. "Conroy called insane." *Sun* (NY), December 13, 1883.
22. "Found worthy of death." *Sun* (NY), December 16, 1883; "Conroy sentenced to be hanged." *Evening Star* (Washington), December 20, 1883.
23. "Policeman Conroy to be imprisoned for life." *Sun* (NY), April 23, 1885.
24. "Got his desserts." *Intelligencer* (Wheeling, WV), December 6, 1883; "Died from his injuries." *New York Times*, December 7, 1883; "Danville." *Dispatch* (Richmond, VA), March 6, 1884.
25. "Listening to a mocking bird." *Evening Critic* (Washington), June 9, 1884; "A costly spree." *Evening Star* (Washington), July 19, 1884; "The brevity basket." *National Republican* (Washington), October 23, 1884.
26. "Officer Ellis acquitted." *National Republican* (Washington), December 18, 1884.
27. "Property more valuable than life." *Emporia Weekly News* (KS), February 26, 1885.
28. "Captain Burt's murderer." *Salt Lake Herald*, May 12, 1885.
29. "The defendant's testimony." *Salt Lake Herald*, May 14, 1885.
30. "Not guilty." *Salt Lake Herald*, May 15, 1885.
31. "City and suburban news." *New York Times*, December 23, 1885; "City and suburban news." *New York Times*, December 24, 1885.
32. "Mr. Schwarzler's assailants." *New York Times*, February 19, 1886.
33. "Robbery in the first degree." *New York Times*, February 20, 1886.
34. "Two years extra for McInerney." *New York Times*, February 27, 1886.
35. "Bits of local news." *New York Tribune*, July 29, 1886.

36. "Killed by a policeman." *National Republican* (Washington), December 25, 1885; "Charged with manslaughter." *New York Times*, December 26, 1885.
37. "A death struggle." *Herald-Tribune* (Lawrence, KS), January 1, 1886.
38. "Lecturing policemen." *New York Tribune*, January 7, 1886.
39. "His aim excellent." *St. Paul Globe*, November 15, 1886.
40. "Murderous policeman." *New York Tribune*, January 22, 1887.
41. "A bullet wildly aimed." *New York Times*, January 22, 1887.
42. "City and suburban news." *New York Times*, January 27, 1887.
43. "Capt. Jack Hussey shot." *New York Times*, June 3, 1887.
44. "Hahn's cowardly shot." *New York Times*, June 4, 1887.
45. "Jack Hussey's murderer." *Evening World* (NY), October 10, 1887.
46. "Hahn tells his story." *New York Times*, October 13, 1887.
47. "Cross-examining Hahn." *Evening World* (NY), October 13, 1887.
48. "Hahn's neck saved." *Evening World* (NY), October 14, 1887.
49. "Jack Hussey's slayer missed his train." *Sun* (NY), January 12, 1888.
50. "Acquitted of a charge of perjury." *New York Tribune*, May 23, 1888.
51. "Several policemen dismissed." *New York Times*, September 5, 1895.
52. "A narrow conviction." *Memphis Appeal* (TN), November 27, 1887; "Caught in the courts." *Memphis Appeal* (TN), November 29, 1887.
53. "Local paragraphs." *Memphis Appeal* (TN), March 14, 1888.
54. "An officer shot." *Evening Bulletin* (Maysville, KY), December 31, 1887.
55. "Brevities." *Fort Wayne Weekly Sentinel* (IN), January 11, 1888.
56. "Policeman Glennon suspended." *Sacramento Record-Union*, September 28, 1888; "The metropolis." *Sacramento Record-Union*, October 2, 1888; "San Francisco and vicinity." *Sacramento Record-Union*, November 30, 1888; "Murderous policeman convicted." *Seattle Post-Intelligencer*, February 7, 1889.
57. "A well-deserved sentence." *Los Angeles Herald*, February 10, 1889.
58. "Bloodthirsty Barrett." *St. Paul Globe*, October 28, 1888.
59. "Barrett's sentence." *Indianapolis Journal*, April 27, 1889.
60. "Pacific coast." *Los Angeles Herald*, December 6, 1888; "Charged with murder." *Los Angeles Herald*, December 11, 1888.
61. "The murderous policeman." *Los Angeles Herald*, April 23, 1889; "Served right." *Los Angeles Herald*, May 12, 1889.
62. "A policeman convicted of assault." *Evening Star* (Washington), July 5, 1889.
63. "A policeman kills the wrong man." *Evening Star* (Washington), May 18, 1889; "Shot the wrong man." *Pittsburgh Dispatch* (PA), May 19, 1889.
64. "Dying of his wound." *New York Times*, October 23, 1889.
65. "Pronounced an accident." *New York Times*, November 1, 1889.
66. "The bartender contradicts Morris." *Sun* (NY), November 14, 1889; "Five policemen broken." *Sun* (NY), November 13, 1889.
67. "An unconvinced jury." *Evening World* (NY), February 13, 1890; "Indictment dismissed." *Evening World* (NY), May 2, 1894.
68. "A policeman's bad shot." *New York Times*, October 21, 1889; "Trying two policemen." *New York Times*, October 31, 1889; "Five policemen broken." *Sun* (NY), November 13, 1889.
69. "Five policemen broken." *Sun* (NY), November 13, 1889.

Chapter 3

1. "A suspended sentence." *Evening Star* (Washington), January 22, 1890.
2. "Hutchinson's tale of woe." *Evening Star* (Washington), June 4, 1890.
3. "Conflicting testimony." *Evening Star* (Washington), July 11, 1890.
4. "Officer Dean acquitted." *Sunday Herald* (Washington), July 13, 1890; "Policeman Dean acquitted." *Evening Star* (Washington), July 14, 1890
5. "Sam Hutchinson denounced." *Evening Star* (Washington), July 18, 1890.
6. "Assaulted in her cell." *Evening World* (NY), June 21, 1890.
7. "A disgraced policeman imprisoned." *Sun* (NY), July 9, 1890.
8. "He aimed too low." *St. Paul Globe*, October 1, 1890.

9. "Kearney condemned." *Boston Globe*, October 24, 1890.
10. "Story of the shooting." *Boston Globe*, December 30, 1890; "Kearney's tears." *Boston Globe*, January 1, 1891.
11. "Kearney not guilty." *Boston Globe*, January 3, 1891; "Kearney out." *Boston Globe*, January 5, 1891.
12. "Policeman killed by brother officer." *Climax* (Richmond, KY), October 22, 1890; "Shot by a brother officer." *New York Times*, October 16, 1890; "A brutal murder." *Seattle Post-Intelligencer*, October 16, 1890.
13. "Officers on trial for assault." *Pittsburgh Dispatch*, December 11, 1890; "Given their medicine." *Pittsburgh Dispatch*, December 21, 1890.
14. "Officer Cross suspended." *Pittsburgh Dispatch*, March 4, 1892; "Winding up jury trials." *Pittsburgh Dispatch*, July 16, 1892.
15. "Wild police shooting." *Evening World* (NY), December 23, 1890; "Policeman Holsworth at bar." *Evening World* (NY), December 24, 1890.
16. "Officer Holsworth." *Brooklyn Eagle*, January 30, 1891.
17. "For wife murder." *Evening World* (NY), January 9, 1891.
18. "On trial for wife murder." *New York Times*, April 16, 1891.
19. "Convicted of manslaughter." *Sun* (NY), April 18, 1891.
20. "Policeman Smith guilty." *New York Times*, April 18, 1891.
21. "City and suburban news." *New York Times*, April 22, 1891; "City and suburban news." *New York Times*, May 21, 1891; "Prison now for Smith." *Evening World* (NY), June 19, 1891.
22. "Clubbed to death." *Pittsburgh Dispatch*, April 24, 1891.
23. Ibid.
24. "Held for murder." *Pittsburgh Dispatch*, April 26, 1891.
25. "Four homicide indictments." *Pittsburgh Dispatch*, June 6, 1891; "Three indictments for murder." *Pittsburgh Dispatch*, June 13, 1891; "Criminal court's grind for a day." *Pittsburgh Dispatch*, October 2, 1891; "Saturday sentences in criminal court." *Pittsburgh Dispatch*, October 4, 1891.
26. "Bell's trial begins." *Pittsburgh Dispatch*, July 16, 1891.
27. "Bell is acquitted." *Pittsburgh Dispatch*, July 17, 1891.
28. "Matthew Bell at liberty." *Pittsburgh Dispatch*, July 21, 1891.
29. "Couldn't convict the copper." *Pittsburgh Dispatch*, August 9, 1890.
30. "Shot husband and wife." *New York Times*, July 15, 1891.
31. "A policeman kills two assailants." *Seattle Post-Intelligencer*, July 15, 1891; "Inquest on the Brennans." *Evening World* (NY), July 15, 1891.
32. "Denied a Catholic burial." *Pittsburgh Dispatch*, July 17, 1891.
33. "The Brennan inquest." *New York Times*, July 18, 1891.
34. No title. *Hickman Courier* (KY), January 29, 1892.
35. "Slapped his face." *San Francisco Call*, July 18, 1893; "A police officer sentenced." *San Francisco Call*, July 19, 1893.
36. "Will probably die." *Evening Star* (Washington), November 22, 1893.
37. "Condition serious." *Evening Star* (Washington), November 23, 1893.
38. "Suspended without pay." *Evening Star* (Washington), December 27, 1893.
39. "Terry to be tried." *Evening Star* (Washington), May 11, 1894.
40. "The officer guilty." *Evening Star* (Washington), May 23, 1894.
41. "Three years at hard labor." *Evening Star* (Washington), June 9, 1894.
42. "May be tried again." *Evening Star* (Washington), October 10, 1894; "Terry not held." *Evening Star* (Washington), October 12, 1894; "The week." *Evening Star* (Washington), February 13, 1897.
43. "Shot in the left temple." *St. Paul Globe*, December 10, 1893; "For manslaughter." *Princeton Union* (MN), December 14, 1893.
44. "Killed by policemen." *Sun* (NY), December 26, 1893.
45. "Brutal cops sentenced." *St. Paul Globe*, February 10, 1895.
46. "Sues a policeman." *Evening World* (NY), October 1, 1894.
47. "Clubbers summoned." *Evening World* (NY), October 2, 1894.
48. Ibid.
49. "A gang of police ruffians." *New York Tribune*, October 3, 1894.
50. Ibid.
51. Ibid.

52. Ibid.
53. "Another policeman accused of misconduct." *Sun* (NY), October 26, 1894.
54. "A policeman indicted for assault." *New York Tribune*, November 3, 1894; "Policeman Bernard Murphy vindicated." *Sun* (NY), November 1, 1895.
55. "Shot his prisoner." *Evening Star* (Washington), March 4, 1895.
56. "Death was instant." *Evening Star* (Washington), March 5, 1895; "Accidental shooting." *Evening Star* (Washington), March 6, 1895.
57. "It was murder." *Washington Times*, March 6, 1895.
58. "Indignation meetings." *Evening Star* (Washington), March 7, 1895.
59. "Two district verdicts." *Washington Times*, March 7, 1895.
60. "Green's pistol." *Evening Star* (Washington), March 12, 1895.
61. Ibid.
62. "A strange verdict." *Washington Times*, March 15, 1895.
63. "Ignored again." *Evening Star* (Washington), April 19, 1895.
64. "Denounce Foster's slayer." *Evening Star* (Washington), May 7, 1895.
65. "Green to be tried." *Evening Star* (Washington), May 6, 1895; "Officer Green's revolver." *Evening Star* (Washington), May 28, 1895.
66. "Police outrage." *Advocate* (Topeka, KS), September 4, 1895.
67. No title. *Advocate* (Topeka, KS), April 22, 1896; "Some news about Kansas." *Advocate* (Topeka, KS), August 5, 1896.
68. "Slap costs three lives." *Abbeville Press and Banner* (SC), October 14, 1896; "Scraps and facts." *Yorkville Enquirer* (SC), September 30, 1896.
69. "Exchange gleanings." *Ocala Evening Star* (FL), November 25, 1896.
70. "Policeman kills a tormentor." *Times* (Washington), August 1, 1897.
71. "Killed by a policeman." *New York Tribune*, August 1, 1897.
72. "Killed by a policeman." *New York Times*, August 1, 1897
73. "The shooting of Devine." *New York Times*, August 2, 1897; "Police board and O'Brien." *New York Times*, August 12, 1897.
74. "Policeman kills a burglar." *Evening Star* (Washington), September 6, 1897; "Roundsman Goughran exonerated." *New York Times*, September 11, 1897.
75. "Chase after a policeman." *New York Times*, March 14, 1898.
76. "A policeman indicted." *Evening Times* (Washington), March 26, 1898; "Verdict for McAuliffe." *New York Times*, April 20, 1898.
77. "Beat him to death." *Evening Bulletin* (Maysville, KY), April 7, 1898.
78. "Policeman's awful crime." *New York Tribune*, August 12, 1898.
79. "One policeman kills another." *Rock Island Argus* (IL), February 11, 1899; "Killed a brother officer." *Salt Lake Herald*, May 18, 1899.
80. "Policeman indicted." *Semi-Weekly Messenger* (Wilmington, NC), June 9, 1899.
81. "Personals." *Little Falls Weekly Transcript* (MN), September 1, 1899.

Chapter Four

1. "Policeman kills pugilist." *Evening Star* (Washington), June 16, 1900.
2. "Homicide in Alexandria." *Richmond Dispatch* (VA), August 3, 1900.
3. "A policeman's fatal shot." *Times* (Richmond, VA), August 3, 1900.
4. "Alexandria." *Richmond Dispatch* (VA), August 4, 1900.
5. "Affair in Alexandria." *Evening Star* (Washington), August 4, 1900.
6. "A fatal accident." *Evening Star* (Washington), March 11, 1902.
7. "Policeman indicted." *Times* (Richmond, VA), March 22, 1901; "A policeman fined." *Times* (Richmond, VA), May 16, 1901.
8. "Policeman kills a gambler." *Omaha Daily Bee*, November 12, 1900; "Policeman kills a gambler." *St. Louis Republic*, November 12, 1900.
9. "The right to club." *New York Tribune*, March 15, 1901.
10. "Policeman killed him." *Pullman Herald* (WA), May 4, 1901; "Want to mob him." *Indianapolis Journal*, April 30, 1901.
11. "Killed by officer." *Topeka State Journal*, April 27, 1901.

12. "Hall is arrested." *Topeka State Journal,* April 29, 1901.
13. "Hall pleads guilty." *Topeka State Journal,* July 6, 1901.
14. "Hall must go." *Topeka State Journal,* July 23, 1901; "Hall let out." *Topeka State Journal,* July 29, 1910; "Police jottings." *Topeka State Journal,* December 9, 1901; "Troutman loses fight." *Topeka State Journal,* December 24, 1901.
15. "Policeman kills minister's son." *Yale Expositor* (MI), August 30, 2001; "In self-defence." *Minneapolis Journal,* August 26, 1901.
16. "Officer Frank Ellis becomes a murderer." *Guthrie Leader* (OK), August 30, 1901.
17. "Capture effected last evening." *Guthrie Leader* (OK), August 31, 1901.
18. "The jury decides Frank Ellis sane." *Guthrie Leader* (OK), February 17, 1902; "A life sentence for Frank Ellis." *Guthrie Leader* (OK), March 21, 1902.
19. "Mrs. Frank Ellis dead at Bridgeport." *Guthrie Leader* (OK), May 19, 1903.
20. "Witnessed signing of pardon." *Guthrie Leader* (OK), January 28, 1908.
21. "Policeman convicted of assault." *New York Tribune,* April 19, 1902.
22. "General domestic." *St. Louis Republic,* October 26, 1901.
23. "Fired to frighten." *Ohio Democrat* (Logan, Ohio), November 14, 1901.
24. "Policeman killed him." *Salt Lake Herald,* December 29, 1901.
25. "Policeman kills two men." *Butte Inter Mountain* (MT), January 13, 1902; "Policeman kills two." *St. Paul Globe,* January 14, 1902; "Killed by a policeman." *Bryan Morning Eagle* (TX), January 15, 1902.
26. "Shoots two in bed." *New York Tribune,* January 15, 1902.
27. "Policeman kills wife; planned a triple crime." *Evening World* (NY), January 7, 1902.
28. "Ex-policeman a murderer." *New York Times,* May 23, 1902; "Ennis to die in chair July 7." *Evening World* (NY), May 26, 1902.
29. "Daft from remorse." *St. Paul Globe,* June 6, 1902; "Murderer Ennis's condition." *New York Times,* November 25, 1903.
30. "How a murderer was cunningly caught and executed." *Deseret Evening News* (Salt Lake), December 14, 1903.
31. "Trials soon." *Paducah Sun* (KY), February 19, 1902; "Who killed Bill Dooley." *Hickman Courier* (KY), February 28, 1902.
32. "Policeman indicted." *Paducah Sun* (KY), May 12, 1902; "Case was continued." *Paducah Sun* (KY), September 8, 1902.
33. "Policeman kills his wife." *Bismarck Tribune* (ND), April 4, 1902; "Policeman kills his wife." *New York Times,* April 3, 1902.
34. "Policeman guilty of manslaughter." *New York Times,* June 11, 1902; "Policeman O'Brien sentenced." *New York Times,* June 22, 1902.
35. "Walter Brown exonerated." *St. Louis Republic,* June 13, 1902; "Policeman's victim dies." *St. Louis Republic,* April 21, 1902.
36. "Policeman held for murder." *St. Louis Republic,* April 30, 1902; "Walter Brown exonerated." *St. Louis Republic,* June 13, 1902; "Patrolman Brown dismissed." *St. Louis Republic,* June 21, 1902.
37. "Kills the fugitive who refuses to halt." *San Francisco Call,* May 2, 1902; "Shot dead at Roseburg." *Journal* (Salem, OR), May 1, 1902.
38. "A tragedy at Roseburg." *Rogue River Courier* (Grants Pass, OR), May 8, 1902.
39. "Policeman kills a politician." *Princeton Union* (MN), September 4, 1902.
40. "Killed in struggle with a policeman." *St. Louis Republic,* September 3, 1902.
41. "Policeman is held for Manning's death." *St. Louis Republic,* September 4, 1902.
42. "Warrant issued for O'Hearn." *St. Louis Republic,* September 7, 1902; "Policemen to receive no furloughs this summer." *St. Louis Republic,* April 23, 1904.
43. "Patrolman O'Hearn suspended." *St. Louis Republic,* October 23, 1904.
44. "Policeman kills himself and wife." *Times* (Richmond, VA), October 26, 1901.
45. "Political feud." *Evening Bulletin* (Maysville, KY), November 14, 1902; "Large funeral." *Kentucky Irish American* (Louisville), November 22, 1902; "Brown found guilty." *Evening Bulletin* (Maysville, KY), April 18, 1904; "Robert Brown sentenced." *Evening Bulletin* (Maysville, KY), April 21, 1904.
46. "Killed in a man hunt." *New York Times,* February 6, 1903; "Capt. Colby killed." *Evening Star* (Washington), February 5, 1903; "Shot dead by mistake." *Arizona Republican* (Phoenix), February 12, 1903.
47. "Policeman kills policeman." *Washington Times,* February 9, 1903; "One policeman kills

another." *Houston Post*, February 9, 1903; "Virginia news." *Alexandria Gazette* (VA), February 10, 1903; "Shock caused her death." *Bolivar Bulletin* (TN), June 26, 1903.
  48. "Former policeman guilty." *Daily Press* (Newport News, VA), October 1, 1910; "New trial refused." *Tazewell Republican* (VA), November 24, 1910.
  49. "Policeman convicted of assaulting neighbor." *Evening World* (NY), February 25, 1903.
  50. "Convicted after long delay." *New York Times*, February 26, 1903.
  51. "Ex-policeman sentenced." *New York Times*, February 28, 1903.
  52. "Killed by a policeman." *Alexandria Gazette* (VA), March 25, 1903.
  53. "Fleeing man killed." *Evening Star* (Washington), March 25, 1903.
  54. "Held for grand jury." *Evening Star* (Washington), April 1, 1903; "Week ending May 9, 1903." *Evening Star* (Washington), May 9, 1903.
  55. "One policeman shots another." *Evening World* (NY), March 28, 1903; "Brother cops to air troubles." *Sun* (NY), May 23, 1903.
  56. "Policeman kills." *Cameron County Press* (Emporium, PA), July 2, 1903.
  57. "Judge Mayer's charge." *Lock Haven Express* (PA), January 9, 1904; "The final summons calls Michael Crowley." *Lock Haven Express* (PA), March 13, 1905.
  58. "Shenandoah man shot." *Freeland Tribune* (PA), June 29, 1903
  59. "Policeman kills thief." *San Francisco Call*, July 5, 1903.
  60. "A policeman kills a man." *Semi-Weekly Messenger* (Wilmington, NC), October 2, 1903.
  61. "Monday morning murder." *Comet* (Johnson City, TN), October 1, 1903.
  62. "George Allen case remanded." *Comet* (Johnson City, TN), October 12, 1905.
  63. "Denver detective guilty of murder." *Salt Lake Tribune*, May 14, 1904; "To be tried for murder." *Evening Star* (Washington), March 1, 1904.
  64. "Says policeman killed man." *Evening World* (NY), March 30, 1904.
  65. "Think policeman killed bartender." *New York Times*, March 31, 1904.
  66. "Policeman freed on murder charge." *Evening World* (NY), May 12, 1904.
  67. "Some recent occurrences." *Laurens Advertiser* (SC), May 4, 1904; "Record of a year." *Yorkville Enquirer* (SC), November 1, 1904.
  68. "Died of his wounds." *Edgefield Advertiser* (SC), May 4, 1904; "The circuit court." *Yorkville Enquirer* (SC), November 18, 1904.
  69. "Policeman shot in a Bowery tussle." *New York Times*, May 9, 1904.
  70. Ibid.
  71. Ibid.
  72. "Policeman held for first degree murder." *New York Times*, August 5, 1904.
  73. "Policeman on trial." *New York Times*, December 7, 1904.
  74. "Says police shielded him." *New York Times*, December 9, 1904.
  75. "Verdict of guilty found against Mallon." *New York Times*, December 10, 1904; "Long sentence for policeman." *Evening World* (NY), December 16, 1904.
  76. "Saw O'Brien shooting; calls police derelict." *New York Times*, December 31, 1904.
  77. "Mallon out on bail." *New York Times*, March 18, 1905; "City news in brief." *New York Tribune*, December 22, 1906; "Patrolman must serve sentence." *New York Tribune*, June 15, 1907.
  78. "Say he shot O'Brien." *New York Tribune*, April 18, 1909.
  79. "To free ex-policeman." *Sun* (NY), January 27, 1916.
  80. "Policeman killed him as he ran." *Evening World* (NY), June 4, 1904.
  81. "Mystery in shooting of supposed burglar." *New York Times*, June 5, 1904.
  82. "Two verdicts in shooting of Daly." *Evening World* (NY), August 9, 1904.
  83. "Disagreed on Daly killing." *Sun* (NY), August 10, 1904.
  84. "Thief shot on street by Harlem detective." *New York Times*, July 28, 1904; "Daly dead; sleuth held who shot him." *New York Times*, July 29, 1904.
  85. "Detective kills man." *New York Times*, August 4, 1904.
  86. "Newark detective held." *Sun* (NY), August 5, 1904; "Detective who shot man suspended." *Sun* (NY), August 7, 1904; "Newark a little wet." *New York Tribune*, July 23, 1906.
  87. "Two years." *Paducah Sun* (KY), August 24, 1904.
  88. "Policeman kills another." *Manning Times* (SC), October 5, 1904; "Eight years for Goodman." *Bamberg Herald* (SC), October 27, 1904.
  89. "Policeman killed at pistol practice." *Evening Statesman* (Walla Walla, WA), October 22, 1904; "Killed by his friend." *Hocking Sentinel* (Logan, Ohio), October 27, 1904.

90. "Policeman kills a man." *New York Tribune*, November 3, 1904.
91. "Policeman kills man." *New York Times*, November 3, 1904.
92. "Policeman kills his best friend." *Evening World* (NY), November 3, 1904.
93. "Verdict favored policeman." *New York Times*, November 5, 1904.
94. "Policeman held for murder." *New York Times*, December 24, 1904; "Two policemen guilty." *New York Times*, January 21, 1905; "20 years for policeman." *New York Times*, February 1, 1905.
95. "Clubber will be suspended." *Evening World* (NY), December 21, 1904.
96. "To arrest a patrolman." *New York Tribune*, December 22, 1904.
97. "Clubber spends night in cell." *Evening World* (NY), December 23, 1904.
98. "Charged with murder." *Times Dispatch* (Richmond, VA), December 29, 1904.
99. "Men and women shot in riot." *Evening World* (NY), May 27, 1904.
100. "Two policemen are on trial for murder." *Evening World* (NY), January 17, 1905.
101. "New trial for cop who killed." *Sun* (NY), April 1, 1905; "Policeman scot-free." *Sun* (NY), March 8, 1906.
102. "Policeman shot in rifle range." *Evening World* (NY), January 16, 1905; "Swift trials for the cops." *Sun* (NY), February 17, 1905.
103. "Blew brains out for refusing." *Los Angeles Herald*, February 28, 1905.
104. "Atrocious crime in Chicago street." *Paducah Sun* (KY), February 28, 1905; "Teacher shot in street." *Abbeville Press and Banner* (SC), March 22, 1905.
105. "Cop kills manager Mississippi Club." *Daily Press* (Newport News, VA), March 19, 1905; "A tragedy at Hattiesburg." *Bee* (Earlington, KY), March 23, 1905.
106. "Policeman indicted on assault charge." *St. Louis Republic*, May 11, 1905.
107. "Tomasso's penalty prison and a fine." *St. Louis Republic*, June 24, 1905.
108. "Policeman killed box." *Daily Press* (Newport News, VA), April 26, 1905; "Kills Herbert's protégé." *New York Times*, April 26, 1905.
109. "Hartje offers a million to wife." *New York Times*, October 8, 1907.
110. "A policeman kills a soldier." *Times Dispatch* (Richmond, VA), May 12, 1905; "Virginia news." *Alexandria Gazette* (VA), May 13, 1905.
111. "Policeman indicted for murder." *Evening Star* (Washington), May 17, 1905; "Virginia news." *Alexandria Gazette* (VA), September 21, 1905.
112. "Shot by girl's father." *New York Times*, June 25, 1905; "Jno Dockery shot." *Semi-Weekly Messenger* (Wilmington, NC), June 27, 1905; "Shooting policeman indicted." *Daily Press* (Newport News, VA), October 1, 1905.
113. "The Dockery-Rogers case." *Semi-Weekly Messenger* (Wilmington, NC), January 12, 1906.
114. "Policeman killed a politician." *Evening Star* (Washington), July 6, 1905; "July 4th casualties." *Evening Star* (Washington), July 5, 1905.
115. "Policeman kills young man." *Omaha Daily Bee*, August 5, 1905; "Young Easley shot by officer." *Times Dispatch* (Richmond, VA), August 5, 1905.
116. "Policeman kills three." *Salt Lake Tribune*, August 11, 1905.
117. Policeman killed a burglar." *Cameron County Press* (Emporium, PA), February 8, 1906.
118. "Policeman kills drummer." *Paducah Sun* (NY), February 9, 1906; "Drunken policeman kills traveling man." *Salt Lake Tribune*, February 10, 1906.
119. "Denver murder." *Clayton Enterprise* (NM), February 16, 1906.
120. "Guilty of murder." *Salt Lake Herald*, March 28, 1906; "Secrest goes to prison." *Evening Statesman* (Walla Walla, WA), April 16, 1906.
121. "Spokane policeman kills a burglar." *Deseret Evening News* (Salt Lake), April 4, 1906; "Burglar dies from his wounds." *Spokane Press*, April 4, 1906; "Local news." *East Oregonian* (Pendleton), April 5, 1906; "Briley claims whiskey saved his life." *Spokane Press*, July 18, 1906.
122. "Policeman jailed as girl's assailant." *Minneapolis Journal*, July 13, 1906.
123. "Accidentally shot." *Evening Star* (Washington), July 30, 1906.
124. "Charges preferred." *Evening Star* (Washington), August 2, 1906.
125. "Policeman under charges." *Evening Star* (Washington), October 3, 1906.
126. "Hearing of testimony." *Evening Star* (Washington), October 19, 1906.
127. "Trial board meets." *Evening Star* (Washington), October 27, 1906.
128. "Lipscomb loses place on force." *Washington Times*, February 14, 1907.
129. "Action in police cases." *Evening Star* (Washington), March 13, 1907; "Policeman Lipscomb resigns from force." *Washington Times*, March 17, 1907.

130. "Charges revived." *Evening Star* (Washington), May 16, 1907; "Verdict not guilty." *Evening Star* (Washington), October 25, 1907; "Court acquits policeman." *Washington Herald*, October 26, 1907.
131. "Policeman kills actor." *Albuquerque Morning Journal*, August 3, 1906; "Hightower killed." *Bryan Morning Eagle* (TX), August 1, 1906.
132. "Shot by a policeman." *Titusville Herald* (PA), August 27, 1906.
133. "Policeman goes to jail." *Sun* (NY), October 20, 1907; "Manslaughter if cop kills." *Columbian* (Bloomsburg, PA), October 24, 1907.
134. "Cop kills his assailant." *Sun* (NY), September 19, 1906.
135. "Tragedy at Concord." *Evening Star* (Washington), September 25, 1906.
136. "Double tragedy in Concord, N.H." *Vermont Phoenix* (Brattleboro, VT), September 28, 1906.
137. "Prisoner's struggle to escape fatal." *Minneapolis Journal*, September 30, 1906.
138. "Death of a police prisoner probed." *Minneapolis Journal*, October 1, 1906.
139. "Blame for death on two policemen." *Minneapolis Journal*, October 6, 1906.
140. "Accused patrolmen are now suspended." *Minneapolis Journal*, October 7, 1906.
141. "Accuser of police cleared in court." *Minneapolis Journal*, October 13, 1906; "Higgins sent up." *Minneapolis Journal*, October 22, 1906.
142. "Minneapolis policemen indicted." *Bemidji Pioneer* (MN), October 19, 1906; "News in Minnesota." *Little Falls Herald* (MN), March 15, 1907.
143. "Policeman convicted of assault." *New York Tribune*, March 2, 1907.
144. "Police clubber convicted." *New York Times*, March 3, 1907.
145. "Policeman sentenced." *New York Tribune*, March 7, 1909.
146. "Policeman kills captain." *Evening Star* (Washington), February 5, 1907.
147. "Others share blame." *Elkhart Daily Review* (IN), December 11, 1907.
148. "Policeman kills bread-box robber." *Times Dispatch* (Richmond, VA), March 28, 1907.
149. "Policeman badly beaten." *Sun* (NY), May 3, 1907.
150. "Policemen guilty of assault." *New York Tribune*, May 8, 1907.
151. "Perjury fails to save them." *Sun* (NY), June 8, 1907.
152. "Ask for jobs lost on story of a coward." *Evening World* (NY), September 21, 1907; "Sharp attack on Hanson." *Sun* (NY), January 11, 1908.
153. "Sharp attack on Hanson." *Sun* (NY), January 11, 1908; "Alleged police hazers restored." *New York Tribune*, April 7, 1908.
154. "Policeman kills escaping bandit." *Washington Times*, May 11, 1907.
155. "Mob demanded officer's life." *Salt Lake Herald*, May 11, 1907; "Butte roused." *Pullman Herald* (WA), May 18, 1907.
156. "Policeman kills fugitive." *Rock Island Argus* (IL), May 24, 1907; "Officer held for shooting." *Rock Island Argus* (IL), May 25, 1907; "Sterling policeman indicted." *New York Times*, October 10, 1907.
157. No title. *Burlington Hawk Eye* (Iowa), January 11, 1908; "Manlius." *Princeton Bureau County Tribune* (IL), January 31, 1908.
158. "Policeman kills man in running battle." *Salt Lake Tribune*, August 14, 1907; "Killed for stealing a bottle of whisky." *Rogue River Courier* (Grants Pass, OR), August 16, 1907.
159. "Fatal billy blow." *St. Landry Clarion* (Opelousas, LA), October 5, 1907.
160. "Policeman kills cigar man." *Washington State Journal* (Ritzville, WA), October 9, 1907.
161. "Shoots down youth in crowded park." *New York Times*, October 7, 1907; "Accused policeman bailed." *New York Times*, October 8, 1907.
162. "Policeman dies of grief." *New York Times*, July 22, 1908.
163. "Policeman kills innocent man." *Los Angeles Herald*, November 25, 1907; "Fatal battle with gang of tramps." *Capital Journal* (Salem, OR), November 25, 1907.
164. "Tragedies of Christmas day." *Semi-Weekly Messenger* (Wilmington, NC), December 31, 1907.
165. "New policeman kills his dearest friend." *San Francisco Call*, February 13, 1908; "Killed for a fool joke." *Wenatchee World* (WA), February 14, 1908.
166. "Police officer convicted." *Daily Ardmoreite* (Ardmore, OK), February 16, 1908.
167. "Shot down in depot." *Bryan Morning Eagle* (TX), November 3, 1908; "Former policeman killed." *Daily Ardmoreite* (Ardmore, OK), November 5, 1908.

168. "Joy turned to sadness." *Salt Lake Herald*, March 2, 1908; "Crime charged to hasty officer." *Billings Gazette* (MT), March 3, 1908.
169. "Policeman jailed for killing man." *Washington Times*, May 24, 1908.
170. "Policeman held for death." *New York Times*, May 24, 1908; "Policeman who admits killing of boy is held." *Evening World* (NY), May 23, 1908.
171. "Policeman killed a teamster." *Marion Daily Mirror* (Ohio); "Free patrolman who slew." *Broad Ax* (Salt Lake), July 11, 1908.
172. "Policeman's pistol killed Barbara Reig." *New York Times*, July 24, 1908.
173. Ibid.
174. "Policeman Shellard held without bail." *New York Times*, July 25, 1908; "Crowd hoots police at slain girl's bier." *New York Times*, July 26, 1908.
175. "Verdict is that she shot herself." *New York Times*, July 30, 1908; "Shellard must stay in jail." *New York Times*, July 31, 1908; "Policeman Shellard out on bail." *New York Times*, August 14, 1908.
176. "Shellard off the force." *New York Times*, August 22, 1908.
177. "Shellard in cell to await trial as girl's slayer." *Evening World* (NY), September 10, 1908.
178. "Shellard murder trial." *New York Times*, January 19, 1909.
179. "The Shellard murder case." *New York Times*, January 20, 1909; "Shellard a witness." *New York Times*, January 21, 1909.
180. "Jury disagrees in Shellard case." *New York Times*, January 22, 1909; "Shellard out on $15,000 bail." *New York Times*, March 20, 1909.
181. "Police try to kill a cowboy." *Los Angeles Herald*, August 27, 1908.
182. "Policeman kills bad negro." *Red Cloud Chief* (Red Cloud, NE), September 4, 1908.
183. "Kills captain." *Washington Herald*, March 6, 1909; "Motive is advanced for Mathews murder." *Washington Times*, March 7, 1909.
184. "Dismissed from the force." *Evening Star* (Washington), April 1, 1909.
185. "Collier is bound over to grand jury today." *Washington Times*, March 6, 1909; "Fund is started for accused man." *Washington Herald*, March 9, 1909.
186. "Justifies the deed." *Evening Star* (Washington), August 3, 1909.
187. "Collier is cool telling of crime." *Washington Times*, December 3, 1909; "Find Collier guilty." *Evening Star* (Washington), December 5, 1910; "Collier out on bail." *Weekly News* (Washington), December 11, 1909.
188. "Long term in prison." *Evening Star* (Washington), January 7, 1910; "Abandons appeal in manslaughter case." *Evening Star* (Washington), March 16, 1910; "Collier off to prison." *Evening Star* (Washington), March 31, 1910.
189. "Act of a deranged man." *Daily News* (Newport News, VA), March 9, 1909.
190. "Policeman kills man for burglar." *Los Angeles Herald*, March 21, 1909.
191. "In name of charity." *Topeka State Journal* (KS), April 1, 1909; "Killing by mistake." *Deseret Evening News* (Salt Lake), April 5, 1909.
192. "Verdict against policeman." *Freeport Journal* (IL), March 25, 1909.
193. "Pocatello policeman kills fighting negro." *Deseret Evening News* (Salt Lake), April 28, 1909; "Dining car waiter shot." *Ogden Standard* (Utah), April 28, 1909.
194. "Gus Travis was accidentally killed." *Ogden Standard* (Utah), April 29, 1909.
195. "Policeman guilty of assault with club." *Spokane Press*, May 4, 1909; "Wallace has turned in his star." *Spokane Press*, July 20, 1909.
196. "Shot by policeman in Sunday law row." *New York Times*, May 3, 1909.
197. Ibid.
198. "Young Probber dead, policeman in cell." *New York Times*, May 4, 1909.
199. "Say policeman shot boy for revenge." *New York Times*, June 23, 1909.
200. "Dillon goes to Sing Sing." *New York Times*, June 30, 1909; "Gamblers keep off." *Sun* (NY), July 8, 1909; "Dillon convicted." *New York Tribune*, June 26, 1909.
201. "Policeman kills a negro." *Daily News* (Newport News, VA), May 29, 1909.
202. "Here and there." *Interior Journal* (Stanford, KY), June 15, 1909.
203. "Double tragedy." *Times and Democrat* (Orangeburg, SC), June 19, 1909.
204. "Police officer kills man." *Daily Press* (Newport News, VA), June 24, 1909; "Police captain shoots to kill." *Evening Statesman* (Walla Walla, WA), June 23, 1909.
205. "Conboy jailed and his victim dying." *San Francisco Call*, June 24, 1909.

206. Ibid.
207. "Conboy released on giving bond." *San Francisco Call*, June 25, 1909; "Charges preferred against Conboy." *San Francisco Call*, June 27, 1909.
208. "Locked up on charge of murder." *San Francisco Call*, October 7, 1909.
209. "Grief stricken sister complains." *San Francisco Call*, October 12, 1909.
210. "Jury charges Conboy with Lagan murder." *San Francisco Call*, October 14, 1909.
211. "Conboy on trial for Lagan's death." *San Francisco Call*, November 17, 1909; "Conboy found guilty." *San Francisco Call*, April 19, 1912.
212. "Perjury is charged in Conboy case." *San Francisco Call*, February 9, 1910; "Thought Lagan meant murder says Conboy." *San Francisco Call*, February 12, 1910; "Paints Conboy as defending his life." *San Francisco Call*, February 16, 1910.
213. No title. *Evening Herald* (Klamath Falls, OR), April 22, 1912; "Conboy resigned." *San Francisco Call*, May 12, 1912; "Michael Conboy loses fight for ticket of leave." *San Francisco Call*, August 24, 1913.
214. "Policeman kills girl." *Marion Daily Mirror* (Ohio), June 29, 1909.
215. "Policeman kills negro." *Bamberg Herald* (SC), September 16, 1909; No title. *Watchman and Southron* (Sumter, SC), September 29, 1909.
216. "Policeman kills negress." *Bamberg Herald* (SC), November 18, 1909; "Policeman kills negro woman." *Tensas Gazette* (St. Joseph, LA), November 19, 1909.
217. "A policeman of Monroe." *Caucasian* (Shreveport, LA), November 16, 1909; No title. *Tensas Gazette* (St. Joseph, LA), May 13, 1910.
218. "Italians determined to get facts." *Seattle Star*, December 22, 1909.
219. "Innocent man, shot by police, is dying." *Seattle Star*, December 23, 1909.
220. "Italians say policeman killed boy; riot feared." *Los Angeles Herald*, January 19, 1910; "Fellow officers will aid Walsh." *Seattle Star*, January 21, 1910; "Patrolman is on trial for killing." *Seattle Star*, June 22, 1910; "Walsh jury can't agree." *Seattle Star*, June 25, 1910; "Hurt, man walks around for days." *Seattle Star*, July 1, 1910.

Chapter Five

1. "Antonio Guavara will not wear prison stripes." *Albuquerque Morning Journal*, July 22, 1910; "Policeman Antonio Guavara still carries his ready gun." *Albuquerque Morning Journal*, January 10, 1910.
2. "Council declines to suspend Guavara." *Albuquerque Morning Journal*, February 8, 1910.
3. "Vargas dies from a policeman's pistol." *Roswell Recorder* (NM), April 4, 1910; "Guavara guilty of assault with weapon." *Albuquerque Morning Journal*, May 1, 1910; "Antonio Guavara will not wear prison stripes." *Albuquerque Morning Journal*, July 22, 1910.
4. "Gaynor nullifies system." *Thibodaux Sentinel* (LA), February 26, 1910.
5. "Policeman kills rioter." *Daily News* (Newport News, VA), March 1, 1910.
6. "Lewis gets ten year sentence." *Paducah Sun* (KY), March 23, 1910; No title. *Hickman Courier* (KY), March 28, 1912.
7. "Policeman kills young man." *Bemidji Daily Pioneer* (MN), March 29, 1910.
8. "Policeman kills a drunkard." *Greenville Journal* (Ohio), June 30, 1910; "Policeman guilty of manslaughter." *Marion Daily Mirror* (Ohio), February 27, 1911; "Two years for murder." *Democratic Banner* (Mt. Vernon, Ohio), March 7, 1911.
9. "Gaynor and the police." *Norfolk Weekly News-Journal* (VA), September 2, 1910.
10. "Policeman kills a woman." *Columbus Journal* (NE), September 21, 1910.
11. "Policeman kills wife on street." *Washington Herald*, October 2, 1910.
12. "Happy baby knows nothing of tragedy in Baston home." *Washington Times*, October 2, 1910.
13. "Slayer's money found in shoes." *Washington Herald*, October 4, 1910.
14. "Former policeman seeks a new trial." *Washington Times*, February 10, 1911; "Declares he is sorry; makes plea for mercy." *Evening Star* (Wa shington), March 10, 1911.
15. "Baston will appeal to Taft after going to prison." *Washington Times*, June 16, 1911; "Clemency for policeman." *Evening Star* (Washington), January 5, 1917.
16. "Policeman kills himself." *New York Tribune*, October 28, 1910; "Policeman on a rampage." *New York Times*, October 25, 1910.

17. "More policemen in trouble." *Sun* (NY), March 24, 1910; "Policeman Kelly on trial." *New York Times*, May 13, 1910.
18. "San Francisco policeman kills escaping suspect." *Los Angeles Herald*, November 7, 1910; "Policeman's victim known to police." *San Francisco Call*, November 8, 1910.
19. "Say policeman killed girl." *Sun* (NY), November 26, 1910; "Bail for patrolman Welsh." *New York Tribune*, November 29, 1910.
20. "Held for stray bullet death." *Sun* (NY), January 14, 1911; "Lieut. Foody dismissed." *New York Times*, March 1, 1911.
21. "Policeman Armstrong before police judge." *Evening Star* (Washington), December 14, 1910; "Armstrong faces trial before board." *Washington Times*, December 22, 1910; "Armstrong pays fine for Weaver assault." *Washington Times*, January 10, 1911; "Former officer nabbed at a fire." *Washington Herald*, March 29, 1911.
22. "Policeman accused of assault to murder." *San Francisco Call*, December 2, 1910; "Birdsall good officer gets queer reward." *San Francisco Call*, August 9, 1911.
23. "Policeman kills youthful rioter." *Washington Herald*, December 26, 1910.
24. "Policeman kills infantry bandman." *Logan Republican* (Utah), January 24, 1911; "Is killed by a policeman as he eats." *El Paso Herald*, January 24, 1911.
25. "Bernauer on the witness stand tells why he shot Frank Richard." *El Paso Herald*, March 21, 1911; "Bernauer acquitted by jury on the charge of murdering Richard." *El Paso Herald*, March 22, 1911.
26. "Policeman kills a boy by mistake." *New York Times*, May 28, 1911.
27. "No evidence given that policeman killed student." *Evening World* (NY), May 30, 1911.
28. "More indictments for burning of negro." *Norwich Bulletin* (CT), September 21, 1911; "Coatesville is scene of attempted outrage." *El Paso Herald*, November 21, 1911.
29. "Policeman kills soldier." *East Oregonian* (Pendleton), September 20, 1911.
30. "Policeman kills fugitive." *New York Tribune*, October 13, 1911.
31. "Policeman fells woman in street." *New York Times*, November 14, 1911.
32. "Woman appears against policeman." *New York Times*, November 15, 1911.
33. "Guilty of clubbing woman." *New York Times*, February 16, 1912.
34. "Policeman kills liveryman." *Washington Herald*, December 25, 1911.
35. "Policeman kills negro." *Bamberg Herald* (SC), May 2, 1912.
36. "Policeman kills negro." *Herald and News* (Newberry, SC), May 21, 1912.
37. "Policeman killed mill operative." *Bamberg Herald* (SC), June 20, 1912.
38. "Slain man's friends active." *Bamberg Herald* (SC), June 27, 1912.
39. "General Sessions." *Yorkville Enquirer* (SC), December 3, 1912.
40. "Waldo will ask police inquiry." *Sun* (NY), July 15, 1912.
41. "New York startled by murder of gambler." *Day Book* (Chicago), July 16, 1912.
42. "Becker at city hall." *New York Tribune*, July 19, 1912; Wikipedia entries; Rosenthal murder case, Francisco Cirofici, Charles Becker, downloaded August 4, 1915.
43. No title. *Day Book* (Chicago), October 31, 1912; No title. *Seattle Star*, November 27, 1912; "Limit powers." *Evening Times* (Grand Forks, ND), December 11, 1912.
44. "Seattle detective wounds man by mistake." *El Paso Herald*, January 22, 1913; "Detective guilty of assault." *Tacoma Times*, January 22, 1913; "You'll find it here." *Tacoma Times*, January 23, 1913; "Judge lauds M'Namee in fining him for shooting." *Seattle Star*, February 3, 1913.
45. "Patrolman kills deputy police." *Salt Lake Tribune*, December 16, 1912.
46. "Patrolman confesses he killed his chief." *San Francisco Call*, December 17, 1912.
47. "Central City policeman kills negro." *Record* (Greenville, KY), December 19, 1912.
48. "Jailbreak effort is futile." *Daily Missoulian* (Missoula, MT), January 5, 1913; "Mysterious shooting explained." *Manchester Democrat* (IA), January 29, 1913.
49. "Policeman guilty of manslaughter in killing youth." *Evening Public Ledger* (Philadelphia), October 27, 1914; "Policeman sentenced to jail." *Star-Independent* (Harrisburg, PA), October 31, 1914.
50. "Heard own pardon case presented." *Harrisburg Telegraph* (PA), November 18, 1914; "Dauphin man pardoned." *Star-Independent* (Harrisburg, PA), November 19, 1914.
51. "Policeman kills relative." *Pioneer Express* (Pembina, ND), March 21, 1913; "Local doings in tabloid form." *Day Book* (Chicago), March 17, 1913; "News of the day concerning Chicago." *Day Book* (Chicago), December 20, 1913.

52. "Policeman kills negro." *Day Book* (Chicago), June 16, 1913.
53. "No pardon yet for policeman." *El Paso Herald*, August 7, 1913.
54. "Policeman kills a tobacco agent." *Ogden Standard* (Utah), September 25, 1913.
55. "Policemen kill and wound men." *Ogden Standard* (Utah), November 3, 1913; "Man is shot dead in chase for steer." *Bemidji Daily Pioneer* (MN), November 4, 1913.
56. "Policeman kills fleeing robber." *Sun* (NY), February 5, 1914; "Downie was thug killed." *New York Times*, February 6, 1914; "Kills fleeing thug; remains on duty." *Sun* (NY), February 5, 1914.
57. "Police officers convicted." *Arizona Republican* (Phoenix), March 11, 1914.
58. "Policeman kills fugitive." *Sun* (NY), June 13, 1914.
59. "Fulton policeman kills a negro." *Hickman Courier* (KY), July 23, 1914.
60. "Policeman kills big negro." *Bamberg Herald* (SC), August 6, 1914.
61. "Will hear cop who shot man tomorrow." *Harrisburg Telegraph* (PA), August 3, 1914.
62. "Jury picked for trial of Scott." *Star-Independent* (Harrisburg, PA), January 16, 1915.
63. "Jury may give verdict to-night." *Star-Independent* (Harrisburg, PA), January 18, 1915.
64. "Patrolman found guilty of second degree murder." *Star-Independent* (Harrisburg, PA), January 19, 1915; "Bluecoat to pen, for 12 to 20 years." *Star-Independent* (Harrisburg, PA), February 18, 1915.
65. "Swords Creek man instantly killed." *Bluefield Telegraph* (VA), August 2, 1914; "News of Pounding Mill." *Clinch Valley News* (Jeffersonville, VA), January 12, 1915.
66. "Greenville policeman kills." *Keowee Courier* (Pickens, SC), November 4, 1914; "South Carolina news." *Yorkville Enquirer* (SC), January 12, 1915.
67. "Policeman kills negro." *Manning Times* (SC), October 28, 1914.
68. "Cop kills cop–queer tale." *Day Book* (Chicago), January 28, 1915.
69. "Policeman kills brother officer." *Washington Times*, February 25, 1915; "Policeman held as slayer of another." *Sun* (NY), February 26, 1915; "Policeman gets 30 years for murder." *Evening World* (NY), May 13, 1915.
70. "Policeman kills wife and himself." *Sun* (NY), April 7, 1915; "Policeman kills sleeping wife and himself." *New York Tribune*, April 7, 1915; "Pet dogs and cats guard slain couple." *New York Times*, April 7, 1915.
71. "Youth flees police, is shot and killed." *Evening Public Ledger* (Philadelphia), June 12, 1915; "Police victim a convict." *Evening Public Ledger* (Philadelphia), June 14, 1915.
72. "Policeman kills negro." *Mt. Sterling Advocate* (KY), August 25, 1915.
73. No title. *Pickens Sentinel* (SC), October 14, 1915.
74. "Policeman kills two boys with one shot." *East Oregonian* (Pendleton), October 27, 1915.
75. "Shooting of boys is held unjustifiable." *Omaha Daily Bee*, October 26, 1915; "Released on bond." *Bisbee Daily Review* (AZ), October 31, 1915; "Murder charge not sustained." *Arizona Republican* (Phoenix), February 3, 1916.
76. "Policeman kills children and self." *Omaha Daily Bee*, January 16, 1916; "Kills children then self." *Evening Star* (Washington), January 16, 1916.
77. "Detective convicted of assault in subway." *Evening World* (NY), December 14, 1916.
78. "Cop killed fleeing negro." *Kansas City Sun* (MO), November 25, 1916.
79. "Four cops convicted for beating sailors." *Evening Public Ledger* (Philadelphia), June 26, 1917.
80. "Policeman kills another." *Bemidji Pioneer* (MN), February 9, 1917.
81. "Policeman kills fugitive." *Evening World* (NY), March 1, 1917; "Dying, he runs two blocks." *Evening World* (NY), February 28, 1917.
82. "Policeman kills his chief." *Tulsa Daily World*, July 13, 1917.
83. "Policeman kills father." *New York Tribune*, August 15, 1917; "Condensed telegraphs." *Norwich Bulletin* (CT), August 16, 1917.
84. "Cop kills negro holdup." *Topeka State Journal* (KS), October 12, 1917.
85. "Policeman kills coroner." *Bamberg Herald* (SC), October 18, 1917.
86. "Policeman kills baby." *New York Times*, November 14, 1917; "Stray bullet kills baby at mother's side." *New York Times*, November 14, 1917; "Arrested for 33rd time." *New York Times*, August 2, 1925.
87. "Cops kill 2 robbers." *Topeka State Journal* (KS), November 19, 1917.
88. "Cop kills boy who tried to steal." *Guthrie Leader* (OK), January 11, 1918.

89. "Policeman kills 13-year-old bandit." *Evening Public Ledger* (Philadelphia), March 9, 1918.
90. "Mill City policeman kills alleged holdup." *Little Falls Herald* (MN), April 5, 1918.
91. "Fifth Ward cop indicted." *Evening Public Ledger* (Philadelphia), June 6, 1918; "Two years for Auerbach." *Evening Public Ledger* (Philadelphia), June 25, 1918.
92. "Boy killed in chase over roofs after raid on crap game." *New York Tribune*, July 15, 1918.
93. "Two policemen indicted for first-degree murder." *Times-Dispatch* (Richmond, VA), February 11, 1921; "2 policemen indicted for killing boy." *New York Tribune*, February 11, 1921.
94. "New York policeman guilty of manslaughter." *Norwich Bulletin* (CT), March 19, 1921; "Flood is given 3 years." *New York Tribune*, March 25, 1921; "Governor pardons Cornelius J. Flood." *New York Times*, December 9, 1925.
95. "Policeman kills one of two assailants." *Evening Public Ledger* (Philadelphia), September 13, 1918.
96. "Policeman shoots boy in gambling quarrel." *Maui News* (Wailuku, HI), November 1, 1918; "Policeman sentenced to 2 years hard labor." *Maui News* (Wailuku, HI), December 6, 1918.
97. "Policeman is indicted." *Evening Star* (Washington), March 4, 1919; "Former policeman sentenced." *Evening Star* (Washington), March 7, 1920.
98. "Policeman guilty of assault and drunkenness." *Norwich Bulletin* (CT), December 17, 1918.
99. "Policeman kills burglar." *Bisbee Daily Review* (AZ), April 26, 1919.
100. "Prlja to be tried on charge of assault." *Butte Bulletin* (MT), April 29, 1919; "Prlja's fate goes in hands of jury today." *Butte Bulletin* (MT), May 2, 1919; "Prlja convicted of assault on Burzan." *Butte Bulletin* (MT), May 3, 1919; "Prlja sentenced to term in penitentiary." *Butte Bulletin* (MT), May 8, 1919.
101. "Butte policemen rally to the aid of convicted officer." *Great Falls Tribune* (MT), May 13, 1919; "Convicted officer of Butte released under $5,000 bail." *Great Falls Tribune* (MT), June 30, 1919.
102. "Kelley takes care of faithful." *Butte Bulletin* (MT), July 12, 1919; "Convicted Butte cop is denied new trial in district court." *Great Falls Tribune* (MT), August 6, 1919; "Butte mayor ordered to reinstate Prlja or show cause why." *Great Falls Tribune* (MT), October 23, 1919; "Supreme Court decides that Phil Prlja must serve pen sentence." *Butte Bulletin* (MT), March 29, 1920.
103. "Governor recommends a pardon for Prlja." *Great Falls Tribune* (MT), April 8, 1920; "An unconditional pardon is granted former policeman." *Great Falls Tribune* (MT), May 1, 1920.
104. "Court orders Prlja to be reinstated upon police force." *Great Falls Tribune* (MT), September 12, 1920; "Will take an appeal." *Great Falls Tribune* (MT), September 15, 1920.
105. "Former officer shot six times at Butte." *Great Falls Tribune* (MT), March 21, 1922; "Burzan acquitted of murder charge." *Great Falls Tribune* (MT), November 11, 1921; "Dismiss appeal of former officer after his death." *Great Falls Tribune* (MT), March 15, 1922.
106. "Policeman kills man in scuffle." *Oklahoma City Times*, May 13, 1919.
107. "Tragedy in Columbia." *Watchman and Southron* (Sumter, SC), May 31, 1919; "South Carolina news," *Yorkville Enquirer* (SC), May 30, 1919.
108. "Lancaster freed by jury's verdict." *Manning Times* (SC), September 24, 1919; "Lancaster freed by jury's verdict." *Abbeville Press and Banner* (SC), September 23, 1919.
109. "Boy, 16, killed by rookie policeman." *Washington Times*, July 9, 1919.
110. "$532 and cop who killed boy missing." *Washington Times*, September 19, 1919.
111. "H. A. Starr accused of manslaughter." *Evening Star* (Washington), October 1, 1919; "Ex-bluecoat freed by jury." *Washington Herald*, October 20, 1920.
112. "Policeman kills dog; same bullet hits boy." *New York Tribune*, July 24, 1919.
113. "Policeman kills soldier." *Daily Gate City* (Keokuk, Iowa), August 7, 1919.
114. "Terrel gets even." *Evening Times-Republican* (Marshalltown, Iowa), September 16, 1919.
115. "Policeman kills innocent boy, 15." *Washington Times*, September 19, 1919; "Cop kills youth fleeing from gunman." *Sun* (NY), September 19, 1919.
116. "Boy's slayer is freed." *Evening World* (NY), September 24, 1919; "Application for full pay." *Sun* (NY), October 8, 1919.
117. "Policeman kills sergeant." *Seattle Star*, November 3, 1919.
118. "Brown will prosecute patrolman." *Seattle Star*, November 4, 1919; "Jury out only 20 minutes." *Seattle Star*, January 7, 1920.
119. "Detective guilty of flogging man." *Sun and Herald* (NY), February 10, 1920; "Wants

Rowan off force." *New York Times*, March 7, 1920; "Crowd in panic." *New York Tribune*, April 4, 1921.

120. "Policeman kills fleeing robber." *Evening World* (NY), March 31, 1920; "Gunman murdered asleep with wife." *New York Times*, April 1, 1920; "Woman knocked down and robbed in street." *New York Times*, April 26, 1929.

121. "Policeman kills student." *Richmond Times-Dispatch* (VA), May 29, 1920; "Wisconsin student is shot dead by policeman." *New York Tribune*, May 29, 1920.

122. "Policeman who killed student must face trial." *Rock Island Argus* (IL), June 2, 1920; "Policeman who killed student held for trial." *Ogden Standard-Examiner* (Utah), June 18, 1920; "Officer is freed." *Evening Star* (Washington), January 14, 1921.

123. "Policeman indicted as an eye gouger." *Sun and Herald* (NY), September 2, 1920; "2 lay loss of eyes to same policeman." *New York Times*, August 14, 1920.

124. "Cop's case goes over seventh time." *Evening World* (NY), June 15, 1921; "Jury disagrees in case of Coleman, ex-detective." *Evening World* (NY), June 28, 1921.

125. "Mt. Sterling policeman kills man attacking him." *Richmond Daily Register* (KY), September 15, 1920; "Self-defense proven–Stockdale is cleared." *Mt. Sterling Advocate* (KY), September 18, 1920.

126. "Bloodshed in Chicago vote" *Seattle Star*, September 15, 1920.

127. "Policeman kills negro prisoner in St. Louis." *Dallas Express*, November 27, 1920.

Bibliography

Newspaper Articles with Titles

"A. A. Starr accused of manslaughter." *Evening Star* (Washington), October 1, 1919.
"Abandons appeal in manslaughter case." *Evening Star* (Washington), March 16, 1910.
"Accidental shooting." *Evening Star* (Washington), March 6, 1895.
"Accidentally shot." *Evening Star* (Washington), July 30, 1906.
"Accused patrolmen are now suspended." *Minneapolis Journal*, October 7, 1906.
"Accused policeman bailed." *New York Times*, October 8, 1907.
"Accuser of police cleared in court." *Minneapolis Journal*, October 13, 1906.
"Acquitted of a charge of perjury." *New York Tribune*, May 23, 1888.
"Act of a deranged man." *Daily News* (Newport News, VA), March 9, 1909.
"Action in police cases." *Evening Star* (Washington), March 13, 1907.
"Affair in Alexandria." *Evening Star* (Washington), August 4, 1900.
"Alexandria." *Richmond Dispatch* (VA), August 4, 1900.
"Alleged police hazers restored." *New York Tribune*, April 7, 1908.
"Another policeman accused of misconduct." *Sun* (NY), October 26, 1894.
"Antonio Guavara will not wear prison stripes." *Albuquerque Morning Journal*, July 22, 1910.
"Application for full pay." *Sun* (NY), October 8, 1919.
"Armstrong faces trial before board." *Washington Times*, December 22, 1910.
"Armstrong pays fine for Weaver assault." *Washington Times*, January 10, 1911.
"Arrested for 33rd time." *New York Times*, August 2, 1925.
"Ask for jobs lost on story of a coward." *Evening World* (NY), September 21, 1907.
"Assault and battery." *Charleston News* (SC), March 28, 1872.
"Assaulted in her cell." *Evening World* (NY), June 21, 1890.
"Atrocious crime in Chicago street." *Paducah Sun* (KY), February 28, 1905.
"Attorneys for Ellis waive examination." *Guthrie Leader* (OK), September 5, 1901.
"Bail for patrolman Welsh." *New York Tribune*, November 29, 1910.
"Barrett's sentence." *Indianapolis Journal*, April 27, 1889.
"The bartender contradicts Morris." *Sun* (NY), November 14, 1889.
"Baston will appeal to Taft after going to prison." *Washington Times*, June 16, 1911.
"Beat him to death." *Evening Bulletin* (Maysville, KY), April 7, 1898.
"Becker at city hall." *New York Tribune*, July 19, 1912.
"Becker in agony as he hears his doom." *New York Tribune*, October 31, 1912.
"Bell is acquitted." *Pittsburgh Dispatch*, July 17, 1891.
"Bell's trial begins." *Pittsburgh Dispatch*, July 16, 1891.
"Bernauer acquitted by jury on the charge of murdering Richard." *El Paso Herald*, March 22, 1911.
"Bernauer on the witness stand tells why he shot Frank Richard." *El Paso Herald*, March 21, 1911.
"Birdsall good officer gets queer reward." *San Francisco Call*, August 9, 1911.
"Bits of local news." *New York Tribune*, July 29, 1886.

"Blame for death on two policemen." *Minneapolis Journal*, October 6, 1906.
"Blew her brains out for refusing." *Los Angeles Herald*, February 28, 1905.
"Blood again." *New Orleans Daily Democrat*, March 9, 1880.
"Bloodshed in Chicago vote." *Seattle Star*, September 15, 1920.
"Bloodthirsty Barrett." *St. Paul Globe*, October 28, 1888.
"Bloody deeds." *Omaha Daily Bee*, March 12, 1883.
"Bluecoat to pen, for 12 to 20 years." *Star-Independent* (Harrisburg, PA), February 18, 1915.
"Boy killed in chase over roofs after raid on crap game." *New York Tribune*, July 15, 1918.
"Boy, 16, killed by rookie policeman." *Washington Times*, July 9, 1919.
"Boy's slayer is freed." *Evening World* (NY), September 24, 1919.
"The Brennan inquest begun." *New York Times*, July 18, 1891.
"Brevities." *Fort Wayne Weekly Sentinel* (IN), January 11, 1888.
"The brevity basket." *National Republican* (Washington), October 23, 1884.
"Briley claims whiskey saved his life." *Spokane Press*, July 18, 1906.
"Brooklyn." *New York Tribune*, August 17, 1880.
"Brother cops to air troubles." *Sun* (NY), May 23, 1903.
"Brown found guilty." *Evening Bulletin* (Marysville, KY), April 18, 1904.
"Brown will prosecute patrolman." *Seattle Star*, November 4, 1919.
"Brutal cops sentenced." *St. Paul Globe*, February 10, 1895.
"A brutal murder." *Seattle Post-Intelligencer*, October 16, 1890.
"A brute gets off with a ridiculous sentence." *New Albany Ledger* (IN), October 18, 1883.
"A brute with a billy." *Omaha Daily Bee*, November 5, 1883.
"A bullet wildly aimed." *New York Times*, January 22, 1887.
"Burglar dies from wound." *Spokane Press*, April 4, 1906.
"Burzan acquitted of murder charge." *Great Falls Tribune* (MT), November 11, 1921.
"Butte mayor ordered to reinstate Prlja or show cause why." *Great Falls Tribune* (MT), October 23, 1919.
"Butte policeman rally to the aid of convicted officer." *Great Falls Tribune* (MT), May 13, 1919.
"Butte roused." *Pullman Herald* (WA), May 18, 1907.
"Captain Burt's murderer." *Salt Lake Herald*, May 12, 1885.
"Capt. Colby killed." *Evening Star* (Washington), February 5, 1903.
"Capt. Jack Hussey shot." *New York Times*, June 3, 1887.
"Capture effected last evening." *Guthrie Leader* (OK), August 31, 1901.
"Case was continued." *Paducah Sun* (KY), September 8, 1902.
"The Casey jury disagree." *New York Times*, April 26, 1883.
"Casey to have new trial." *New York Times*, May 10, 1884.
"Caught in the courts." *Memphis Appeal* (TN), November 29, 1887.
"Central City policeman kills negro." *Record* (Greenville, KY), December 19, 1912.
"Charged with manslaughter." *New York Times*, December 26, 1885.
"Charged with murder." *Los Angeles Herald*, December 11, 1888.
"Charged with murder." *Times Dispatch* (Richmond, VA), December 29, 1904.
"Charges preferred." *Evening Star* (Washington), August 2, 1906.
"Charges preferred against Conboy." *San Francisco Call*, June 27, 1909.
"Charges revived." *Evening Star* (Washington), May 16, 1907.
"Chase after a policeman." *New York Times*, March 14, 1898.
"The Chattanooga police. *Knoxville Chronicle* (TN), July 27, 1871.
"Chattanooga road." *Knoxville Chronicle* (TN), July 27, 1871.
"The circuit court." *Yorkville Enquirer* (SC), November 18, 1904.
"City and suburban news." *New York Times*, June 24, 1884.
"City and suburban news." *New York Times*, December 23, 1885.
"City and suburban news." *New York Times*, December 24, 1885.
"City and suburban news." *New York Times*, January 27, 1887.
"City and suburban news." *New York Times*, April 22, 1891.
"City and suburban news." *New York Times*, May 21, 1891.
"City news in brief." *New York Times*, December 22, 1906.
"Clemency for policeman." *Evening Star* (Washington), January 5, 1917.
"Clubbed to death." *Pittsburgh Dispatch*, April 24, 1891.

"Clubber spends night in cell." *Evening World* (NY), December 23, 1904.
"Clubber will be suspended." *Evening World* (NY), December 21, 1904.
"Clubbers summoned." *Evening World* (NY), October 2, 1894.
"Coatesville is scene of attempted outrage." *El Paso Herald*, November 21, 1911.
"Collier is bound over to grand jury today." *Washington Times*, March 6, 1909.
"Collier is cool telling of crime." *Washington Times*, December 3, 1909.
"Collier off to prison." *Evening Star* (Washington), March 31, 1910.
"Collier out on bail." *Weekly News* (Washington), December 11, 1909.
"The Comiskey inquest." *New York Times*, March 16, 1883.
"Conboy found guilty." *San Francisco Call*, April 19, 1912.
"Conboy jailed and his victim dying." *San Francisco Call*, June 24, 1909.
"Conboy on trial for Lagan's death." *San Francisco Call*, November 17, 1909.
"Conboy released on giving bond." *San Francisco Call*, June 25, 1909.
"Conboy resigned." *San Francisco Call*, May 12, 1912.
"Condensed locals." *Evening Star* (Washington), July 25, 1872.
"Condensed telegrams." *Norwich Bulletin* (CT), August 16, 1917.
"Condition serious." *Evening Star* (Washington), November 23, 1893.
"Conflicting testimony." *Evening Star* (Washington), July 11, 1890.
"Conroy called insane." *Sun* (NY), December 13, 1883.
"Conroy sentenced to be hanged." *Evening Star* (Washington), December 20, 1883.
"Convicted after a long delay." *New York Times*, February 26, 1903.
"Convicted Butte cop is denied new trial in district court." *Great Falls Tribune* (MT), August 6, 1919.
"Convicted of manslaughter." *Sun* (NY), April 18, 1891.
"Convicted officer of Butte released under $5000 bail." *Great Falls Tribune* (MT), June 30, 1919.
"Conviction of a policeman." *Evening Star* (Washington), February 6, 1874.
"Cop killed fleeing negro." *Kansas City Sun* (MO), November 25, 1916.
"Cop kills boy who tried to steal." *Guthrie Leader* (OK), January 11, 1918.
"Cop kills cop—queer tale." *Day Book* (Chicago), January 28, 1915.
"Cop kills his assailant." *Sun* (NY), September 19, 1906.
"Cop kills manager Mississippi Club." *Daily Press* (Newport News, VA), March 19, 1905.
"Cop kills negro holdup." *Topeka State Journal* (KS), October 12, 1917.
"Cop kills youth fleeing from gunman." *Sun* (NY), September 19, 1919.
"Cop's case goes over seventh time," *Evening World* (NY), June 15, 1921.
"Cops kill 2 robbers." *Topeka State Journal* (KS), November 19, 1917.
"A costly spree." *Evening Star* (Washington), July 19, 1884.
"Couldn't convict the copper." *Pittsburgh Dispatch*, August 9, 1890.
"Council declines to suspend Guavara." *Albuquerque Morning Journal*, February 8, 1910.
"Court acquits policeman." *Washington Herald*, October 26, 1909.
"Court orders Prlja to be reinstated upon police force." *Great Falls Tribune* (MT), September 12, 1920.
"Crime." *Weekly Chillicothe Crisis* (MO), May 13, 1880.
"Crime charged to hasty officer." *Billings Gazette* (MT), March 3, 1908.
"Criminal court's grind for a day." *Pittsburgh Dispatch*, October 2, 1891.
"Cross-examining Hahn." *Evening World* (NY), October 13, 1887.
"Crowd hoots police at slain girl's bier." *New York Times*, July 26, 1908.
"Crowd in panic." *New York Tribune*, April 4, 1921.
"Daft from remorse." *St. Paul Globe*, June 6, 1902.
"Daly dead; sleuth held who shot him." *New York Times*, July 29, 1904.
"Danville." *Dispatch* (Richmond, VA), March 6, 1884.
"Dauphin man pardoned." *Star-Independent* (Harrisburg, PA), November 19, 1914.
"Death of police prisoner probed." *Minneapolis Journal*, October 1, 1906.
"A death struggle." *Herald-Tribune* (Lawrence, KS), January 1, 1886.
"Death was instant." *Evening Star* (Washington), March 5, 1895.
"Declares he is sorry; makes plea for mercy." *Evening Star* (Washington), March 10, 1911.
"The defendant's testimony." *Salt Lake Herald*, May 14, 1885.
"Denied a Catholic burial." *Pittsburgh Dispatch*, July 17, 1891.
"Denounce Foster's slayer." *Evening Star* (Washington), May 7, 1895.

"Denver detective guilty of murder." *Salt Lake Tribune*, May 14, 1904.
"Denver murder." *Clayton Enterprise* (NM), February 16, 1906.
"Detective convicted of assault in subway." *Evening World* (NY), December 14, 1916.
"Detective guilty of assault." *Tacoma Times*, January 22, 1913.
"Detective guilty of flogging man." *Sun and Herald* (NY), February 10, 1920.
"Detective kills man." *New York Times*, August 4, 1904.
"Detective who shot man suspended." *Sun* (NY), August 7, 1904.
"Died from his injuries." *New York Times*, December 7, 1883.
"Died of his wounds." *Edgefield Advertiser* (SC), May 4, 1904.
"Dillon convicted." *New York Tribune*, June 26, 1909.
"Dillon goes to Sing Sing." *New York Times*, June 30, 1909.
"Dining car waiter shot." *Ogden Standard* (UT), April 28, 1909.
"Disagreed on Daly killing." *Sun* (NY), August 10, 1904.
"A disgraced policeman imprisoned." *Sun* (NY), July 9, 1890.
"Dismiss appeal of former officer after his death." *Great Falls Tribune* (MT), March 15, 1922.
"Dismissed from the force." *Evening Star* (Washington), April 1, 1909.
"The Dockery-Rogers case." *Semi-Weekly Messenger* (Wilmington, NC), January 12, 1906.
"Double tragedy." *Times and Democrat* (Orangeburg, SC), June 19, 1909.
"Double tragedy in Concord, N.H." *Vermont Phoenix* (Brattleboro, VT), September 28, 1906.
"Downie was thug killed." *New York Times*, February 6, 1914.
"Drunken policeman kills traveling man." *Salt Lake Tribune*, February 10, 1906.
"Dying of his wound." *New York Times*, October 23, 1889.
"Dying, he runs two blocks." *Evening World* (NY), February 28, 1917.
"Eight years for Goodman." *Bamberg Herald* (SC), October 27, 1904.
"Ending with a murder." *Sun* (NY), November 5, 1883.
"Ennis to die in chair July 7." *Evening World* (NY), May 26, 1902.
"Ex-bluecoat freed by jury." *Washington Herald*, October 20, 1920.
"Exchange gleanings." *Ocala Evening Star* (FL), November 25, 1896.
"Ex-policeman a murderer." *New York Times*, May 23, 1902.
"Ex-policeman sentenced." *New York Times*, February 28, 1903.
"Facts and figures." *Plymouth Democrat* (IN), April 7, 1870.
"A fatal accident." *Evening Star* (Washington), March 11, 1902.
"Fatal battle with gang of tramps." *Capital Journal* (Salem, OR), November 25, 1907.
"Fatal billy blow." *St. Landry Clarion* (Opelousas, LA), October 5, 1907.
"Fellow officers will aid Walsh." *Seattle Star*, January 21, 1910.
"Fifth Ward cop indicted." *Evening Public Ledger* (Philadelphia), June 6, 1918.
"The final summons calls Michael Crowley." *Lock Haven Express* (PA), March 13, 1905.
"Find Collier guilty." *Evening Star* (Washington), December 5, 1909.
"Fired to frighten." *Ohio Democrat* (Logan, Ohio), November 14, 1901.
"First degree Becker verdict." *Forest Republican* (Tionesta, PA), October 30, 1912.
"$532 and cop who killed boy missing." *Washington Times*, September 19, 1919.
"Five policemen broken" *Sun* (NY), November 13, 1889.
"Fleeing man killed." *Evening Star* (Washington), March 25, 1903.
"Flood is given 3 years." *New York Times*, March 25, 1921.
"For manslaughter." *Princeton Union* (MN), December 14, 1893.
"For wife murder." *Evening World* (NY), January 9, 1891.
"Former officer nabbed at a fire." *Washington Herald*, March 29, 1911.
"Former officer shot six times at Butte." *Great Falls Tribune* (MT), March 22, 1921.
"Former policeman guilty." *Daily News* (Newport News, VA), October 1, 1910.
"Former policeman killed." *Daily Ardmoreite* (Ardmore, OK), November 5, 1908.
"Former policeman seeks a new trial." *Washington Times*, February 10, 1911.
"Former policeman sentenced." *Evening Star* (Washington), March 7, 1920.
"Found guilty of manslaughter." *New Orleans Democrat*, November 8, 1879.
"Found worthy of death." *Sun* (NY), December 18, 1883.
"Four cops convicted for beating sailors." *Evening Public Ledger* (Philadelphia), June 26, 1917.
"Four homicide indictments." *Pittsburgh Dispatch*, June 6, 1891.
"Free patrolman who slew." *Broad Ax* (Salt Lake), July 11, 1908.

"Fulton policeman kills a negro." *Hickman Courier* (KY), July 23, 1914.
"Fund is start for accused man." *Washington Herald*, March 9, 1909.
"Gamblers keep off." *Sun* (NY), July 8, 1909.
"A gang of police ruffians." *New York Tribune*, October 3, 1894.
"Gaynor and the police." *Norfolk Weekly News-Journal* (VA), September 2, 1910.
"Gaynor nullifies system." *Thibodaux Sentinel* (LA), February 26, 1910.
"General domestic." *St. Louis Republic*, October 26, 1901.
"General sessions." *Yorkville Enquirer* (SC), December 3, 1912.
"George Allen case remanded." *Comet* (Johnson City, TN), October 12, 1905.
"The Georgetown tragedy." *Evening Star* (Washington), July 17, 1872.
"Given their medicine." *Pittsburgh Dispatch*, December 21, 1890.
"Got his desserts." *Wheeling Intelligencer* (WV), December 6, 1883.
"Governor pardons Cornelius J. Flood." *New York Times*, December 9, 1925.
"Governor recommends a pardon for Prlja." *Great Falls Tribune* (MT), April 8, 1920.
"Green to be tried." *Evening Star* (Washington), May 6, 1895.
"Green's pistol." *Evening Star* (Washington), March 12, 1895.
"Greenville policeman kills." *Keowee Courier* (Pickens, SC), November 4, 1914.
"Grief stricken sister complains." *San Francisco Call*, October 12, 1909.
"Guavara guilty of assault with weapon." *Albuquerque Morning Journal*, May 1, 1910.
"Guilty of clubbing woman" *New York Times*, February 16, 1912.
"Guilty of murder." *Salt Lake Herald*, March 28, 1906.
"Gunman murdered asleep with wife." *New York Times*, April 1, 1920.
"Gus Travis was accidentally killed." *Ogden Standard* (Utah), April 29, 1909.
"Hahn tells his story." *New York Times*, October 13, 1887.
"Hahn's cowardly shot." *New York Times*, June 4, 1887.
"Hahn's neck saved." *Evening World* (NY), October 14, 1887.
"Hall is arrested." *Topeka State Journal* (KS), April 29, 1901.
"Hall let out." *Topeka State Journal* (KS), December 9, 1901.
"Hall must go." *Topeka State Journal* (KS), July 23, 1901.
"Hall pleads guilty." *Topeka State Journal* (KS), July 6, 1901.
"Happy baby knows nothing of tragedy in Baston home." *Washington Times*, October 2, 1910.
"Hartje offers a million to wife." *New York Times*, October 8, 1907.
"He aimed too low." *St. Paul Globe*, October 1, 1890.
"Heard own pardon case presented." *Harrisburg Telegraph* (PA), November 18, 1914.
"Hearing of testimony." *Evening Star* (Washington), October 19, 1906.
"Held for a murder." *Pittsburgh Dispatch*, April 26, 1891.
"Held for grand jury." *Evening Star* (Washington), April 1, 1903.
"Held for stray bullet death." *Sun* (NY), January 14, 1911.
"Here and there." *Interior Journal* (Stanford, KY), June 15, 1909.
"Higgins sent up." *Minneapolis Journal*, October 22, 1906.
"Hightower killed." *Bryan Morning Eagle* (TX), August 1, 1906.
"His aim excellent." *St. Paul Globe*, November 15, 1886.
"Homicide in Alexandria." *Richmond Dispatch* (VA), August 3, 1900.
"How a murderer was cunningly caught and executed." *Deseret Evening News* (Salt Lake), December 14, 1903.
"Hurt, man walks around for days." *Seattle Star*, July 1, 1910.
"Hutchinson's tale of woe." *Evening Star* (Washington), June 4, 1890.
"Ignored again." *Evening Star* (Washington), April 19, 1895.
"In name of charity." *Topeka State Journal* (KS), April 1, 1909.
"In quest on the Brennans." *Evening World* (NY), July 15, 1891.
"In self-defence." *Minneapolis Journal*, August 26, 1901.
"Indictment dismissed." *Evening World* (NY), May 2, 1894.
"Indignation meetings." *Evening Star* (Washington), March 7, 1895.
"Innocent man, shot by police is dying." *Seattle Star*, December 23, 1909.
"Is killed by policeman as he eats." *El Paso Herald*, January 19, 1911.
"It was manslaughter." *New Orleans Daily Democrat*, March 10, 1880.
"It was murder." *Washington Times*, March 6, 1895.

"Italians determined to get facts." *Seattle Star*, December 22, 1909.
"Italians say policeman killed boy; riot feared." *Los Angeles Herald*, January 19, 1910.
"Jack Hussey's murderer." *Evening World* (NY), October 10, 1887.
"Jailbreak is futile." *Daily Missoulian* (Missoula, MT), January 5, 1913.
"JtDockery shot." *Semi-Weekly Messenger* (Wilmington, NC), June 27, 1905.
"John Hussey's slayer missed his train." *Sun* (NY), January 12, 1888.
"Joy turns to sadness." *Salt Lake Herald*, March 2, 1908.
"Judge lauds McNamee in fining him for shooting." *Seattle Star*, February 3, 1913.
"Judge Mayer's charge." *Lock Haven Express* (PA), January 9, 1904.
"July 4th casualties." *Evening Star* (Washington), July 5, 1905.
"Jury charges Conboy with Lagan murder." *San Francisco Call*, October 14, 1909.
"The jury decides Frank Ellis Sane." *Guthrie Leader* (OK), February 17, 1902.
"Jury disagrees in case of Coleman, ex-detective." *Evening World* (NY), June 28, 1921.
"Jury disagrees in Shellard case." *New York Times*, January 22, 1909.
"Jury may give verdict to-night." *Star-Independent* (Harrisburg, PA), January 18, 1915.
"Jury out only 20 minutes." *Seattle Star*, January 7, 1920.
"Jury picked for trial of Scott." *Star-Independent* (Harrisburg, PA), January 16, 1915.
"Justifies the deed." *Evening Star* (Washington), August 3, 1909.
"Kearney condemned." *Boston Globe*, October 24, 1890.
"Kearney not guilty." *Boston Globe*, January 3, 1891.
"Kearney out." *Boston Globe*, January 5, 1891.
"Kearney's tears." *Boston Globe*, January 1, 1891.
"Kelley takes care of faithful." *Butte Bulletin* (MT), July 12, 1919.
"Killed." *Knoxville Chronicle* (TN), July 25, 1871.
"Killed a brother officer." *Salt Lake Herald*, May 18, 1899.
"Killed by a policeman." *Alexandria Gazette* (VA), March 25, 1903.
"Killed by a policeman." *Bryan Morning Eagle* (TX), January 15, 1902.
"Killed by a policeman." *National Republican* (Washington), December 25, 1885.
"Killed by a policeman." *New York Times*, August 1, 1897.
"Killed by a policeman." *New York Tribune*, November 5, 1883.
"Killed by a policeman." *St. Paul Globe*, September 22, 1882.
"Killed by his friend." *Hocking Sentinel* (Logan, Ohio), October 27, 1904.
"Killed by officer." *Topeka State Journal* (KS), April 27, 1901.
"Killed by policemen." *Sun* (NY), December 26, 1893.
"Killed for a fool joke." *Wenatchee World* (WA), February 14, 1908.
"Killed for stealing a bottle of whisky." *Rogue River Courier* (Grants Pass, OR), August 16, 1907.
"Killed in a man hunt." *New York Times*, February 6, 1903.
"Killed in struggle with a policeman." *St. Louis Republic*, September 3, 1902.
"Killing by mistake." *Deseret Evening News* (Salt Lake), April 5, 1909.
"Kills captain." *Washington Herald*, March 6, 1909.
"Kills children then self." *Evening Star* (Washington), January 16, 1916.
"Kills fleeing thug; remains on duty." *Sun* (NY), February 5, 1914.
"Kills Herbert's protégé." *New York Times*, April 26, 1905.
"Kills the fugitive who refuses to halt." *San Francisco Call*, May 2, 1902.
"Lancaster freed by jury's verdict." *Abbeville Press and Banner* (SC), September 23, 1919.
"Lancaster freed by jury's verdict." *Manning Times* (SC), September 24, 1919.
"Large funeral." *Kentucky Irish American* (Louisville), November 22, 1902.
"Latest local." *Star* (Cincinnati), February 18, 1875.
"Latest telegraphic brevities." *National Republican* (Washington), April 29, 1870.
"Law report." *Star* (Cincinnati), January 25, 1875.
"Lecturing policemen." *New York Tribune*, January 7, 1886.
"Lewis gets ten year sentence." *Paducah Sun* (NY), March 23, 1910.
"Lieut. Foody dismissed." *New York Times*, March 1, 1911.
"A life sentence for Frank Ellis." *Guthrie Leader* (OK), March 21, 1902.
"Limit powers." *Evening Times* (Grand Forks, ND), December 11, 1912.
"Lipscomb loses place on force." *Washington Times*, February 14, 1907.
"Listening to a mocking bird." *Evening Critic* (Washington), June 9, 1884.

"Local doings in tabloid form." *Day Book* (Chicago), March 17, 1913.
"Local items." *Charlotte Democrat* (NC), October 18, 1875.
"Local items." *State Journal* (Jefferson City, MO), January 5, 1877.
"Local news." *East Oregonian* (Pendleton), April 5, 1906.
"Local paragraphs." *Memphis Appeal* (TN), March 14, 1888.
"Locked up on charge of murder." *San Francisco Call*, October 7, 1909.
"Long sentence for policeman." *Evening World* (NY), December 16, 1904.
"Long term in prison." *Evening Star* (Washington), January 7, 1910.
"Mallon out on bail." *New York Times*, March 18, 1905.
"Man is shot dead in chase for steer." *Bemidji Daily Pioneer* (MN), November 4, 1913.
"Manlius." *Princeton Bureau County Tribune* (IL), January 31, 1908.
"Manslaughter if cop kills." *Columbian* (Bloomsburg, PA), October 24, 1907.
"Matthew Bell at liberty." *Pittsburgh Dispatch*, July 21, 1891.
"May be tried again." *Evening Star* (Washington), October 10, 1894.
"McNamara admitted to bail." *Sun* (NY), September 11, 1883.
"Men and women shot in riot." *Evening World* (NY), May 27, 1904.
"The metropolis." *Sacramento Record-Union*, October 2, 1884.
"Michael Conboy loses fight for ticket of leave." *San Francisco Call*, August 24, 1913.
"Mill City policeman kills alleged holdup." *Little Falls Herald* (MN), April 5, 1918.
"Minneapolis policemen indicted." *Bemidji Pioneer* (MN), October 19, 1906.
"Mr. Schwarzler's assailants." *New York Times*, February 19, 1886.
"Mob demanded officer's life." *Salt Lake Herald*, May 11, 1907.
"Monday morning murder." *Comet* (Johnson City, TN), October 1, 1903.
"More indictments for burning of negro," *Norwich Bulletin* (CT), September 21, 1911.
"More policemen in trouble." *Sun* (NY), March 24, 1910.
"The morning's news." *Sacramento Record-Union*, January 2, 1882.
"Motive is advanced for Mathews murder." *Washington Times*, March 7, 1909.
"Mrs. Frank Ellis dead at Bridgeport." *Guthrie Leader* (OK), May 19, 1903.
"Mt. Sterling policeman kills man attacking him." *Richmond Daily Register* (KY), September 15, 1920.
"Murder charge not sustained." *Arizona Republican* (Phoenix, AZ), February 3, 1916.
"Murder in Columbia." *Anderson Intelligencer* (SC), June 26, 1879.
"Murder in the first degree." *New York Times*, May 24, 1883.
"Murdered by a policeman." *Boston Post*, August 31, 1883.
"Murdered by a policeman." *Nashville Union and American*, August 26, 1869.
"Murdered by a policeman." *New York Times*, March 12, 1883.
"Murderer Ennis's condition." *New York Times*, November 25, 1903.
"Murderers bailed." *Evening Star* (Washington), November 20, 1878.
"A murdering policeman dismissed." *New York Tribune*, September 13, 1883.
"The murderous policeman." *Los Angeles Herald*, April 23, 1889.
"Murderous policeman." *New York Tribune*, January 22, 1887.
"A murderous policeman arrested." *Bismarck Tribune* (ND), August 31, 1883.
"Murderous policeman convicted." *Seattle Post-Intelligencer*, February 7, 1889.
"Mysterious shooting explained." *Manchester Democrat* (Iowa), January 29, 1913.
"Mystery of shooting of supposed burglar." *New York Times*, June 5, 1904.
"A narrow conviction." *Memphis Appeal* (TN), November 27, 1887.
"New policeman kills his dearest friend." *San Francisco Call*, February 13, 1908.
"New trial for cop who killed." *Sun* (NY), April 1, 1905.
"New trial refused." *Tazewell Republican* (VA), November 24, 1910.
"New York policeman guilty of manslaughter." *Norwich Bulletin* (CT), March 19, 1921.
"New York startled by murder of gambler." *Day Book* (Chicago), July 16, 1912.
"Newark a little wet." *New York Tribune*, July 23, 1906.
"Newark detective held." *Sun* (NY), August 5, 1904.
"News in brief." *Bolivar Bulletin* (TN), November 19, 1886.
"News in Minnesota." *Little Falls Herald* (MN), March 15, 1907.
"News of Pounding Mill." *Clinch Valley News* (Jeffersonville, VA), August 7, 1914.
"News of the day concerning Chicago." *Day Book* (Chicago), December 20, 1913.
"No evidence given that policeman killed student." *Evening World* (NY), May 30, 1911.

"No jurisdiction." *Brooklyn Eagle*, August 21, 1880.
"No pardon yet for policeman." *El Paso Herald*, August 7, 1913.
"Not even suspended." *Stark County Democrat* (Canton, Ohio), February 21, 1878.
"Not guilty." *Salt Lake Herald*, May 15, 1885.
"O'Brien's commutation." *Evening Star* (Washington), March 26, 1873.
"Officer Cross suspended." *Pittsburgh Dispatch*, March 4, 1892.
"Officer Dean acquitted." *Sunday Herald* (Washington), July 13, 1890.
"Officer Ellis acquitted." *National Republican* (Washington), December 18, 1884.
"Officer Frank Ellis becomes a murderer." *Guthrie Leader* (OK), August 30, 1901.
"Officer Green's revolver." *Evening Star* (Washington), May 28, 1895.
"The officer guilty." *Evening Star* (Washington), May 23, 1894.
"Officer held for shooting." *Rock Island Argus* (IL), May 25, 1907.
"Officer Holsworth." *Brooklyn Eagle*, January 30, 1891.
"Officer is freed." *Evening Star* (Washington), January 14, 1921.
"Officer McNamara dismissed." *New York Times*, September 13, 1883.
"An officer shot." *Evening Bulletin* (Maysville, KY), December 31, 1887.
"Officers on trial for assault." *Pittsburgh Dispatch*, December 11, 1890.
"On trial for wife murder." *New York Times*, April 16, 1891.
"One policeman kills another." *Houston Post*, February 9, 1903.
"One policeman kills another." *Rock Island Argus* (IL), February 11, 1899.
"One policeman shoots another." *Evening World* (NY), March 28, 1903.
"Others share blame." *Elkhart Daily Review* (IN), December 11, 1907.
"Our letter from Broadbrim." *Donaldson Chief* (LA), November 17, 1883.
"Pacific coast." *Los Angeles Herald*, December 6, 1888.
"Paints Conboy as defending his life." *San Francisco Call*, February 16, 1910.
"A pardoned convict's child." *Evening Star* (Washington), January 16, 1879.
"Patrolman Brown dismissed." *St. Louis Republic*, June 21, 1902.
"Patrolman confesses he killed his chief," *San Francisco Call*, December 17, 1912.
"Patrolman found guilty of second degree murder." *Star-Independent* (Harrisburg, PA), January 19, 1915.
"Patrolman is on trial for killing." *Seattle Star*, June 22, 1910.
"Patrolman kills deputy police." *Salt Lake Tribune*, December 16, 1912.
"Patrolman must serve sentence." *New York Tribune*, June 15, 1907.
"Patrolman O'Hearn suspended." *St. Louis Republic*, October 23, 1904.
"Perjury fails to save them." *Sun* (NY), June 8, 1907.
"Perjury is charged in Conboy case." *San Francisco Call*, February 9, 1910.
"Personals." *Little Falls Weekly Transcript* (MN), September 1, 1899.
"Pet dogs and cats guard slain couple." *New York Times*, April 7, 1915.
"A Philadelphia policeman kills two men." *Evening Star* (Washington), April 27, 1870.
"Pocatello policeman kills fighting negro." *Deseret Evening News* (Salt Lake), April 28, 1909.
"Police board and O'Brien." *New York Times*, August 12, 1897.
"Police captain shoots to kill." *Evening Statesman* (Walla Walla, WA), June 23, 1909.
"Police clubber convicted." *New York Times*, March 2, 1907.
"Police court." *Cincinnati Star*, October 9, 1876.
"Police court." *Star* (Cincinnati), January 5, 1875.
"Police jottings." *Topeka State Journal* (KS), December 9, 1901.
"Police murders." *New Albany Daily Ledger* (IN), August 30, 1869.
"Police officer convicted." *Daily Ardmoreite* (Ardmore, OK), February 16, 1908.
"Police officer kills man." *Daily Press* (Newport News, VA), June 24, 1909.
"A police officer sentenced." *San Francisco Call*, July 19, 1893.
"Police officers convicted." *Arizona Republican* (Phoenix, AZ), March 11, 1914.
"Police outrage." *Advocate* (Topeka, KS), September 4, 1895.
"Police try to kill a cowboy." *Los Angeles Herald*, August 27, 1908.
"Police victim a convict." *Evening Public Ledger* (Philadelphia), June 14, 1915.
"Policeman accused of assault to murder." *San Francisco Call*, December 2, 1910.
"Policeman Antonio Guavara still carries his ready gun." *Albuquerque Morning Journal*, January 10, 1910.

"Policeman Armstrong before police judge." *Evening Star* (Washington), December 14, 1910.
"Policeman badly beaten." *Sun* (NY), May 3, 1907.
"Policeman Bernard Murphy vindicated." *Sun* (NY), November 1, 1895.
"Policeman Conroy to be imprisoned for life." *Sun* (NY), April 23, 1885.
"A policeman convicted of assault." *Evening Star* (Washington), July 5, 1889.
"Policeman convicted of assault." *New York Tribune*, April 19, 1902.
"Policeman convicted of assault." *New York Tribune*, March 2, 1907.
"Policeman convicted of assaulting neighbor." *Evening World* (NY), February 25, 1903.
"Policeman convicted of manslaughter." *Globe-Republican* (Dodge City, KS), February 13, 1896.
"Policeman Dean acquitted." *Evening Star* (Washington), July 14, 1890.
"Policeman dies of grief." *New York Times*, July 22, 1908.
"A policeman fined." *Times* (Richmond, VA), May 16, 1901.
"Policeman fells woman in street." *New York Times*, November 14, 1911.
"Policeman freed on murder charge." *Evening World* (NY), May 12, 1904.
"Policeman gets 30 years for murder." *Evening World* (NY), May 13, 1915.
"Policeman Glennon suspended." *Sacramento Record-Union*, September 28, 1888.
"Policeman goes to jail." *Sun* (NY), October 20, 1907.
"Policeman guilty of assault." *New York Tribune*, May 8, 1907.
"Policeman guilty of assault and drunkenness." *Norwich Bulletin* (CT), December 17, 1918.
"Policeman guilty of assault with club." *Spokane Press*, May 4, 1909.
"Policeman guilty of manslaughter." *New York Times*, June 11, 1902.
"Policeman guilty of manslaughter." *Marion Daily Mirror* (Ohio), February 27, 1911.
"Policeman guilty of manslaughter in killing youth." *Evening Public Ledger* (Philadelphia), October 27, 1914.
"Policeman held as slayer of another." *Sun* (NY), February 26, 1915.
"Policeman held for death." *New York Times*, May 24, 1908.
"Policeman held for first degree murder." *New York Times*, August 5, 1904.
"Policeman held for murder." *New York Times*, December 24, 1904.
"Policeman held for murder." *St. Louis Republic*, April 30, 1902.
"Policeman Holsworth at bar." *Evening World* (NY), December 24, 1890.
"A policeman indicted." *Evening Times* (Washington), March 26, 1898.
"Policeman indicted." *Paducah Sun* (KY), May 12, 1902.
"Policeman indicted." *Semi-Weekly Messenger* (Wilmington, NC), June 9, 1899.
"Policeman indicted." *Times* (Richmond, VA), March 22, 1910.
"Policeman indicted as an eye gouger." *Sun and Herald* (NY), September 2, 1920.
"A policeman indicted for assault." *New York Tribune*, November 3, 1894.
"Policeman indicted for murder." *Evening Star* (Washington), May 17, 1905.
"Policeman indicted on assault charge. *St. Louis Republic*, May 11, 1905.
"Policeman is held for Manning's death." *St. Louis Republic*, September 4, 1902.
"Policeman is indicted." *Evening Star* (Washington), March 4, 1919.
"Policeman jailed as girl's assailant." *Minneapolis Journal*, July 13, 1906.
"Policeman jailed for killing man." *Washington Times*, May 24, 1908.
"Policeman Kelly on trial." *New York Times*, May 13, 1910.
"Policeman killed a burglar." *Cameron County Press* (Emporium, PA), February 8, 1906.
"Policeman killed a politician." *Evening Star* (Washington), July 6, 1905.
"Policeman killed a teamster." *Marion Daily Mirror* (Ohio), June 30, 1908.
"Policeman killed at pistol practice." *Evening Statesman* (Walla Walla, WA), October 22, 1904.
"Policeman killed boy." *Daily Press* (Newport News, VA), April 26, 1905.
"Policeman killed by brother officer." *Climax* (Richmond, VA), October 22, 1890.
"Policeman killed him." *Pullman Herald* (WA), May 4, 1901.
"Policeman killed him." *Salt Lake Herald*, December 29, 1901.
"Policeman killed him as he ran." *Evening World* (NY), June 4, 1904.
"Policeman killed mill operative." *Bamberg Herald* (SC), June 20, 1912.
"Policeman kills." *Cameron County Press* (Emporium, PA), July 2, 1903.
"Policeman kills a boy by mistake." *New York Times*, May 28, 1911.
"Policeman kills a burglar." *Evening Star* (Washington), September 6, 1897.
"Policeman kills a drunkard." *Greenville Journal* (Ohio), June 30, 1910.

"Policeman kills a gambler." *Omaha Daily Bee*, November 12, 1900.
"Policeman kills a man." *New York Tribune*, November 3, 1904.
"A policeman kills a man." *Semi-Weekly Messenger* (Wilmington, NC), October 2, 1903.
"A policeman kills a man, and then shoots himself." *Stark County Democrat* (Canton, Ohio), August 28, 1879.
"Policeman kills a negro." *Daily News* (Newport News, VA), May 29, 1909.
"A policeman kills a planter." *Evening Star* (Washington), June 24, 1879.
"Policeman kills a politician." *Princeton Union* (MN), September 4, 1902.
"A policeman kills soldier." *Times Dispatch* (Richmond, VA), May 12, 1905.
"Policeman kills a student." *Richmond Times-Dispatch* (VA), May 29, 1920.
"Policeman kills a tobacco agent." *Ogden Standard* (Utah), September 25, 1913.
"Policeman kills a tormentor." *Times* (Washington), August 1, 1897.
"Policeman kills a woman." *Columbus Journal* (NE), September 21, 1910.
"Policeman kills actor." *Albuquerque Morning Journal*, August 3, 1906.
"Policeman kills another." *Bemidji Pioneer* (MN), February 9, 1917.
"Policeman kills another." *Manning Times* (SC), October 5, 1904.
"Policeman kills baby." *New York Tribune*, November 14, 1917.
"Policeman kills bad negro." *Red Cloud Chief* (NE), September 4, 1908.
"Policeman kills big negro." *Bamberg Herald* (SC), August 6, 1914.
"Policeman kills bread-box robber." *Times Dispatch* (Richmond, VA), March 28, 1907.
"Policeman kills brother officer." *Washington Times*, February 25, 1915.
"Policeman kills burglar." *Bisbee Daily Review*, April 26, 1919.
"Policeman kills captain." *Evening Star* (Washington), February 5, 1907.
"Policeman kills children and self." *Omaha Daily Bee*, January 16, 1916.
"Policeman kills cigar man." *Washington State Journal* (Ritzville, WA), October 9, 1907.
"Policeman kills coroner." *Bamberg Herald* (SC), October 18, 1917.
"Policeman kills dog; same bullet hits boy." *New York Tribune*, July 24, 1919.
"Policeman kills drummer." *Paducah Sun* (KY), February 9, 1906.
"Policeman kills escaping bandit." *Washington Times*, May 11, 1907.
"Policeman kills father." *New York Times*, August 15, 1917.
"Policeman kills fleeing robber." *Evening World* (NY), March 31, 1920.
"Policeman kills fleeing robber." *Sun* (NY), February 5, 1914.
"Policeman kills fugitive." *Evening World* (NY), March 1, 1917.
"Policeman kills fugitive." *New York Tribune*, October 13, 1911.
"Policeman kills fugitive." *Rock Island Argus* (IL), May 24, 1907.
"Policeman kills fugitive." *Sun* (NY), June 13, 1914.
"Policeman kills gambler." *St. Louis Republic*, November 12, 1900.
"Policeman kills girl." *Marion Daily Mirror* (OH), June 29, 1909.
"Policeman kills himself." *New York Tribune*, October 28, 1910.
"Policeman kills himself and wife." *Times* (Richmond, VA), October 26, 1902.
"Policeman kills his best friend." *Evening World* (NY), November 3, 1904.
"Policeman kills his chief." *Tulsa Daily World*, July 13, 1917.
"Policeman kills his wife." *Bismarck Tribune* (ND), April 4, 1902.
"Policeman kills his wife." *New York Times*, April 3, 1902.
"Policeman kills infantry bandman." *Logan Republican* (Utah), January 24, 1911.
"Policeman kills innocent boy, 15." *Washington Times*, September 19, 1919.
"Policeman kills innocent man." *Los Angeles Herald*, November 25, 1907.
"Policeman kills liveryman." *Washington Herald*, December 25, 1911.
"Policeman kills man." *New York Times*, November 3, 1904.
"Policeman kills man for burglar." *Los Angeles Herald*, March 21, 1909.
"Policeman kills man in running battle." *Salt Lake Tribune*, August 14, 1907.
"Policeman kills man in scuffle." *Oklahoma City Times*, May 13, 1919.
"Policeman kills minister's son." *Yale Expositor* (MI), August 30, 1901.
"Policeman kills negress." *Bamberg Herald* (SC), November 18, 1909.
"Policeman kills negro." *Bamberg Herald* (SC), September 16, 1909.
"Policeman kills negro." *Bamberg Herald* (SC), May 2, 1912.
"Policeman kills negro." *Day Book* (Chicago), June 16, 1913.

"Policeman kills negro." *Herald and News* (Newberry, SC), May 21, 1912.
"Policeman kills negro." *Manning Times* (SC), October 28, 1914.
"Policeman kills negro." *Mt. Sterling Advocate* (KY), August 25, 1915.
"Policeman kills negro prisoner in St. Louis." *Dallas Express*, November 27, 1920.
"Policeman kills negro woman." *Tensas Gazette* (St. Joseph, LA), November 19, 1909.
"Policeman kills one of two assailants." *Evening Public Ledger* (Philadelphia), September 13, 1918.
"Policeman kills policeman." *Evening World* (NY), January 31, 1894.
"Policeman kills policeman." *Washington Times*, February 9, 1903.
"Policeman kills pugilist." *Evening Star* (Washington), June 16, 1900.
"Policeman kills relative." *Pioneer Express* (Pembina, ND), March 21, 1913.
"Policeman kills rioter." *Daily News* (Newport News, VA), March 1, 1910.
"Policeman kills sergeant." *Seattle Star*, November 3, 1919.
"Policeman kills sleeping wife and himself." *New York Tribune*, April 7, 1915.
"Policeman kills soldier." *Daily Gate City* (Keokuk, Iowa), August 7, 1919.
"Policeman kills soldier." *East Oregonian* (Pendleton, OR), September 20, 1911.
"A policeman kills the wrong man." *Evening Star* (Washington), May 18, 1889.
"Policeman kills thief." *San Francisco Call*, July 5, 1903.
"Policeman kills 13-year-old bandit." *Evening Public Ledger* (Philadelphia), March 9, 1918.
"Policeman kills three." *Salt Lake Tribune*, August 11, 1905.
"Policeman kills two." *St. Paul Globe*, January 14, 1902.
"A policeman kills two assailants." *Seattle Post-Intelligencer*, July 15, 1891.
"Policeman kills two boys with one shot." *East Oregonian* (Pendleton, OR), October 27, 1915.
"Policeman kills two men." *Butte Inter Mountain* (MT), January 13, 1902.
"Policeman kills wife and himself." *Sun* (NY), April 7, 1915.
"Policeman kills wife on street." *Washington Herald*, October 2, 1910.
"Policeman kills wife; planned a triple crime." *Evening World* (NY), January 14, 1902.
"Policeman kills young man." *Bemidji Daily Pioneer* (MN), March 29, 1910.
"Policeman kills young man." *Omaha Daily Bee*, August 5, 1905.
"Policeman kills youthful rioter." *Washington Herald*, December 26, 1910.
"Policeman Lipscomb resigns from force." *Washington Times*, March 17, 1907.
"Policeman McNamara held." *Sun* (NY), September 4, 1883.
"Policeman O'Brien sentenced." *New York Times*, June 22, 1902.
"A policeman of Monroe." *Caucasian* (Shreveport, LA), November 16, 1909.
"Policeman on a rampage." *New York Times*, October 25, 1910.
"Policeman on trial." *New York Times*, December 7, 1904.
"Policeman scot-free." *Sun* (NY), March 8, 1906.
"Policeman sentenced." *New York Tribune*, March 7, 1907.
"Policeman sentenced to jail." *Star-Independent* (Harrisburg, PA), October 31, 1914.
"Policeman sentenced to 2 years hard labor." *Maui News* (Wailuku, HI), December 6, 1918.
"Policeman Shellard held without bail." *New York Times*, July 25, 1908.
"Policeman Shellard out on bail." *New York Times*, August 14, 1908.
"Policeman shoots boy in gambling quarrel." *Maui News* (Wailuku, HI), November 1, 1918.
"Policeman shot in rifle range." *Evening World* (NY), January 16, 1905.
"Policeman shot man in a Bowery tussle." *New York Times*, May 9, 1904.
"Policeman Smith guilty." *New York Times*, April 18, 1891.
"Policeman under charges." *Evening Star* (Washington), October 3, 1906.
"Policeman who admits killing of boy is held." *Evening World* (NY), May 23, 1908.
"Policeman who killed student held for trial." *Ogden Standard-Examiner* (Utah), June 18, 1920.
"Policeman who killed student must face trial." *Rock Island Argus* (IL), June 2, 1920.
"Policeman's awful crime." *New York Tribune*, August 12, 1898.
"A policeman's bad shot." *New York Times*, October 21, 1889.
"A policeman's fatal shot." *Times* (Richmond, VA), August 3, 1900.
"Policeman's pistol killed Barbara Reig." *New York Times*, July 24, 1908.
"Policeman's victim dies." *St. Louis Republic*, April 21, 1902.
"Policeman's victim known to police." *San Francisco Call*, November 8, 1910.
"Policemen arrested for murder." *New York Times*, November 18, 1878.
"Policemen held in boy's death stay in Tombs." *New York Tribune*, February 12, 1921.

"Policemen kill and wound men." *Ogden Standard* (Utah), November 3, 1913.
"Policemen to receive no furloughs this summer." *St. Louis Republic*, April 23, 1904.
"Political feud." *Evening Bulletin* (Maysville, KY), November 14, 1902.
"Prison now for Smith." *Evening World* (NY), June 19, 1891.
"Prisoner's struggle to escape fatal." *Minneapolis Journal*, September 30, 1906.
"Prlja convicted of assault on Burzan." *Butte Bulletin* (MT), May 3, 1919.
"Prlja is sentenced to term in penitentiary." *Butte Bulletin* (MT), May 8, 1919.
"Prlja to be tired on charge of assault." *Butte Bulletin* (MT), April 29, 1919.
"Prlja's fate goes in hands of jury today." *Butte Bulletin* (MT), May 2, 1919.
"Pronounced an accident." *New York Times*, November 1, 1889.
"Property more valuable than life." *Emporia Weekly News* (KS), February 26, 1885.
"Record of a year." *Yorkville Enquirer* (SC), November 1, 1904.
"Released on bond." *Bisbee Daily Review* (AZ), October 31, 1915.
"Renewed efforts to save O'Brien from the gallows." *Evening Star* (Washington), February 12, 1873.
"The revolver and the club." *National Republican* (Washington), September 13, 1884.
"The right to club." *New York Tribune*, March 15, 1901.
"Robbery in the first degree." *New York Times*, February 20, 1886.
"Robert Brown sentenced." *Evening Bulletin* (Maysville, KY), April 21, 1904.
"Roundsman Goughran exonerated." *New York Times*, September 11, 1897.
"Sad tragedy in Georgetown." *Evening Star* (Washington), July 16, 1872.
"Sam Hutchinson denounced." *Evening Star* (Washington), July 18, 1890.
"San Francisco and vicinity." *Sacramento Record-Union*, November 30, 1888.
"San Francisco policeman kills escaping suspect." *Los Angeles Herald*, November 7, 1910.
"Saturday sentences in criminal court." *Pittsburgh Dispatch*, October 4, 1891.
"Saw O'Brien shooting, calls police derelict." *New York Times*, December 31, 1904.
"Say policeman killed girl." *Sun* (NY), November 26, 1910.
"Say policeman shot boy for revenge." *New York Times*, June 23, 1909.
"Says he shot O'Brien." *New York Tribune*, April 18, 1909.
"Says police shielded him." *New York Times*, December 9, 1904.
"Says policeman killed man." *Evening World* (NY), March 30, 1904.
"Scraps and facts." *Yorkville Enquirer* (SC), September 30, 1896.
"Seattle detective wounds man by mistake." *El Paso Herald*, January 22, 1913.
"Secrest goes to prison." *Evening Statesman* (Walla Walla, WA), April 16, 1906.
"Self-defense proven—Stockdale is cleared." *Mt. Sterling Advocate* (KY), September 18, 1920.
"Sentenced to be hanged." *New York Times*, May 25, 1883.
"Served right." *Los Angeles Herald*, May 12, 1889.
"Several policemen dismissed." *New York Times*, September 5, 1895.
"Sharp attack on Hanson." *Sun* (NY), January 11, 1908.
"Shellard a witness." *New York Times*, January 21, 1909.
"Shellard in cell to await trial as girl's slayer." *Evening World* (NY), September 10, 1908.
"The Shellard murder case." *New York Times*, January 20, 1909.
"Shellard murder trial." *New York Times*, January 19, 1909.
"Shellard must stay in jail." *New York Times*, July 31, 1908.
"Shellard off the force." *New York Times*, August 22, 1908.
"Shellard out on $15,000 bail." *New York Times*, March 20, 1909.
"Shenandoah man shot." *Freeland Tribune* (PA), June 29, 1903.
"Shock caused her death." *Bolivar Bulletin* (TN), June 26, 1903.
"Shooting at Chico." *Los Angeles Herald*, August 28, 1891.
"Shooting of boys is held unjustifiable." *Omaha Daily Bee*, October 26, 1915.
"The shooting of Devine." *New York Times*, August 2, 1897.
"Shooting policeman indicted." *Daily Press* (Newport News VA), October 1, 1905.
"Shoots down youth in crowded park." *New York Times*, October 7, 1907.
"Shoots two in bed." *New York Tribune*, January 15, 1902.
"Shot by a policeman." *Titusville Herald* (PA), August 27, 1906.
"Shot by brother officer." *New York Times*, October 16, 1890.
"Shot by girl's father." *New York Times*, June 25, 1905.
"Shot by policeman in Sunday law row." *New York Times*, May 3, 1909.

"Shot dead at Roseburg." *Journal* (Salem, OR), May 1, 1902.
"Shot dead by mistake." *Arizona Republican* (Phoenix, AZ), February 12, 1903.
"Shot down in depot." *Bryan Morning Eagle* (TX), November 3, 1908.
"Shot his prisoner." *Evening Star* (Washington), March 4, 1895.
"Shot husband and wife." *New York Times*, July 15, 1891.
"Shot in the left temple." *St. Paul Globe*, December 10, 1893.
"Shot the wrong man." *Pittsburgh Dispatch*, May 19, 1889.
"Slain man's friends active." *Bamberg Herald* (SC), June 27, 1912.
"Slap costs three lives." *Abbeville Press and Banner* (SC), October 14, 1896.
"Slapped his face." *San Francisco Call*, July 18, 1893.
"Slayer's money found in shoes." *Washington Herald*, October 4, 1910.
"Some news about Kansas." *Advocate* (Topeka, KS), August 5, 1896.
"Some recent occurrences." *Laurens Advertiser* (SC), May 4, 1904.
"South Carolina news." *Yorkville Enquirer* (SC), January 12, 1915.
"South Carolina news." *Yorkville Enquirer* (SC), May 30, 1919.
"South Carolina news." *Yorkville Enquirer* (SC), November 20, 1879.
"Sparks from the wire." *Charleston News* (SC), May 23, 1871.
"Spokane policeman kills a burglar." *Deseret Evening News* (Salt Lake), April 4, 1906.
"Sterling policeman indicted." *Rock Island Argus* (IL), October 10, 1907.
"Story of the shooting." *Boston Globe*, December 30, 1890.
"A strange verdict." *Washington Times*, March 15, 1895.
"Stray bullet kills baby at mother's side." *New York Times*, November 14, 1917.
"Sues a policeman." *Evening World* (NY), October 1, 1894.
"Supreme Court decides that Phi Prlja must serve pen sentence." *Butte Bulletin* (MT), March 29, 1920.
"A suspended sentence." *Evening Star* (Washington), January 22, 1890.
"Suspended without pay." *Evening Star* (Washington), December 27, 1893.
"Swift trials for the cops." *Sun* (NY), February 17, 1905.
"Swords Creek man instantly killed." *Bluefield Telegraph* (VA), August 2, 1914.
"Teacher shot in street." *Abbeville Press and Banner* (SC), March 22, 1905.
"Terel gets even." *Evening Times-Republican* (Marshalltown, Iowa), September 16, 1919.
"Terry not held." *Evening Star* (Washington), October 12, 1894.
"Terry to be tried." *Evening Star* (Washington), May 11, 1894.
"Thief shot on street by Harlem detective." *New York Times*, June 28, 1904.
"Thinks policeman killed bartender." *New York Times*, March 31, 1904.
"Thought Lagan meant murder says Conboy." *San Francisco Call*, February 12, 1910.
"Three indictments for murder." *Pittsburgh Dispatch*, June 13, 1891.
"The three men convicted of murder." *Evening Star* (Washington), November 16, 1872.
"Three years at hard labor." *Evening Star* (Washington), June 9, 1894.
"To arrest patrolman." *New York Tribune*, December 22, 1904.
"To be tried for murder." *Evening Star* (Washington), March 1, 1904.
"To free ex-policeman." *Sun* (NY), January 27, 1916.
"Tomasso's penalty prison and a fine." *St. Louis Republic*, June 24, 1905.
"Tragedies of Christmas Day." *Semi-Weekly Messenger* (Wilmington, NC), December 31, 1907.
"Tragedy at Concord." *Evening Star* (Washington), September 25, 1906.
"The tragedy in Columbia." *Anderson Intelligencer* (SC), July 3, 1879.
"Tragedy in Columbia." *Watchman and Southron* (Sumter, SC), May 31, 1919.
"A tragedy at Hattiesburg." *Bee* (Earlington, KY), March 23, 1905.
"A tragedy at Roseburg." *Rogue River Courier* (Grants Pass, OR), May 8, 1902.
"Trial board meets." *Evening Star* (Washington), October 27, 1906.
"Trials soon." *Paducah Sun* (KY), February 19, 1902.
"Troutman loses fight." *Topeka State Journal* (KS), December 24, 1901.
"Trying two policemen." *New York Times*, October 31, 1889.
"20 years for policeman." *New York Times*, February 1, 1905.
"Two district verdicts." *Washington Times*, March 7, 1895.
"2 lay loss of eyes to same policeman." *New York Times*, August 16, 1920.
"Two policemen are on trial for murder." *Evening World* (NY), January 17, 1905.

"Two policemen guilty." *New York Times*, January 21, 1905.
"Two policemen indicted for first-degree murder." *Times-Dispatch* (Richmond, VA), February 11, 1921.
"2 policemen indicted for killing boy." New York Tribune, February 11, 1921.
"Two verdicts in shooting of Daly." *Evening World* (NY), August 9, 1904.
"The verdict in the Keenan inquest." *New York Tribune*, November 9, 1883.
"Two years." *Paducah Sun* (NY), August 24, 1904.
"Two years extra for McInerney." *New York Times*, February 27, 1886.
"Two years for Auerbach." *Evening Public Ledger* (Philadelphia), June 25, 1918.
"Two years for murder." *Democratic Banner* (Mt. Vernon, Ohio), March 7, 1911.
"An unconditional pardon is granted former policeman." *Great Falls Tribune* (MT), May 1, 1920.
"An unconvinced jury." *Evening World* (NY), February 13, 1890.
"Vargas dies from a policeman's pistol." *Roswell Record* (NM), April 4, 1910.
"Verdict against policeman." *Freeport Journal* (IL), March 25, 1909.
"Verdict favored policeman." *New York Times*, November 5, 1904.
"Verdict for McAuliffe." *New York Times*, April 20, 1898.
"Verdict is that she shot herself." *New York Times*, July 30, 1908.
"Verdict not guilty." *Evening Star* (Washington), October 25, 1907.
"Verdict of guilty found against Mallon." *New York Times*, December 10, 1904.
"Virginia news." *Alexandria Gazette* (VA), February 10, 1903.
"Virginia news." *Alexandria Gazette* (VA), May 13, 1905.
"Virginia news." *Alexandria Gazette* (VA), September 21, 1905.
"Waldo will ask police inquiry." *Sun* (NY), July 15, 1912.
"Wallace has turned in his star." *Spokane Press*, July 20, 1909.
"Walsh jury can't agree." *Seattle Star*, June 25, 1910.
"Walter Brown exonerated." *St. Louis Republic*, June 13, 1902.
"Want to mob him." *Indianapolis Journal*, April 30, 1901.
"Wants Rowan off force." *New York Times*, March 7, 1920.
"Warrant issued for O'Hearn." *St. Louis Republic*, September 7, 1902.
"Week ending May 9, 1903." *Evening Star* (Washington), May 9, 1903.
"A well-deserved sentence." *Los Angeles Herald*, February 10, 1889.
"What policeman cannot do." *Evening Star* (Washington), September 17, 1879.
"Who killed Bill Dooley." *Hickman Courier* (KY), February 28, 1902.
"Wild police shooting." *Evening World* (NY), December 23, 1890.
"Will hear cop who shot man tomorrow." *Harrisburg Telegraph* (PA), August 3, 1914.
"Will probably die." *Evening Star* (Washington), November 22, 1893.
"Will take an appeal." *Great Falls Tribune* (MT), September 15, 1920.
"Winding up jury trials." *Pittsburgh Dispatch*, July 16, 1892.
"Wisconsin student is shot dead by policeman." *New York Tribune*, May 29, 1920.
"Witnesses signing of pardon." *Guthrie Leader* (OK), January 28, 1908.
"Woman appears against policeman." *New York Times*, November 15, 1911.
"Woman knocked down and robbed on street." *New York Times*, August 26, 1929.
"You'll find it here." *Tacoma Times*, January 23, 1913.
"Young Easley shot by officer." *Times Dispatch* (Richmond, VA), August 5, 1906.
"Young Probber dead, policeman in cell," *New York Times*, May 4, 1909.
"Youth flees police, is shot and killed." *Evening Public Ledger* (Philadelphia), June 12, 1915.

Newspapers with Untitled Articles

Advocate (Topeka, KS), April 22, 1896.
Burlington Hawk Eye (Iowa), January 11, 1908.
Day Book (Chicago), October 31, 1912.
Evening Herald (Klamath Falls, OR), April 22, 1912.
Hickman Courier (KY), January 29, 1892.
Hickman Courier (KY), March 28, 1912.
Highland Weekly News (Hillsborough, Ohio), February 14, 1878.

Indianapolis Journal, December 30, 1869.
Pickens Sentinel (SC), October 14, 1915.
Seattle Star, November 27, 1912.
Sun (NY), January 27, 1878.
Tensas Gazette (St. Joseph, LA), May 13, 1910.
Watchman and Southron (Sumter, SC), September 29, 1909.
Weekly Union Times (Union, SC), November 21, 1879.

Index

Abingdon, VA 169–170
Ackerman, Dorothy 188
acquittals 27, 28, 30, 39, 74, 100
Adams, Charles 32–34
Albuquerque, NM 156–157
alcohol 7, 14–15, 22, 24, 34–38, 39, 40, 50–51, 65, 74, 81–82, 82–84, 85–88, 89–90, 108–110, 113–114, 119, 128, 131, 133, 144, 148–152, 159–161, 161–162, 164, 167–169, 191
Alexandria, VA 77–78
alienists 88
Allen, George S. 98–99
Allen, William 178
Allen, William (TN) 133
Archibald, John 183–184
Armstrong, George H. 163–164
Aspell, Michael J. 167
Atkinson, Weston 77–78
Atlantic City, NJ 120
Auerbach, Emanuel 189
Augusta, GA 93
Aurora, MN 186

Baird, Harry 185
Baird, John R. 174–175
Ballard, John 184
Banks, Nathan 180–181
Barnes, John J. 62–63
Barnes, William 28
Barrett, Bert 174–175
Barrett, Joseph 39–40
Barrett, Whitney D. 124–125
Barwick, Stinoy 97
Basso, Sebato 161–162
Baston, Catherine 159
Baston, Charles G. 159–161
Bateo, J. 32
Baumer, August 32

Beasley, Hardee 88–89
Beattie, George 178
Bebb, John 7–9
Beck, Christian 12
Becker, Charles 171–173
Belcher, B. C. 186
Bell, Matthew 51–53
Bellerby, Edward 186
Bennett, J. W. 19
Benson, Oscar 118
Bernauer, Henry C. 165–166
Bevell, C. M. 38
Bitterlich, Paul 105
black officers 51–53
black protests 44–46, 66–69
blacks 14, 18, 27, 29–30, 44–46, 55–57, 65–69, 71, 75–76, 88–89, 90, 95–96, 100–101, 112–113, 140, 144, 147, 153, 153–154, 159, 166–167, 170 (2), 175, 177, 179–180, 180, 180–181, 182, 184, 186, 187, 200–201
Blumberg, Solomon 198
Bodkin, Nicholas 93
Borgman, Joseph D. 167–169
Bosse, William H. 99–100
Boston 47–48, 143
Bounds, Fred 107
Bourne, George B. 46
Bowles, David 123
Boyle, Daniel J. 120–122
Bradley, John 140
Brandenborg, Sigwald 125–126
Brennan, Robert 101–105
Brennan, William 54–55
bribery 68
Brickner, Paul 105
Briley, Bob 119–120
Bristol, RI 187
Bristol, TN 93
Britt, David 98–99

Brittingham, John C. 164–165
Brooklyn, NY 19
Brooks, Judson 182
Broom, William J. 120
Brown, Robert 93
Brown, Walter 90
Buffalo, NY 32
Bufkin, E. O. 115
Bulkley, John 24
Burchardt, Roy 167
Burke, J. B. 131
Burke, Thomas 196
Burke, Willie 39
Burton, William 39–40
Burzan, Mike 192–194
Butler, I. S. 133–134
Butler, Thomas 13
Butte, MT 129–130, 192–194

Cahill, William 185
Callahan, Michael F. 191
Campbell, Frank 177
Campbell, William F. 41–42
Canale, Louis 33–34
Carleton, Guy 197–198
Carrao, Francis L. 146–147
Carter, Joseph 118
Casey, Patrick 19–21
Cash, Vincent D. 182–183
Cassidy, David 191
Cedar Rapids, IA 196
Central City, KY 175
Ceredo, WV 84
Chabenat, Lucie 162–163
Chadwick, Julia 124–125
charges dismissed 42
Charleston, SC 10, 180
Chattanooga, TN 10
Cheri, Edward 164
Chicago 9, 48, 58–59, 75, 82, 114, 118, 135, 143–144, 177 (2), 178, 185, 187, 188–189, 200
Childress, Houston 93–94
Chipman, William A. 187
Cincinnati 7–9, 13, 14, 153
city councils, discipline 81–82
civil suits 59, 69
Clare, John 113–114
Claremore, OK 147
Clark, Jack 169–170
Clark, Samuel H. 186
Clayton, Farris 82–84
Clayton, Lynn 82–84
Cleary, Michael 117–118
Cleveland, Grover 57
Clifford, Jon 167
Clifton, NJ 188

Cline, Thomas 158
Clinton, Eugene Z. 128–129
Clinton, NC 157
clubbing 7–9, 10, 21–22, 24–26, 43, 44–46, 48–49, 50–51, 51–53, 59–65, 74, 79, 79–80, 80–82, 84, 94–95, 111–113, 115, 125–126, 126–127, 131, 145, 158, 159, 167–169, 177, 186 (2), 189
Coatesville, PA 166–167
Colby, George H. 93
Cole, Harry 129–130
Coleman, Henry J. 199–200
Coleman, John 42–43
Coleman, Lilla 153
Coleman, Thomas 61–62
Collier, John W. 140–143
collusion, police 66–68
Colored Baptists Preachers Union 69
Columbia, SC 15–16, 188, 194–195
Comisky, James 20
Comisky, Richard 19–21
comments, judicial 28, 49, 57, 90, 94–95, 123, 128, 139, 176–177, 181, 182
commutations 13, 104–105
Conboy, Michael 148–152
Concord, NH 124–125
Conkling, Dennis 19
Connelly, Frank 158
Connor, Charles 123–124
Conroy, William 23–27
convictions 8, 12, 13, 15–16, 21, 23, 27, 31, 39, 40, 51, 57, 58, 70, 83, 99, 104, 107–108, 119, 142–143, 147, 158, 181, 183
Cook, Charles 159
Cornelius, Irwin B. 77
Costello, James A. 43
Cottle, John 7–9
Covington, KY 93
Crookston, MN 58
Cross, Edward 48–49
Crowley, Margaret 120
Crowley, Michael 96–97
Cruger, Albert 69–70
Crumpton, J. C. 153
Cruse, Joe 85
Cullom, Raymond 162
Cunningham, Samuel A. 10–13
Cushing, James 189–190

Daly, Dennis 55
Daly, William 106
Danville, VA 27
Davenport, John 47–48
Davis, Florence 154–155
Dawson, John J. 94–95
Dean, Richard L. 44–46
Deering, Harry 189

demonizing, victims 7–8, 13, 21, 34–38, 44–46, 54, 66–68, 70, 81–82, 106, 107, 130, 132–133, 140, 141–143, 160–161, 162, 170, 179, 180–181, 184, 199
Dennis, Edward 78–79
Denver 99, 119, 140, 177
Des Moines, IA 196
Detroit 189
Devanna, Eugene L. 108–110
Devine, Thomas 71–72
De Wald, John 162
Dickins, Tom 144
Dillon, James F. 145–147
Dockery, John 117
Dodd, Thomas 97
Dolan, Henry 74
Donnelly, Edward 119–120
Dooley, Bill 88–89
Dooley, James 186
Dorfman, Abe 72–73
Doster, Spencer 101
Downie, Robert 178–179
Dowrey, George A. 116–117
Dowrick, George 108–110
Drake, Thomas E. 121
Duman, F. A. 131
Dunn, Bernard 63–64

Earl, Herbert 107
Easley, Henry Jr. 118
editorials 8, 10, 13, 16–17, 26, 29, 33, 66–67, 79–80
Edwards, Morris 200–201
Eichelberger, Will 170
Eklund, Ernest 145
El Paso, TX 165–166
Eli, Henry 191
Elkhart, IN 39–40
Ellis, Frank 82–84
Ellis, Samuel H. 28–29
Emrich, Samuel 99
Englewood, NJ 166
English, Joe 15–16
English, John 15–16
Engvall, Albert 132–133
Ennis, Mary Agnes 85–88
Ennis, William H. 85–88
Eubanks. J. A. 101
Evansville, IN 38–39
executions 12–13, 21, 27, 86–88, 173
exonerations 34, 53, 69, 72, 73, 79, 90, 101, 116–117, 118, 153, 185, 197, 199, 201

family victims 50–51, 74–75, 85–88, 89–90, 93, 143, 147, 159, 177, 183, 185, 194–195
Farley, Patrick 77
Farrell, Joseph 107

Farrell, Patrick H. 99–100
Fay, John 200
Fennessey, Michael 200
Ferguson, Hal 179–180
fines 10, 41, 44, 49, 55, 76, 79, 81, 164, 174, 179, 196
Finn, Joseph 143–144
Finnegan, James 30–31
firearms usage, official 95–96
Fitzgerald, Christopher T. 128–129
Flood, Cornelius J. 189–190
Florence, SC 170
Flynn, Bernard 66
Foster, Reuben 65–69
Freeman, W. 84
Fullen, Jake 147
Fulton, KY 88, 179–180
funds raised, for defense 155
Furlong, Patrick 75

Gaines, H. E. 69–70
Gaynor, William 157, 158–159, 161–162, 172
Gillin, Charles P. 175–176
Givens, R. A. 38
Glade Springs, VA 147
Glenn, Robert 175
Glennon, J. F. 39
Goff, John W. 59–65
Golden, James 187
Golden, Nicholas J. 187
Goodwin, W. C. 107–108
Gorman, Alice 85–88
Gosnell, Reuben 182
Gottwald, Frank 179
Goughran, William F. 72–73
Gowland, Herbert 123
Grady, Michael 130
grand juries 68
Grant, Ulysses S. 13
Granville, MS 187
Graves, Nora 133–134
Graves, W. S. 134
Gray, James 191
Green, Alexander 71
Green, Alvin W. 65–69
Green, Arthur 71
Greenville, SC 182, 184–185
Gretna, LA 70–71
Guavara, Antonio 156–157
Gullickson, Julius 186
Guthrie, OK 82–84

Hahn, Edward 34–38
Hall, S. M. 80–82
Hamilton, OH 32
Hanify, Marti 65
Hanley, Michael 48–49

Index

Hanrahan, Daniel E. 96
Hansen, Bert 129
Hansen, William 41
Hanson, Adolph 189
Harless, Ira 181–182
Harper, Edgar B. 55
Harris, Burns 200–201
Harris, Ellick 18
Harris, Percy 187
Harrisburg, PA 180–181
Hart, Della 41
Haselden, J. L. 170
Hattiesburg, MS 115
Hawkins, James 71
Hawley, Henry 74–75
Head, George 80–82
Healy, Michael J. 58–59
Helms, Jesse W. 188
Henry, Brad 169–170
Hepner, F. D. 133
Herman, Daniel 114
Hewlett, E. M. 67
Higgins, Earl 125–126
Higginson, John J. 196
Hightower, Walter Dudley 122–123
Hill, Charles 182–183
Hilton, George 29–30
Hirsch, Aaron 179
Hobbs, Salvador 28
Holland, George 105
Holmes, John 10
Holsworth, John 49–50
Honolulu 191
Horn, Homer 194
Houlihan, Dan 199
Houston, TX 122–123
Howe, Stanley S. 166–167
Hudson, NY 9
Hussey, John 34–38
Hutchinson, Sam 44

imprisonment 13, 16, 21, 23, 27, 38, 39, 40 (2), 46, 50, 51, 58, 70, 75, 83, 90, 94, 94–95, 104, 107, 110, 115, 119, 123, 128, 142–143, 147, 152, 154, 157, 158, 160, 177, 181, 183, 191 (2)
insanity 26–27, 83–84, 86–88

Jackson, Charles 129–130
Jackson, H. B. 18
Jackson, MI 127–128
Jaffe, Harry 199–200
Jaffe, Isaac 131–132
Jandorf, Carl 199
Jeribola, Peter 197
Jersey City, NJ 9, 54–55, 182–183
Johnson, Jack 179–180

Johnson, Thomas 119
Johnson City, TN 98–99
Johnston, Moses 126–127
Joliet, IL 41
Jones, George 157
Jones, Robert 101–104
Jones, Thomas C. 68
Jordan, Carlisle 131
Junge, Albert 48
juries, hung 21, 42, 130, 139
justifiable homicide, passion 165–166, 197–198

Kane, Thomas P. 121
Kansas City, KS 186
Kansas City, MO 159, 188, 194
Kayler, Henry 43
Kearney, Thomas F. 47–48
Keegan, Edward 186
Keenan, Peter 23–27
Kelly, Charles 191
Kelly, Thomas 161–162
Kenny, Alice Smith 190
Kern, James 14–15
Ketten, Nicholas 118
Kilmer, Frederick 176–177
Kinne, Ira B. 113–114
Klingensmith, C. E. 182
Knowles, Robert 133
Knoxville, TN 85
Kohler, Rudolph 136
Kropp, Louis 151
Krug, Mary 137

La Porte, IN 74
Lagan, Bernard 148–152
Lagan, Margaret 150
Lally, Edward 91–92
Lamb, Edwin 193
Lancaster, Eugene M. 194–195
Lancaster, Mrs. E. M. 194–195
Landgren, Albert 117–118
Langston, Z. T. 78–79
Lanning, John 158
Lappe, W. De Forrest 115–116
Laubersheimer, William 84
Laurel, MS 107
Law and Order League 45–46
Leach, Edward 75
Lee, George W. 68
Lee, Harvey 175–176
Legg, Lee 187
Lerk, Doc 170
Levergne, Gerizim 131
Lewendowski, C. A. 123
Lewis, Isaac 127–128
Lewis, John 158

Lexow Committee (NYS) 59–65
Lindskog, David 82
Lipscomb, J B. 120–122
Lisa, Frank G. 197
Llewellyn, Harvey 167
Long, William 32
Lorick, Newton S. 194–195
Lorimer, William 178
Los Angeles 185
Louisville, KY 19
Lowenstein, Monty 153
Lucas, Thomas 63–64
Luhman, Edwin V. 64
lying, police 18, 29–30, 30–31, 35–38, 101–104, 110, 126–127, 128–129, 135–140, 146–147, 157, 174, 189–190
Lynaugh, Matthew 199
lynchings 15, 29–30, 71, 166–167
Lyon, Celia 22

Macon, GA 147–148
Madden, Thomas 48
Madison, WI 199
Maher, George 134–135
Mallon, Arthur J. 101–105
Malone, William 99
Mamer, Matthew 118
Manion, Larry 91–92
Manning, John 186
Manzello, Guiseppe 51–53
Marion, IA 175–176
Martinez, Fecundo 192
Martling, Abraham 199
Marts, Nellie 153
Mathews, William H. 140–143
Matthews, Matt 140
Maude, Thomas F. 99–100
Mayfield, KY 158
McAdoo, William 110–112
McAuliffe, Jeremiah J. 73–74
McAuliffe, Patrick J. 96
McBride, Roger 41
McClure, Hugh 48–49
McConeghy, Alexander 186
McCullough, Mary 167–169
McDonald, John J. 30–31
McElroy, William 128
McEvoy, Edward 106
McGarvey, Charles 130
McGee, Joseph 20
McGinnis, Herman 123
McGuire, William 158
McInerney, John 93
McInerney, Matthew 30–31
McLaughlin, Frank 110–113
McLeod, Leo A. 195–196
McManus, Charles 105

McNamara, Maurice 21–23
McNamee, M. J. 174
McNaughton, George 180
McSherry, John 123–124
Meany, Richard S. 64
media coverage 8, 30, 34, 44–46, 54, 66–68, 71–72, 106, 108–110, 132–133, 137, 150–152
Memphis, TN 38
Miller, Green 27
Mills, Lewis C. 93
Minneapolis 76, 125–126, 189
minors 46, 47, 176–177, 185, 188, 188–189, 189, 189–190, 195–196, 197
Missouri 84
Monroe, LA 153–154
Moran, Thomas J. 58–59
Morgan, James 13
Morley, Frank 14–15
Morris, Patrick T. 41–42
Morris, S. 115
Morris, Thomas 115
Moseley, M. E. 147
Moss, Frank 59–65
Mt. Sterling, KY 200
Muco, Joe 188
Mullens, Wallace 187
Mulveil, Mary Catherine 114
Munger, William 125–126
Murphy, Bernard 65
Murphy, Joe 153
Murphy, William 176–177
Murtaugh, John 183–184
Murthrough, Hugh 9
Muskogee, OK 133–134

Nachman, Leo 191
Nashville 19
Nelson, Alexander 84
Nelson, Bob 55
Nelson, Lon 84
Nelson, Samuel 58–59
Nelsonville, OH 158
New Orleans 18
New York City 19–21, 21–23, 23–27, 30–31, 32–34, 34–38, 41–42, 42–43, 43, 46, 49–50, 50–51, 59, 59–65, 65, 71–72, 72–73, 73–74, 74–75, 77, 79–80, 84, 85–88, 89–90, 94–95, 96, 99–100, 101–105, 106, 108–110, 110–113, 113–114, 123–123, 126–127, 128–129, 131–132, 134–135, 135–140, 145–147, 157, 158–159, 161–162, 162–163, 167, 167–169, 171–173, 178, 178–179, 179, 183, 186, 187, 189–190, 196, 197, 198, 199, 199–200
New York City Police Department 59–65
Newark, NJ 32, 107

Newman, S. D. 153–154
Newport, TN 133
Nohl, Jacob 16
Nolen, Chester 185
Norton, Edward 13

Oakland, CA 131
O'Brien, Charles H. 10–13
O'Brien, Edward 20
O'Brien, John 89–90
O'Brien, Minnie 89–90
O'Brien, Robert 189–190
O'Brien, William 104
Ocala, FL 71
O'Connor, Jeremiah 20
O'Hearn, Thomas 91–92
O'Keefe, Cornelius 71–72
O'Malley, John 131–132
O'Neill, Michael 166
O'Neill, Thomas 65
Osbourne, Clapp 181–182
Owens, Thomas 90–91

pardons 38, 57, 70, 83–84, 157, 158, 161, 177, 190, 193
Paris, TN 55
Parker, Herman 164–165
Parker, Mitrell 135
Parks, W. H. 28
Parsons, KS 140
Patterson, John W. 112–113
Pennington, John{ en}84
Pepper, Leslie 174
perjury 38, 126, 128–129, 150–152
Philadelphia 9, 13 (2), 97–98, 117–118, 118, 128, 158, 176–177, 183–184, 186, 189, 191
Phillips, Robert A. 116–117
Phoebus, VA 116–117
Pike, Blanche 196
Pittsburgh 48–49, 51–53, 108, 115–116, 123
Pittsfield, MA 191
Pittston, PA 14–15
Plymouth, NH 93
Pocatello, ID 144
police attacked, after shooting 144
police boards 12–13, 21, 22, 37–38, 47–48, 84, 111–112, 121–122, 128–129, 137–138, 141, 145
police boards, discipline 23, 39, 43, 62–64, 90
police collusion in lies 34–38
police corruption 44–46, 59–65, 101–104, 126–127, 134–135, 135–140, 146–147, 162–163, 168–169, 171–173, 189–190, 192–194
police victims 19–21, 38–39, 39–40, 48, 49–50, 75, 93, 93–94, 96, 101–105, 107–108, 113–114, 117, 127–128, 128–129, 140–143, 174–175, 182, 182–183, 186, 187, 197–198
political corruption 26
Pomaria, SC 170
Portipillo, Antonio 154–155
Portland, OR 132–133, 133, 134, 182
Posey, Robert 77–78
Posey, Walter 77–78
Potts, R. M. 88–89
Powers, Thomas 200
Prall, Henry 188
Prlja, Philip 192–194
Probber, Isaac 145–147
Probber, Louis 145–147
prosecutorial neglect 33–34, 35–38, 44–46, 58–59, 67–69, 74, 94–95, 113, 150–152, 199–200
Puckett, James 158
Putnam, Henry H. 170–171

Quist, Peter 125–126

racism 44–46, 66–69, 88–89, 166–167
Raleigh, NC 117
Randolph, Ross 22
rape, attempt 46
Raven, VA 181–182
Raymond, Emma 147–148
Reed, Frank 90–91
Reich, Joseph A. 196
Reig, Barbara 135–140
Reig, Eva 136
Rein, Michael J. 64–65
removal, difficulty of 21–22
Renovo, PA 96–97
repeat offenders 8–9, 21–22, 25, 35, 44, 49, 52, 55, 55–56, 81, 92, 111–112, 148–150, 153–154, 181–182, 199–200
resisting arrest 18, 19, 27, 58, 80–82, 84, 101, 107, 116, 118, 128, 140, 144, 156, 167, 170 (2), 175, 180, 182, 189, 192–194
Rice, Bartley 32
Rice, Edgar 166–167
Rice, Fred 15
Rice, Patrick 42
Richard, Frank 165–166
Richardson, Henry B. 170
Ridgeway, SC 153
right to shoot 28–29
Riley, Joseph 49–50
Riverside CA 174–175
Robbins, James P. 110–113
Robinson, Chester 177
Rock, Peter J. 196
Rock Hill, SC 100–101, 170–171
Rogers, Isaac 117
Rogers, W. J. 40–41

Roper, Joseph 180
Rose, William 15–16
Roseburg, OR 90–91
Roselius, Charles A. 197–198
Rosenbrock, Christopher 40
Rosenthal, Herman 171–172
Rowan, Thomas 198
Ruddock, Roland 166
Russell, Joseph 19
Rutherford, NJ 105
Ryan, George H. 164
Ryan, John 32
Ryan, William 96–97
Ryerson, John 54–55

St. Joseph, MO 79
St. Landry, LA 131
St. Louis 18, 90, 91–92, 115, 200–201
Salisbury, MD 164–165
Salt Lake City 29–30
San Francisco 39, 40, 55, 148–152, 162, 164
sanctifying perpetrators 8, 16, 44–46, 47, 78, 101, 109–110, 122, 124, 151–152, 174, 180–181
Sanders, J. W. 182
sanity hearing 83
Saulsbury, Ross 16
Savannah, GA 107–108
Sawyer, John L. H. 94–95
Say, Patrick 118
Schaefer, Mrs. Karl B. 159
Schellenburger, Cornelius 59
Schery, Nicholas 84
Schmidt, Henry 115
Schwarzler, Joseph 30–31
Scott, Alexander 143–144
Scott, Charles S. 79
Scott, Jack A. 188
Scott, Robert F. 180–181
Seattle 154–155, 174, 197–198
Secord, Charles 187
Secrest, Charles 119
Seigler, S. 75–76
Sera, Leon 179
Shaffer, Henry 134
Shammo, Samuel 185
Sheehan, James 130
Shell, Cornelius 182
Shellard, David 135–140
Shenandoah, PA 97
shot while fleeing 14, 18, 28, 32 (2), 47–48, 56, 58, 66, 73, 77, 95, 105, 106, 107, 116, 118, 120, 120–121, 123 (2), 124, 130 (2), 131, 131–132, 135, 144, 153, 154–155, 158 (2), 162, 166, 167 (2), 175, 176–177, 178–179, 179, 180–181, 183–184, 185, 186, 187, 195–196, 199

shots fired, ricochet 120–121
shots fired in crowds 117–118
shots fired in crowds, bystander victims 33–34, 71, 159, 162–163, 178, 188, 196
shots fired, ricochet, bystander victims 43, 178, 179
Shuttleworth 131–132
Simmons, C. A. 132–133
Smith, Edward 135
Smith, Frank 175
Smith, Harry 75–76
Smith, John 21–23
Smith, Joseph 177
Smith, Mary 50–51
Smith, Rosie 177
Smith, Thomas 79
Smith, William 50–51
Smock, Abe 38–39
South Boston, VA 118
Spillman, Daniel G. 143
Spokane, WA 119–120, 145
Stahl, R. H. 182
Stanton, Thomas J. 59
Starr, Henry A. 195–196
Stephens, William P. 140
Sterling, IL 130
Steurman, William 56–57
Stinger, Edward 97–98
Stockdale, Rufus 200
Strode, W. R. 184
Suffolk, VA 78–79
suicides 74–75, 93, 114, 118, 124–125, 147–148, 183, 185
suicides, attempts 143, 159, 174
Suitter, N. H. 134
suspensions 56, 74

Tanife, Jennie 46
Taylor, Michael H. 199–200
Teeling, George 187
Teeters, Albert H. 108
Telfair, Robert 113
Terrel, Henry W. 196
Terry, Charles 55–57
Tew, John K. 157
Thomas, Daniel 90
Thomas, F. 29–30
Thomas, Harrison 186
Thomas, William 191
Thompson, Andrew 58
Thompson, William S. 40
Toledo, OH 16–17
Tomasso, Anton 115
Topeka, KS 69–70, 80–82
Travis, Gus 144
trials, multiple 83–84, 97, 130, 134, 151–152
trials, severed 30, 126

Trotti, Gaetano 134–135
Tucson, AZ 179, 192

Ullom, Rufus 115–116
Umstead, Charles E. 167
Unger, Frederick 128–129
Union, SC 182

Vancouver, WA 167
Vargas, Francisco 156–157

Waddell, William F. 161
Wagenheim, Walter 178
Walk, G. W. 93–94
Walker, Charles H. 93
Walker, Herbert 188–189
Walker, Zachariah 166–167
Wallace, Joseph R. 179
Wallace, Norris 145
Walsh, Edward 42–43
Walsh, George 196
Walsh, Martin T. 189
Walsh, Michael 14–15
Walsh, Stephen S. 128–129
Walsh, Thomas 154–155
Walsh, Thomas G. 126–127
Wangerman, George 178–179
Ward, Frank 185
Washington, DC 10–13, 27–29, 40–41, 44–46, 55–57, 65–69, 95–96, 120–122, 140–143, 159–161, 163–164, 191, 195–196
Washington, Willis 55–57
Watson, Kitty A. 153–154
weapon discharge, accidental 42, 56, 91, 121–122, 130, 133, 135, 144, 145, 162, 175–176, 182
weapon discharge, ricochet 84, 90–91
weapon, nonexistent, response to drawing of 120, 144, 165, 171, 179, 179–180, 195, 197
weapons, usage of 120–121
Weaver, John H. 186
Weaver, William 163–164
Welch, John 107
Welsh, James 9
Welsh, James T. 162–163
West, Michael 84
Wettle, John G. 133
Wheeler, Ernest 191
Wheeler, William 95–96
Wiley, James P. 82
Williams, Ditrion 27
Williams, Frank 107
Williams, John 140
Wilmington, NC 75–76
Wilmington, OH 84
Wilson, Fred 74
Wilson, Woodrow 161
Winchester, KY 184
Winner, S. C. 75–76
Woodward, Fitzhugh F. 191
Wooster, Fred E. 177

Yonowitz, Benjamin 189

Zalena, Andrew 183
Ziegler, Joseph 38–39
Zipperer, E. O. 107–108

www.ingramcontent.com/pod-product-compliance
Ingram Content Group UK Ltd.
Pitfield, Milton Keynes, MK11 3LW, UK
UKHW041941140426
5217IPUK00014B/594